PROMOTING PRODUCTIVITY IN THE PUBLIC SECTOR

Series Standing Order

If you would like to receive future titles in this series as they
are published, you can make use of our standing order
facility. To place a standing order please contact your
bookseller or, in case of difficulty, write to us at the address
below with your name and address and the name of the
series. Please state with which title you wish to begin your
standing order. (If you live outside the UK we may not have
the rights for your area, in which case we will forward your
order to the publisher concerned.)

Standing Order Service, Macmillan Distribution Ltd,
Houndmills, Basingstoke, Hampshire, RG21 2XS, England.

Promoting Productivity in the Public Sector

Problems, Strategies and Prospects

Edited by
Rita Mae Kelly

MACMILLAN PRESS in association with the POLICY STUDIES ORGANIZATION

First published 1988

Published by
THE MACMILLAN PRESS LTD
Houndmills, Basingstoke, Hampshire RG21 2XS
and London
Companies and representatives
throughout the world

Printed in Hong Kong

British Library Cataloguing in Publication Data
Promoting productivity in the public sector:
problems, strategies and prospects.—
(Policy Studies Organization series)
1. Government productivity 2. Industrial productivity
I. Kelly, Rita Mae II. Series
350.1'47 JF1525.P67
ISBN 0–333–42191–4

The Policy Studies Organization gratefully thanks the Henry J. Leir Foundation for developing the set of papers that are included in this book on *Promoting Public Productivity in the Public Sector*. Particular thanks are owed to Henry J. Leir and his concern for increasing national and cross-national productivity. However, no one other than the individual authors is responsible for the ideas advocated here.

Contents

Notes on the Editor and Contributors

The Editor

Rita Mae Kelly is a professor at the School of Public Affairs, Arizona State University, Tempe, Arizona. She holds a PhD in political science from Indiana University, has served on numerous editorial boards, including *Evaluation Review*, *Women & Politics*, *Policy Studies Review*, and was issue editor for the *Journal of Social Issues* symposium, 'Productivity and Satisfaction in the Public Sector: A Socio-Psychological Perspective'. She has written several books, including: *Community Control of Economic Development* and *The Making of Political Women* (with Mary Boutilier). She is currently editor of the Praeger Series on Women and Politics (with Ruth B. Mandel), *Women and Politics: A Journal of Research and Policy Studies*, and is editor of the *Policy Studies Review* Special Symposium 'Productivity, Public Policy, and Societal Well-Being'.

The Contributors

David N. Ammons is Assistant Professor of Public Administration at North Texas State University. He is the author of *Municipal Productivity: A Comparison of Fourteen High-Quality-Service Cities*, and recent journal articles in *Administration and Society*, *The Bureaucrat*, and *Public Administration Review*.

Stephen H. Anderson is a doctoral candidate in the Policy Sciences Program at SUNY–Binghamton. He is currently a program analyst for the New York City Fire Department. His primary research interest is organizational classification.

William P. Brandon is an Associate Professor of Political Science at the Centre for Public Service at Seton Hall University, South Orange, New Jersey. His research focuses on the health care system and health policy.

Jeffrey L. Brudney is Associate Professor in the Department of Political Science at the University of Georgia. His fields of primary interest include public administration, urban politics, and research design and methodology.

Linda C. Dalton is an Associate Professor of City and Regional Planning, California Polytechnic State University, San Luis Obispo, California. Her research interests include public participation in planning and the structure and politics of city planning agencies.

Thomas C. Dalton teaches at California Polytechnic State University, San Luis Obispo, California. He recently completed his PhD in Political Science from the University of Massachusetts, Amherst, and is presently completing a book on *The State Politics of Judicial and Congressional Reform*.

Fred Englander teaches at Fairleigh Dickinson University in Rutherford, NJ, as an Associate Professor of Economics. He received his PhD in Economics from Rutgers University in 1975. He is a member of the editorial board of the *Public Administration Quarterly*. His fields of interest include the economics of crime, education, and anti-poverty programs. His current research is focused on the administration of US public assistance programs, the public employment service and the Unemployment Insurance system.

Valerie Englander is Assistant Professor of Economics at Saint John's University in New York City. She received her PhD in Economics from Rutgers University in 1975. Her fields of interest include the economics of health services, public program evaluation and the incentives generated by public assistance programs. Dr Englander is currently researching the behaviour of individuals who file benefit appeals in several income maintenance programs.

Robert T. Golembiewski is Research Professor of Political Science and Management at the University of Georgia. His research emphasizes designs for organizational change and study of their consequences. He has written or edited over 40 books and 200 professional articles and case studies.

Kim S. Hunt is Assistant Professor of political science at the University of Texas at Arlington. His current interests include state budgetary politics, intergovernmental policy implementation, and health policy.

Patricia W. Ingraham has been Commissioner of Planning and Economic Development in Broome County, New York, and is currently Assistant Professor at the Maxwell School, Syracuse University. She received her PhD from the State University of New York at Binghamton. Her current research interests include civil service reform, strategic planning, and other efforts to change public bureaucracies.

James Latimore is Assistant Professor of Sociology at the University of North Carolina. He received his PhD from the City University of New York. His research interests include the work ethic, employee stock-ownership plans, friendship factors and utopian communities. He is co-editor of a set of syllabuses used in teaching social theory and is the author of *Weeding Out the Target Population: the Law of Accountability in a Manpower Program*.

David J. Molta is a Teaching Fellow, doctoral student, and academic computing consultant at North Texas State University. His fields of research include urban politics, public personnel management, and political behaviour.

David R. Morgan is Director of the Bureau of Government Research and Professor of Political Science at the University of Oklahoma. The second edition of his text, *Managing Urban America*, was published in 1984. His research interests range from urban fiscal stress to school desegregation.

Stuart S. Nagel is a Professor of Political Science at the University of Illinois and a member of the Illinois bar. He is the secretary-treasurer of the Policy Studies Organization. His recent books include *Public Policy: Goals, Means, and Methods* (1984) and *Policy Evaluation: Making Optimum Decisions* (1982). He is the co-editor with Marc Holzer of *Productivity and Public Policy* (1984).

Dorothy I. Riddle is an Associate Professor in the International Studies Department of the American Graduate School of International Management, Glendale, Arizona. She teaches courses on the global service sector (public and private), comparative administration of non-profit organizations, and evaluation of program effectiveness and operations efficiency in services. Her research is focused on the role of services in economic development, with particular attention to the issue of productivity in services. Her most recent book is *Service-led Growth: The Role of the Service Sector in World Development* (1986).

Douglas H. Shumavon is Assistant Professor of Political Science at Miami University (Oxford, Ohio). He teaches a variety of courses in the fields of Public Administration and Public Policy Analysis. His current research interests include administrative discretion, governmental budgeting, and state regulatory politics.

1 Introduction: Success, Productivity and the Public Sector

Rita Mae Kelly

This chapter provides an overview of the anthology and introduces the basic themes and issues that are raised. With a special emphasis on the 1970s and 1980s, trends in promoting productivity in the public sector are reviewed. Emphasis is placed on the need to keep the well-being of the total society in mind when considering the improvement of public sector performance. The difficulties in transferring private sector models to the public sector are enumerated and placed within a framework highlighting the chapters that follow.

In the late 1970s and early 1980s it became commonplace to assert that government as well as business needed to be more efficient and productive. In order to remain competitive the United States needed to produce more goods and services with less. At first glance this suggestion seems simple and reasonable. A second and third look reveals considerable problems for the overall well-being of society if the effort to make the government more productive is implemented in a simple-minded way. Whereas in business productivity is associated with success in the marketplace and, especially, with profitability; in government, where profitability is absent, productivity becomes harder to identify and measure.

In the democratic system of the United States, government promotes and protects the private enterprise system and the liberty, pluralism, and individuality that is associated with that system. Neither the government nor the economic system are ultimate ends in themselves. Rather, each is a means to attain other valued ends (Committee for Economic Development, 1979, p. 10). The political and economic systems work together to produce the goods, services, and values of the society, and each, historically, has been judged by different criteria of success.

MEASURES OF SUCCESS FOR EACH SECTOR

Although we know the private and public sectors must work together and that they are different from each other in meaningful ways, we seldom compare systematically the objectives and criteria for success that exist for each sector. In order to understand productivity improvement efforts in the public sector it is necessary to begin by determining the criteria of success typically used for each sector. Because success is easier to define in the private sector we shall begin there.

THE PRIVATE SECTOR

In the private, market sector the basic unit of production and delivery is the firm. Survival and profit are its major objectives. The core of most strategies seeking success is to enhance the strength of the firm so that it will be more able to compete on its own terms with other firms.

To help managers and investors evaluate how likely the firm is to reach its objectives, various indicators have been developed: liquidity ratios, profitability ratios, activity ratios, and leverage ratios to mention a few key ones.[1] A firm will score high on these indicators and be most likely to achieve its objectives of survival and profitability if production is efficient. The principle of consumer sovereignity – at the heart of the capitalist market economy system – theoretically, at least, guarantees satisfying individual needs while allocating resources rationally among competing demands. The principle of productivity helps to ensure that only those firms which use resources efficiently and produce goods or services at the least cost will survive.

THE PUBLIC SECTOR

In the public sector, the local governmental unit, such as town, city, or county, is the basic unit for production and delivery of public goods and services. Unlike a firm it has no competitors within its legal territory. It is not expected to make a profit. While capturing a greater share of the market in the private sector leads to praise, usually success, expansion of territory by governmental units leads to conflict, sometimes war. Although some cities have expanded their tax base through consolidation with surrounding political entities, governmental units are less able to gain revenue and ensure their survival by 'expanding their market'. What can simply be corporate growth in the private sector becomes imperialism in the public sector. The standards for success are not the same.

How then do we know when our governmental units are successful?

To judge success it is first necessary to set an objective. For governments, broad objectives are usually set in constitutions or political manifestos like the Declaration of Independence. According to Thomas Jefferson, each generation should be required anew to set the objectives and standards of performance for government. Survival alone is insufficient as an objective. Throughout most of America's history succeeding generations have considered the government to be a success if it kept the peace, won the war (if the USA was at war), and promoted liberty and justice.

At its inception the American government was expected to be a relatively passive participant in the process of producing goods and services. George Washington was expected to function as the first president with a handful of administrative staff. 'That government is best which governs least' were Jefferson's watchwords. The government was to provide, basically, for a sound currency and a secure population. Initially these expectations meant that the government was to provide for the national defence, develop and implement foreign policy, a judicial system, and minimal mechanisms for promoting public well-being. While government was expected to create an environment conducive to developing an efficient capitalist economy, it was not expected to be intimately involved in that economy.

Much of the political history of the United States concerns this debate over how extensive the role of the government should be in society. Over 200 years ago Alexander Hamilton argued that a strong role for the national government was needed, particularly in the economy. As Secretary of the Treasury, Hamilton encouraged the national government to establish a bank, to use its taxing power to promote equality among the citizens, and to increase federal revenue. Others, such as Thomas Jefferson, however, argued the contrary: the government should limit itself to keeping citizens from harming each other. It should not become involved in more active efforts of production or distribution of goods and services. Nor should it regulate the economy. '*Laissez-faire*' meant to let the private sector alone, and that is what the United States government has done for most of its existence.

Changes in the Government's Role

A variety of events in the twentieth century have led to the expectation that United States governmental units, the national government in particular, should play a substantial role in the economy. These events included the adoption of the Income Tax Amendment, participation in the First World War, the Depression, the Second World War, the Korean War, the Vietnam War, the Civil Rights Movement, the Women's Movement, the Welfare Rights Movements, the changing role of the United States in world affairs, and continually rising inflation. Each of these major events have contributed to the expanded role of the government in production and distribution allocation decisions.

The turning point in modern American history was the New Deal of Franklin Roosevelt. The private economy was placed under numerous governmental regulations and controls as a means of pulling out of the Depression. The *laissez-faire* approach to economics was scuttled. The Roosevelt Administration recognized a national obligation to provide a cushion under the economic system and a concurrent obligation to protect citizens against the hardships of old age, unemployment, and an unregulated marketplace. Roosevelt was concerned with the preservation of the private market system through public efforts. At this time productivity and efficiency were less important values.

The imposition of the value of productivity on the government stemmed from three other changes. The first was that the sovereign citizenry by the 1960s included several organized and strong minority groups, and by the 1970s a politicized women's movement. Each group demanded that the public sector, the governmental units, compensate its members for past failures and errors made by both private and public sectors. New demands were made on the government and these groups had the political clout to get those demands met, at least partially. Secondly, the electorate was now predominately urban, living in politically important, but not always economically viable, population centres. Thirdly, partly because of the age of the cities, partly because of world economic trends and balance-of-trade problems, government economic policies promoting the market private sector economy, which had so well suited an under-populated nation in the seventeenth, eighteenth, and nineteenth centuries, no longer worked. The public sector was no longer providing an environment conducive to capitalist growth and a healthy non-inflationary productive market economy, particularly in its urban, densely populated North-east. Whereas in previous centuries the government had only to establish a Homestead Act and to stand aside to let development occur, in the twentieth century cities had to be torn down before 'progress' could begin. Urban renewal could not take place with *laissez-faire* policies that worked in an era of 'Manifest Destiny'.

Suddenly, in the 1970s the poor – the 'outs' of almost all descriptions – as well as economic conservatives and the business community were demanding 'productivity' – a business value – from the public sector. Everyone wanted more for less.

The Rising Concern for Productivity in the Public Sector

Americans have always had a practical concern for productivity, and this concern has been an impetus for scientific and technological advancement. In earlier years efficiency experts such as Frederick Taylor began observing, analysing, measuring and evaluating the effectiveness, efficiency and productivity of individuals and groups of industrial production workers.

However, by the 1970s problems of national productivity were receiving attention from the federal government, and some of that attention was devoted to the productivity of public sector workers.

Efforts to improve the performance of the enlarged public sector have been based upon two strategies: a market strategy and a performance evaluation strategy. Until the 1970s the market strategy consisted of two major thrusts. The first was to contract the production and delivery of goods and services to the private sector: The government administration would monitor the contract and pay the bills. In the 1980s the drive to privatize the delivery of public goods and services became intensified. The second thrust was to tax or add user charges on private transactions that had either positive or negative spillover effects on citizens or groups not involved in the private transaction. These levies would give actors in the private sector the incentive to pursue public objectives. Since the 1970s considerable effort has been spent on a third thrust, that being to try to create public sector entities that would be as similar as possible to the characteristics of the private sector firm in terms of intermeshing the demand and supply for public goods (see, for example, Buchanan and Tolleris, 1972; Buchanan and Tullock, 1971; Olson, 1973).

In addition to efforts either to utilize or to imitate the private sector, a performance evaluation strategy has been developed for the public sector, also based substantially on decision analytic techniques used in the private sector. In essence, concrete measurable goals and objectives are set for administrative units; and executives are expected to reward and punish public employees on the basis of their efficient attainment rather than on other, 'political', criteria (see Rivlin, 1971).

In recent years, private sector models of efficiency and productivity have been applied in the public sector by means of a number of different analyses: cost-effectiveness analysis, cost-benefit analysis, planning-programming-budgeting systems, operations research, and introduction of new incentive systems. These applications have been hailed by some as being instrumental in bringing about cost savings, more and better services and goods, and higher standards for workers and managers in the public sector. They have also been the focus of controversy and criticism, on grounds that, at best, they bypass the critical issues involved in the production and delivery of public goods and services, and, at worst, they yield a false precision that is misleading.

Objections to Transferring Private Sector Productivity Analysis to the Public Sector

The objections to transferring private sector notions of productivity to the public sector encompass concerns for conceptual differences regarding the meaning of efficiency in the two sectors, measurement difficulties, and concerns for the impact that ideology and politics have on the implementation of public policy.

Efficiency and effectiveness in the public sector

While arguing that greater productivity and efficiency by public agencies is desirable, some scholars (for example, Van B. Cleveland, 1979) question whether the concept of efficiency can mean the same in the public sector as it does when used in the private economic sphere. Indeed, even in the private sector the meaning of efficiency can vary with the area of application. The light bulb, for example, may be viewed as only 60 per cent efficient in producing light because 40 per cent of its energy is expended in producing unwanted heat. But traditionally economists have used the term 'efficiency' in a much broader way, and in a way that ties it to the utilitarian notion that value is entirely subjective. That notion, in turn, makes the application of the concept of efficiency in the public sector quite problematic.

Van B. Cleveland (1979) states the utilitarian view as follows:

> What has positive value (utility) or negative value (disutility) is entirely a matter of individual choice and taste. Thus, the utilitarians used the term 'satisfaction' and 'value' more or less synonymously. Together, these principles – that economic value is subjective, that it diminishes with the quantity of the goods consumed, and that the disutility of labor increases with the quantity of individual supplies – lead logically to the proposition that a free, competitive exchange of goods in a market will maximize the sum total of satisfactions (the excess of utility over disutility in the community).   (p. 142)

According to this utilitarian theory of value, individual utilities are non-comparable, non-commensurable, and totally subjective. Given these premises, it follows that no objective criteria for distributing social benefits, goods, and services can be established by any entity external to the individual (including government) that will allocate scarce goods and resources efficiently so that the greatest good for the greatest number of individuals will be obtained. Only by interacting in a free market can individual satisfactions be maximized with prices reflecting actual costs, benefits, marginal utilities, disutilities, and trade-offs. As Van B. Cleveland (1979) stresses: '*In short, the notion of economic efficiency includes not only an end (maximizing economic value or utility) but also a necessary means, a freely competitive market*' (p. 142).

It is obvious that the public sector does not constitute a '*freely, competitive market*'. Individuals do not subjectively choose specific public goods. Most public goods and services are delivered to collective units, such as families, firms, neighbourhoods, municipalities, states, and regions (cf. Lineberry, 1977). Socio-spatial political units, not individuals, are the negotiators for public goods and services. Nor do individuals pay for public goods on the basis of marginal utilities or costs. Most taxes (for example, income, property, and sales taxes) are paid independently of receiving specific public goods and services. The most significant decisions that most individuals make to affect what public goods and services they will receive occur when they choose a residence: the location of a house or an apartment within a given legal/political/geographical area determines, to a large extent, both the quantity and the quality of public goods and services that will be available to them.

These differences between 'the individual consumer' and 'the public' mean that, whereas efficiency and effectiveness converge readily in the private sector, they do not converge so readily in the public sector. In classical economics the focus of attention for the private sector is on 'allocative efficiency'; that is, on producing the best mix of types and amounts of goods so that consumer satisfactions are maximized. In this view, administrative or technical efficiency is less crucial and has a narrower focus; it is part of the act of production.

In the public sector, on the other hand, there is no profit and often no tangible product. Here, the term 'effectiveness' is somewhat comparable to the notion of 'allocative efficiency' as applied in the private sector. According to Leathers (1979, p. 65), effectiveness connotes 'maximization of net benefits from available resources'. Presumably these net benefits are received by many. When applied to a public sector organization, 'efficiency' tends to connote a quality of smoothness of internal operation and administration. There is a definite routine, clarity of authority and responsibility. But an 'efficiently' running unit may be completely ineffective in achieving the goals of that organization (say, the amelioration of poverty among the minority members of a particular neighbourhood), just as an efficiently running generator is ineffective if it is not connected to any functioning machine.

In terms of classical economic theory, the goal is to maximize satisfaction of the subjective demands of all citizens. In the public sector of a democracy, however, the rights, needs and wishes of minority groups and individuals need to be reckoned with as well as the needs and desires of the majority. Often the public sector is engaged in creating and delivering public goods and services that are not desired, needed or preferred by the majority, but rather are necessary for some particular group – such as the poor or elderly. Hence, the term 'efficiency' in its allocative sense is not easily applied. In such cases, we need a broader and more objective standard for evaluation than just maximizing the satisfaction of the subjective preferences of the aggregate of individuals as revealed through the market. Indeed, even if there is a strong consensus of individuals, such non-subjective standards are essential for acceptable allocation of public goods, because such allocation must take account of the abstract principles of liberty, merit, equality, and human rights.

Measurement difficulties

In the private sector, productivity is usually expressed as a ratio of outputs over inputs. Final goods or services are divided by resources used in production such as labour, capital, and land. To be useful, the ratio must permit comparisons over time, among competing firms or divisions, or among comparable products.

Attempts to transfer such productivity measures to the public sector have faltered not only because of the conceptual incompatibilities in the meaning of economic efficiency between the two sectors but also because of two unique characteristics of outputs in the public sector. The first characteristic is that public goods and services are often not divisible into discrete units. They cannot always be packaged so that only those citizens who want them, or those who pay their taxes, or those who are deserving, receive them. Once created, they become available to all. Of course, not all public goods are of this nature, but most are to some degree. Therefore, public outputs are harder to describe and price precisely than, say, a ton of coal or a loaf of bread.

A second unique characteristic of many government outputs is that they 'perish' the moment they are created and delivered. Consumption and production are almost simultaneous. Again, measurement becomes difficult and occasionally impossible (Ross and Burkhead, 1974).

To cope with these difficulties productivity experts have recommended distinguishing between direct outputs of the governmental unit and the consequences desired or occurring as the result of those direct outputs. For example, the number of arrests by a police department is a direct output, while having safe streets at night is the desired outcome or consequence. Some productivity experts have argued (see Greytak, Phares and Morley, 1976; Burkhead and Hennigan, 1978; Hatry, 1978; Hayward, 1976) that productivity analyses in the public sector should be limited, as far as possible, to the direct outputs. The rationale for this limitation is basically that the use of such measures is fairest to public employees, and that they are more measurable than the consequences. Government employees cannot control all of the factors contributing to public safety or to public health. The police can control the number of arrests they make, but they cannot force citizens to report crimes or to be witnesses in court. Doctors can vaccinate children against diseases but they cannot ensure that children wash their hands before eating, or do not drink contaminated water, or eat junk food and lead from paint on window sills. If public safety and public health (the desired consequence) do not improve, it is not fair, from this administrative efficiency perspective, to label public employees 'unproductive'. Their productivity, it is argued, should be measured on the basis of what they can do, what they can control, what they can increase or decrease. Productivity improvements cannot be made without such potential for administrative action. Although this last statement is true, citizens cannot be viewed as irrational if they think the government is wasteful, non-responsive and inefficient when the number of policemen and arrests increase but their feelings of safety decline.

Without belabouring the point further, measurement difficulties alone make the transfer of productivity as a dominant value to the public sector questionable. The incorporation of quality control and effectiveness measures with the administrative efficiency ratios can help correct these difficulties. None the less, productivity and efficiency can never attain the dominance in public sector as either decision-making or success criteria that they have in the private sector: the politics of implementation of public policy will not permit it.

The politics of implementing public policy

How one thinks about productivity in the public sector depends on whether or not politics is considered as a part of the implementation process. As Clarence Stone (1980) has pointed out, there are two conflicting paradigms guiding implementation studies: one from the field of political economics; and the other derived from a combined political sociological-psychological perspective. The former tends to concentrate on administrative efficiency and managerial control, and to exclude issues of politics and value trade-offs; the latter tends to see public bureaucracies caught within a swirl of continual politics and to view administrative efficiency as less interesting and less important than the value trade-offs problem. The political economy perspective attempts to translate economic efficiency criteria to the public sector; the political sociological-psychological perspective attempts to incorporate multiple values and effectiveness criteria into productivity analyses. Productivity indices based on output/input ratios and cost-benefit analyses stem from the classical economic perspective; client satisfaction, research and analysis of how citizens and government agencies together produce desired public outcomes stem from the sociological-psychological perspectives.

The political economy approach has a conceptual clarity linked with market and private firm views of efficiency. Its appeal depends on the assumption that goal-setting and the politics of allocating goods and services essentially ends when implementation begins. However, as students of reform movements are aware the 'control of the bureaucracy is itself a political issue and *analysis of the implementation process is an ideological weapon in an ongoing struggle for administrative power*' (Stone, 1980, p. 28). The political economy approach with its stress on productivity justifies the role of new professionals, highly trained middle-class and upper middle-class analysts. It denigrates the role – and value – of more populist approaches to government.

The political psychosociological approach, in contrast, stresses the lack of predictability in the implementation process. From this perspective, implementation implies modifying goals, adapting them to specific groups, places, and interests. The idealistic, vague goal established in policy settings in reinterpreted, made concrete, made liveable in the implementation process. Because of the low visibility at the implementation stage, original goals can be revised in fact, while they are never officially renounced. Political economists tend to view such political bargaining as a failure of bureaucracies, the source of technical inefficiences. Political sociologists and psychologists tend to identify such changes as a necessary part of a political system which claims that public policies are only means to a greater end of serving a sovereign citizenry.

Promoting Productivity in the Public Sector: Problems, Strategies, and Prospects

As can be seen, the topic of public sector productivity is a complex one. Interest in promoting productivity in the public sector has led to new problems and a variety of strategies for improving the implementation of public policy and the delivery of public goods and services. This anthology examines some of the more critical problems and strategies that have become apparent as a result of this effort. We focus attention on the following: organizational structures, policy environmental factors, program design, cost containment, value trade-offs, and human resources. A common theme of the contributors is that promoting productivity in the public sector often produces unintended organizational and programmatic consequences. While efforts to improve productivity appear to be able to flourish in a variety of policy environments, success in achieving policy and program objectives is more problematic. In the eyes of our authors the attempts to transfer efficiency and productivity concepts and tools from the private to the public sector have not been resoundingly successful. None the less, the more sophisticated understanding of the problems and strategies for promoting efficiency and effectiveness in the public sector provide a firmer information base for future implementation efforts.

A unique interdisciplinary policy studies perspective is offered which emphasizes the problems involved in the formation, implementation, and evaluation of alternative public policies designed to increase public sector efficiency and productivity.

In Part I, (*Efficiency, Performance, and Organizational Structures*) Thomas C. Dalton and Linda C. Dalton explore 'The Politics of Measuring Public Sector Performance: Productivity and the Public Organization' (Chapter 2).

This chapter develops a theory that explains why public organizations are subjected to multiple and competing measures of performance, and how the resulting pressures affect their development. The theory emerges from three points. First, the debate on productivity measurement may not be dismissed as simply a basic difference between public and private sector organizations. Not only does the point of measurement in the public sector differ fundamentally from the private sector, but the way organizational performance is measured helps constitute their structure. Second, several elements of organizational structure are identified which yield three models of public organization: bureaucratic routine, professional expertise, and collegial. Each model is associated with particular interpretations of productivity appropriate to its structure. Third, public organizations typically undergo a life cycle in terms of the pattern of ways in which their performance is measured as they alternate between periods of stability and periods of crisis. The extent to which an organization's structural form endures over time will depend on its leadership, political strength, and power within the policy system in which it is located. The authors also identify additional lines of inquiry suggested by the theory, such as the role and effects of federal intervention, factors significant in policy implementation processes, and the nature of institutional change, as well as implications of perform-ance measurement for representation in a democratic state.

Part II focuses on policy environmental factors, program design, and productivity. In Chapter 3, 'Productivity Emphasis in Local Government: an Assessment of the Impact of Selected Policy Environment Factors', David N. Ammons and David J. Molta address the concern for how organizational and policy environmental factors affect productivity efforts at the local level of government. Assessing a variety of organizational and community characteristics in a nationwide sample of jurisdictions, they conclude, as Dalton and Fitzpatrick do at the national level, that productivity improvement efforts are not dependent on any one policy environment or policy system. They also find that a relationship between the source of local government revenues and the degree of involvement of the jurisdictions in providing public utilities is related to the commitment to productivity improvement. Overall, however, they conclude that the policy environmental factors examined in their study explain relatively little of the variation found among jurisdictions in terms of their emphasis on productivity improvement.

In Chapter 4, 'Assessing the Relationships Between Program Design and Productivity', Patricia Ingraham and Stephen H. Anderson argue that accurate assessment of public performance and productivity necessarily includes consideration of those elements of program design and implementation which shape early perceptions of program intent and expectations for program performance. Suggested elements are participation in the design environment of the program, the nature of implementation strategy, and initial criteria for judging effective program performance. The authors also suggest that performance assessment would be simplified if programs had relatively clear, specific objectives and direct administrative controls.

The study in Chapter 5, 'Workfare in New Jersey: A Five-Year Assessment', by Valerie and Fred Englander, examines how changing the objectives and design of social welfare programs affects cost-effectiveness and goal attainment. It reviews the debate on the relative virtues of workfare, and describes the nature of the New Jersey General Assistance Employability Program. The central issue is whether efforts to subject New Jersey's General Assistance (GA) population to work requirements have generated sufficient reductions in transfer payments to justify the resources necessary to administer this reform. The methodology section develops a multiple regression-based model to explain changes in the size of the GA population based on economic and labour market conditions, seasonal variations, secular trends, the relative generosity of GA payments, and the presence of workfare. Although the authors found that the program did reduce the state GA roles substantially and significantly below what they would have been without the program, they suggest that several important issues remain to be addressed.

In Chapter 6 James Latimore explores the consequences of 'Indirect Provision of Government Services: Contracts and Productivity'. In this study the impact of the federal government on productivity in the private sector is examined by focusing on government services provided indirectly through contracts and reimbursement programs. The expressed interest of the federal government in productivity, and its attempts to encourage productivity increases, are contrasted with the more fundamental interests of the political system of the United States and the existing constraints that, at present, limit the federal government's ability to enhance productivity. A case study of a manpower program and an analysis of recent changes in the Medicare program are offered as examples of the 'productivity brake' applied by the federal government. Recommendations for increasing the ability of the federal government to have a favourable impact on productivity are derived from the examination of these two programs.

Part III examines how budgets and cost containment strategies can be used to promote productivity.

In Chapter 7, 'Obstacles to Doing More with Less: Illustrations from the Kansas Experience', Kim S. Hunt explores the connections between productivity and budgeting reforms. State budgeting reforms are often instituted with a strong desire to improve the productivity of state government. A decision-making framework is developed with which to analyze potential obstacles to successful implementation of budget reforms; examples from the Kansas experience illustrate the logic of the effort.

In Chapter 8, 'Why Government Cannot Contain Health Care Costs: An Interpretation of the United States Health Care System', William P. Brandon reviews definitions of concepts such as cost containment, productivity, and health, and examines the context of the health care system in the United States. Although the health care sector is seen as one of the largest 'industries' in the United States, the author thinks it is more appropriate to consider it as a distinct system with its own peculiar political economy. The discussion of 'productivity' and societal well-being provides an opportunity to consider why health care in the United States should be conceptualized as a system and to explore the implementation of the present health policy initiatives.

Part IV addresses some of the value trade-offs involved in promoting productivity versus stressing equity. In Chapter 9, 'Local Government Productivity: Efficiency and Equity', Jeffrey L. Brudney and David R. Morgan examine the possibilities for incorporating measures of equity into performance measurement at the local government level. After reviewing previous efforts to include assessment of quality and effectiveness, they explore two alternative approaches: the use of a measure of the severity of the pre-service problems of clients, and the distribution of services across client groupings. They conclude by asserting that these approaches facilitate the inclusion of equity as a coequal value with efficiency and effectiveness in public sector performance assessments.

Douglas H. Shumavon, in Chapter 10, uses a case study from Cincinnati, Ohio, to highlight the tension between productivity and social goals as they are manifested in procurement processes in local government. Shumavon uses a case study of the procurement function ('housekeeping' activity) to illustrate how a concern for social goals and equity can influence, usually negatively, efficiency efforts. He asserts, though, that social goals can be achieved even in organizational units noted for their efficiency ethos by providing incentives that allow for greater attention to those goals.

Part V of this book focuses on human resources and productivity. In Chapter 11, 'Public Sector Productivity and Role Conflicts', Dorothy I. Riddle describes the critical roles played by clients and employees in service delivery, as well as the common constraints on optimal participation. The author argues that less-than-optimal productivity is attributable to the complex role of the client both as a 'supervisee', coproducing services in a high-contact service delivery environment, and as a 'supervisor', evaluating satisfaction with the services delivered. An analysis of potential problems that arise from conflicting needs is included as well as a proposed framework for resolution. Robert T. Golembiewski, in Chapter 12, studies 'Policy Initiatives in Worksite Research: Implications from Research on a Phase Model of Burn-out'. Golembiewski offers an analysis of burn-out in terms of eight phases and the implications his findings have for policy-making. As individuals are assigned rankings upwards from Phase I through VIII on burn-out, certain patterns of association are evident: the quality of the worksite deteriorates significantly, physiological symptoms increase in non-random ways, and the trend of performance appraisals as well as objectively measured productivity is downward. The author suggests that these relationships imply the significant costs of advanced burn-out and also that they have two policy-relevant implications. First, technical features of the phase model contraindicate in significant particulars the major evolving policy posture concerning work – for example, the emphasis in *Work in America* on improving the quality of working life by job enrichment and heightened participation. Secondly, the data suggest the reasonable expansion of the concept of 'noxious and harmful' work to include psychological burn-out.

In Part VI, Stuart Nagel, in 'The New Productivity', presents some conclusions about promoting productivity in the public sector. Nagel's analysis of productivity leads him to conclude that we are entering a new era of productivity involving a partnership among: (1) the public sector of government agencies using tax reduction incentives to encourage productive behaviour; (2) the private sector of business firms taking advantage of those incentives to increase their productivity; and (3) the not-for-profit sector, including the academic world, seeking to develop new knowledge relative to improved technologies, industrial psychology, public administration, and other relevant fields. The implications of this kind of productive partnership are, the author points out, increased societal benefits and reduced societal costs, which in turn may greatly expand the cornucopia of societal rewards and lead to the next cycle of equalization and growth.

Note

1. The liquidity ratio provides information on how much working capital and ready cash a firm has available to respond to opportunities and changes in the market. The profitability ratios indicate the actual and potential earnings of a firm relative to total assets, total debt, and/or interest and taxes depending on the specific ratio used. The activity ratios offer insights into the relationship between the firm's net sales inventory, or tangible net worth, and total assets or total sales. The leverage ratios provide information on the firm's liabilities, net worth, and likelihood of obtaining additional debt and operating capital as needed.

References

Buchanan, J. M. and R. D. Tolleris (1972), *Theory of public choice* (Ann Arbor, MI: University of Michigan Press).

Buchanan, M. M. and G. Tullock (1971), *The calculus of consent* (Ann Arbor, MI: University of Michigan Press).

Burkhead, J. and P. J. Hennigan (1978), 'Productivity analysis: A search for definition and order', *Public Administration Review*, 38(1), pp. 34–40.

Committee for Economic Development, Research and Policy Committee (1979), *Redefining government's role in the market system* (New York: Committee for Economic Development).

Greytak, D., D. Phares and E. Moreley (1976), *Municipal output and performance in New York City* (Lexington, MA: Lexington Books).

Hatry, H. P. (1978), 'The status of productivity measurement in the public sector', *Public Productivity Review*, 38(1), pp. 28–33.

Hayward, N. (1976), 'The productivity challenge', *Public Administration Review*, 36(5), pp. 544–50.

Leathers, C. G. (1979), 'Language barriers in public productivity analysis: The case of efficiency and effectiveness', *Public Productivity Review*, 3(4), pp. 63–8.

Lineberry, R. (1977), *Equality and urban policy* (Beverly Hills, CA: Sage).

Olson, M. (1973), 'Public services on the assembly line', *Evaluation*, 1(1), pp. 37–41.

Rivlin, A. M. (1971), *Systematic thinking for social action* (Washington, DC: Brookings Institution).

Ross, J. P. and J. Burkhead (1974), *Productivity in the local government sector* (Lexington, MA: Lexington Books).

Stone, C. N. (1980), 'The implementation of social programs: Two perspectives', *Journal of Social Issues*, 36(4), pp. 13–34.

Van B. Cleveland, H. (1979), 'The meaning of efficiency', in T. Geiger, *Welfare and efficiency*, pp. 141–4 (New York: Macmillan).

Part I
Efficiency, Performance and Organizational Structures

Part II

2 The Politics of Measuring Public Sector Performance: Productivity and the Public Organization

Thomas C. Dalton and Linda C. Dalton

At a time when government budgets are being reduced and public organizations are being exhorted to improve their productivity, a probe of the language of performance appraisal is in order, for the way contests over the measurement of public performance affect the conduct of public organizations raises issues that are central to representation in a democratic state.

This chapter develops a theory to explain why public organizations are subjected to multiple and competing measures of performance, and how the resulting pressures affect their development. It considers 'productivity' as the latest in a historical sequence of terms used to address the question of how well public organizations function. The theory emerges around three points.

First, widely-debated questions about how to measure productivity cannot be dismissed simply as a basic difference between public and private sector organizations, nor as an issue tangential to organizational conduct. Not only does the point of measurement in the public sector differ fundamentally from the private sector, but the way organizational performance is measured helps constitute their organizational structure. Moreover, a typology of different interpretations of productivity may be applied to measure public sector organizational performance. Among these interpretations, there is no single best measure of performance; rather, the measures adopted serve some interests as opposed to others.

Second, several elements of organizational structure are identified which yield three models of public organization: bureaucratic routine, professional expertise, and collegial. Each model is associated with particular interpretations of productivity appropriate to its structure. The political environment and policy system with which organizations must contend limit their leverage over how their performance is measured. Consequently, since organizations may not appear to be successful according to measures which are imposed externally or by system counterparts, they will bargain for interpretations of productivity which best serve their interest. Third, public organizations typically undergo a life-cycle in terms of the pattern of ways in which their performance is measured as they alternate between periods of stability or equilibrium, and crisis. The extent to which an organization's structural form endures over time will depend upon its leadership, political strength and power within the policy system in which it is located.

Finally, we identify additional lines of inquiry suggested by the theory, such as the role and effects of federal intervention, factors significant in policy implementation processes, and the nature of institutional change, as well as implications of performance measurement for representation in a democratic state. The theory is developed from a wide range of literature from the fields of political science, economics, public administration and planning, and is illustrated by examples from three policy areas: criminal justice, employment and training, and higher education.

PUBLIC PERFORMANCE UNDER PRESSURE

Waste! duplication! overlap! red tape! In recent years the cacophony of voices raised in criticism of government performance has increased. Strident remarks surface from every political persuasion – ranging from Senator William Proxmire's 'Golden Fleece' awards through President Jimmy Carter's efforts to reform the federal bureaucracy, to Budget Director David Stockman's attempts to dismantle it. While the specific points of the critique may be debated, two basic questions are common:

(1) Why does government not perform its tasks more productively?
(2) What are the tasks of government?

Since the New Deal, liberal interests have been guided by the assumption that government has broad social responsibilities. Part of the agenda of liberal reform has been to improve government's ability to eliminate the sources of human misery. In contrast, conservative thought, most recently expressed by the Reagan administration, argues that government has failed either because it has tried to do too much, or because it has not been effective in doing what it is supposed to do.

Over the last few decades observers have tried to understand past social policy failures in order to improve future performance. Of course, lack of success in the effort to rectify past errors stems from the intractability of poverty, insufficient knowledge about specific problems, rising expectations, and inadequate commitment of resources. But even if we accept these limitations, we remain dissatisfied with deficiencies in delivery systems (for example, that clients do not get what they need when they need it, even when it is available in their communities) and with the use of public funds (for example, that so much goes into administration, duplicate services, or activities which do not appear to yield clear improvements in conditions).

In recent years, the assessment of public sector performance has been increasingly construed in productivity terms. First, strategies may be sustained to increase the effectiveness of social programs through administrative rather than programmatic change and still be consistent with the liberal reform agenda. Second, according to emergent conservative thought, public performance must be measured against the same standards as those used in the private sector.[1]

The assumption that government should work better has led to an exhortation to run government like a business. While this view dates back to populist and progressive reform of the early twentieth century, it expanded with MacNamara's application of private sector management principles to the US Department of Defense. Systems analysis, operations research, and program budgeting (PPBS) were introduced to government, followed more recently by Management by Objectives (MBO) and Zero-based Budgeting (ZBB). Thus, the recent focus on public sector productivity improvement is rooted in the administrative reform tradition in which structural reforms in representation processes have been combined with efficiency and effectiveness measures to make government more accountable and rational (Silverman, 1973, pp. 145–7).

Another impetus to the increased interest in productivity has been the need to evaluate public programs. Program evaluation has broadened the measurement of government performance to include questions about whether the purpose of public programs are appropriate, as well as how well program objectives are met as a result of the use of public resources (Deniston, *et al.*, 1972, pp. 142–3). Implementation analysis has been introduced to examine the extent to which intended results are achieved and why. Thus, interest in why programs succeed or fail has run concurrently with the introduction of managerial reforms, especially since the dramatic expansion of public sector social programs in the 1960s (Rivlin, 1971; Williams, 1971).

The contention has been, until more recently, that some *neutral* measure or combination of measures may be discovered and strategies deployed that will enable the creation of the broad-based political consensus necessary to achieve the ideals of efficiency *and* representation embodied in the administrative reform tradition. While critics of these efforts continue to penetrate appearances to uncover the biases and shortcomings inherent in such endeavours, the subtle ways in which the language of appraisal of public performance is implicated in the politics of administrative reform has generally gone unnoticed and unexamined.

Productivity improvement has been announced in many quarters as the preferred, if not inevitable, goal of the public organization of the 1980s. However, there is, as we shall show, far from universal agreement on what the term 'productivity' means. We present a review here of alternative uses or interpretations of productivity, in order to probe the sources of political contests over the application of the term to private and public contexts.

INTERPRETATIONS OF PRODUCTIVITY

While political demands for increased productivity in the public sector have grown, the term has assumed multiple meanings. In this section we present six distinct interpretations of productivity. The first five are derived from the literature about productivity and the sixth emerges as a logical addition to the set of meanings. We use the following terms to distinguish the six interpretations (ranging from most simple to most complex):

(1) Technical efficiency
(2) Instrumental efficiency
(3) Organizational effectiveness
(4) Allocative efficiency
(5) Social effectiveness
(6) Political allocation

Technical Efficiency

First, productivity may be defined in economic terms as the attempt to maximize output in relation to input. Economists generally call this notion of productivity technical efficiency, where efficiency is measured by the ratio of products or outputs to resources or inputs[2] or cost per unit (Balk, 1975; Ervin, 1978, p. 16; Quinn, 1978, pp. 41–2; Yamada, 1972, p. 765). Importantly, this definition *assumes* that the various production activities are relevant to the final products, but does not deal with them directly. Further, technical efficiency is concerned with increasing production or supply of goods and services, without regard to demand (Leathers, 1979, p. 64).

Instrumental Efficiency

Instead of characterizing productivity in terms of maximizing output with respect to input the emphasis can be reversed so that it is placed on manipulating inputs to achieve a given output. Stated this way, what is important is not so much the output itself but the various activities or processes by which inputs or factors of production may be combined to achieve *any given output* (Gilder, 1975, p. 7; Hamilton, 1972, p. 792; Hatry, 1980, p. 320; Hayward, 1976, p. 544; Kull, 1978, p. 6).

Although outputs will vary according to the combination of input factors, standards are required to compare or justify why one combination of input factors and the resulting level of output is more appropriate or desirable than another. There can be honest differences over what is appropriate, and thus the constituents of productivity may be complicated by normative variation.

In the private sector a new struggling firm that is heavily capitalized (for example, it carries substantial short-term debts in relation to other costs such as labour) will be most rational by choosing to make a return just below or at the break-even point in order, for example, to maximize tax breaks for depreciation of capital. Although it appears counter-intuitive not to maximize efficient use of inputs, maximization is not compatible with viable operation in the short run (Van de Ven, 1980, p. 126).

In the public sector, empirical evidence supports the idea that public service agencies will manipulate various input factors only to the extent that the results maximize or optimize agency self-interests (Yin, Heald and Vogel, 1977). Thus, the actual incorporation or adoption of an innovation (as one way to combine inputs) may be accomplished, but at the expense of maximizing output or service improvements.

Organizational Effectiveness

Human factors are of particular importance in examining how inputs are used to achieve results. Employee or staff motivation, the degree of staff development, participation, and consensus processes are all crucial to maximizing organizational effectiveness (Argyris, 1964). Incentive mechanisms do not just reward employees for increased output but provide recognition as a valuable person and encouragement of further self-development and respect. In the social services this implies retention of employees who are motivated not just for personal gain or security, but who are inspired by a sense of public mission to improve the status and circumstances of the less fortunate among us.

In the short run, it is probably rational for the new entrant into a product market to institute incentives and rewards system for its employees in order to obtain the loyalty and labour stability requisite to organizational effectiveness and short-run survival. However, over the long run, as the firm's fixed capital costs are absorbed (that is, paid off), prices for input factors, except labour, become more flexible. The inflexibility of labour costs (for example, because of unionization, cost of living increases) will prompt the firm to seek ways to reduce the fixed costs of labour through the introduction of capital-intensive technologies that produce cost-savings and productivity increases over the long run.

In contrast, over the long run, public sector organizations are constrained precisely in the area of labour costs savings. Civil service rules and public service unions constrain the fulfilment of legislative mandates and the stability of public agency budgets.

Allocative Efficiency

This notion of productivity has to do with the extent to which production processes approximate supply and demand conditions within the marketplace (Leathers, 1979, p. 64). This notion may be distinguished from other uses of the term 'productivity' in that efficiency may be maximized in the production of a good but its allocation may not reflect or satisfy actual demand conditions. Thus, productivity as technical efficiency or instrumental efficiency appears to be more directly applicable to explain the logic of short-run choices of private and public organizations to achieve a given level of output, but allocative efficiency is a long-run concept.

For instance, the fact that the production of US automobiles has reached 'saturation' point many times in our recent economic history is one such compelling example of mismatch between supply and demand. Moreover, the rush of new firms into a promising product area can produce short-run distortions or gluts that lead to unsold inventories and signal massive failure of new enterprises. In these instances, impersonal economic forces normally act to prune the market of excessive entrants and bring back eventual equilibrium of supply and demand (Whetten, 1980, pp. 347–8).

A public sector example here is the production of mass transit services for the benefit of low-income, lower-class, inner city residents, where actual ridership patterns appear to benefit middle-income and upper-income suburban dwellers, who escape bonds or other forms of taxation for payment of development of the service (Best and Connolly, 1976).

Social Effectiveness

One of the reasons public sector productivity is such an elusive term is because the idea captures not just efficiency considerations but those of effectiveness as well. In the public sector, effectiveness incorporates the direct measurement of quality or level of service (Adam, 1979, p. 27; Adams, 1975, p. 36) which is handled indirectly in the marketplace when poor quality ultimately reduces profitability (Balk, 1975, p. 9). Effectiveness goes beyond consumer satisfaction to include achievement of external or societal outcomes or objectives (for example, placement of clients in unsubsidized jobs, reduction of crime) rather than outputs (Deniston, *et al.*, 1972, p. 162; Ervin, 1978, p. 17; Mark, 1972, p. 748; Yamada, 1972, p. 765). Importantly, while consumer satisfaction with private sector goods and services cannot be reduced any further than to wants or preferences, it is commonly argued that what the public wants can be reduced to 'need' or 'interest'. Thus, the heroine addict or heavy cigarette smoker may want to continue the habit but society and public health organizations have found this not to be in the individual's interest.

Moreover, there can be tremendous variations in public attitude and opinion as to what is essential or necessary to ensure a viable and productive economy and liveable, desirable society, and thus, serve the public interest. Admittedly, honest differences in interpretation and morality arise here just because public programs typically serve multiple and sometimes conflicting goals and values. For example, employment and training programs are designed not just to find jobs for the 'disadvantaged' but to help employers fill job vacancies, reduce pressure on public schools to educate unmotivated and disinterested students, reduce opportunities for juvenile crime and, in an aggregate sense, increase economic and social stability.

Political Allocation

Given these cross-pressures and political realities that confront the public sector, it is evident that another way to view productivity is in terms of political accountability – or the composition of interests served by an organization or program. This definition of productivity depends upon the perspective, circumstances, goals and interests of the affected parties. The way that the burdens and benefits are actually distributed as a result of the political exchange and what that implies about the distribution of power is what is both essential about politics and what sets it apart from market activities.

In this regard, not only do persons or groups enter the political arena to advance or protect their interests but public organizations as well as private enterprises have compelling incentives to ensure their interests are represented in the political process. For example, private interests have criticized the delivery of social and economic services for ideological and practical reasons. In recent years criticism of 'welfarism' (for example, AFDC, Jobs programs) has escalated for both its insidious effects upon self-reliance and the 'work ethic' and for the perceived waste and dismal productivity record of such programs (for example, duplication, and fragmentation – Salamon, 1981). Thus, the private sector is wont to point out the ideological boundaries of acceptable public policy.

More pragmatically, private proprietary firms (such as OIC, Urban League, SER) have long attempted, but with little success, to break up the governmental, administrative monopoly of social services programs in order to increase their control of the delivery of such services. The extent to which such firms are discontented with such a secondary contractual status finds expression in the political process in which private service deliverers join the chorus of criticism emanating from the private sector that unrelentlessly chastizes public agencies for waste, fraud and, importantly, dismal productivity (for example, excessive, handcuffing regulations that prevent innovative service delivery, and contribute to duplication, overlap and the like).[3]

Interestingly, what is significant about this political exchange, upon closer inspection, is what it reveals about the interests of the contestants. For example, the Comprehensive Employment and Training Act of 1973 was designed to assist the disadvantaged through training, work experience, and pre-employment counselling to obtain unsubsidized employment. Until more recently, with the addition of the Private Sector Initiative Program (Title VII, CETA, 1978 – intended to increase co-operation between CETA and private employers), businesses have been reluctant to hire CETA participants primarily because the disadvantaged are not viewed as assets to increased productivity. To this day, business participation in CETA has been negligible for this and perhaps other reasons, such as red tape and costly regulations.

COMPARING THE USES OF PRODUCTIVITY: A RECAPITULATION

So far, several uses or senses of what we mean by productivity have been explicated. Each successive interpretation, while not intended to be an improvement over its predecessor, complicates the last in the sense that our notions about and the demonstrable comparability between private and public sector productivity become more attenuated and problematic. As shown in Table 2.1, we can distinguish the first four concepts as applicable to either the private or public sector (technical, instrumental, and allocative efficiency and organizational effectiveness) from the latter two as suited just to the public sector (social effectiveness and political allocation). Also, we can distinguish productivity measures which focus on internal operations of organizations (technical and instrumental efficiency and organizational effectiveness) from those that address the external relationships among organizations or between organizations and other social institutions (allocative efficiency, social effectiveness, and political allocation). Finally, we can characterize certain definitions as reflecting attempts to maximize outputs or outcomes with respect to inputs (technical efficiency and social effectiveness) or manipulate inputs (instrumental efficiency and organizational effectiveness), while others imply trade-offs or balancing (allocative efficiency and political allocation). As we move across the table the number and variety of variables included in the measurement of productivity increases.

THE POLITICS OF MEASUREMENT OF PUBLIC PERFORMANCE

As our review of alternative interpretations of productivity suggests, there is considerable debate today over the extensiveness of the definition. We contend that this debate is largely a function of the contested character of the concept itself (Connolly, 1974). Conceptual disputes arise when there is some play between the point, use and context. Thus, we argue that it is misleading to say that there is a right or wrong definition of productivity (or, for that matter, right or wrong way to measure performance). Rather, the conventions that regulate the use of the concept need to be identified in order to reconcile the contested elements of productivity, as they are utilized in private and public

Table 2.1 Interpretations of productivity – summary

	Technical efficiency	Instrumental efficiency	Organizational effectiveness	Allocative efficiency	Social effectiveness	Political allocation
applicability to public vs. private sector	private or public	private or public	private or public	private or public	public only	public only
measurement of internal operations vs. external relationships	internal	internal	internal	external	external	external
variety of complexity of factors measured	maximize output	manage inputs and activities or processes	emphasize human input factors	balance supply and demand	emphasize multiple outcomes	balance benefits and burdens among interests

contexts, to permit a deeper understanding of the politics involved in the measurement of public performance.

In this section we shall demonstrate how competing uses of productivity originate from conventions which regulate their application in particular contexts. That analysis will uncover how each interpretation of productivity isolates certain contextual features or meanings rather than others; show how the point explains application to market and non-market contexts; and demonstrate how political forces help explain why some of the measures used to appraise public performance must necessarily entail values which are central to a democratic state.

Finally, we shall examine how political contests over the meaning and point of productivity contribute to an explanatory theory of the structural transformations that public organizations undergo in response to conflicts over their performance.

The term 'productivity', like other measures of public performance is used differently depending upon the context. Conventions help govern correct and incorrect usage and ensure that intended meanings are communicated. However, the fact that linguistic conventions are tacitly held rather than explicitly acknowledged makes violations both likely and soluble (Wittgenstein, 1953). Further, it is possible for rules or conventions to change over time, as contexts change (for example, environmental, organizational, cultural, political, or economic conditions), but the process is gradual and, at times imperceptible.[4] In fact, as our later discussion will suggest, changes in the political forces and economic conditions with which public organizations must contend, combined with pressures to establish new measures of public performance, may precipitate changes in structural factors which account for an organization's characteristic form.

Most of the concepts from which we draw to measure or evaluate private or public performance serve to *appraise* the value of some acknowledged accomplishment (Connolly, 1974, p. 10). Contests over such terms are particularly interminable for two related reasons. First, terms of appraisal permit a variation in application to the *same* context because of the lack of consensus on their normative content. Second, as a consequence, such terms exhibit an open texture, in which new uses or interpretations may be added to existing ones to justify characterizing a situation from the point of view of some interests rather than others. Proponents of a political ideology, for example, often argue for a change or expansion of existing political vocabularies in order to gain recognition of a burden or injustice that otherwise would go unacknowledged. We may characterize a firm's performance as profitable or unprofitable, its utilization of resources (such as labour, capital, energy) as productive or unproductive, or innovative or non-innovative. While some of our ways of appraising private sector performance find expression in public sector contexts (for example, productivity, innovation, and others), we may characterize an organization's implementation of public policies as just or unjust, equitable or non-equitable, coercive or non-coercive, or representative or unrepresentative. While most of these values may be utilized as measures of public performance and embody in varying ways what we consider to be essential to the governance of a democratic state, the exact features of what constitutes a 'just' or 'representative' state, for example, remain essentially contested.

There are at least two features of the logic of appraisal that help capture the 'point' of a concept in relation to use in context. First, as we have noted, there are several alternative ways to appraise performance. But importantly, what distinguishes one from the other, is not just the context. For the features of the context pertain only to broad conventions which govern the way we distinguish between, say, profitable individual actions and those of a firm (in these two cases it is a matter of scale and complexity). And as we have argued, context is only of limited value in these instances. Rather, what comes into play to distinguish alternative appraisals is the point of why one measure of performance is chosen over the other.[5] The point of measuring the conduct of a firm in terms of profitability is, for example, to isolate those aspects of performance that permit certain judgements about the conduct of firms which inhabit the same industry. In these instances, profit refers to the net earnings of each firm or firms within an industry. But the point changes when productivity is used instead of profitability. For productivity refers not to earnings but rather, broadly, to the ratio between inputs and outputs or the efficient and effective use of resources to achieve any given output. Moreover, to characterize the entire economy as productive or unproductive involves contextual features which are different again from the behaviour of a given firm. Thus, the point of the two terms differs precisely because they isolate different features of a shared context. Moreover, as we shall argue below, the participants in a political conflict trade upon this variability of the point of focus in a particular context to advance their favoured measures of performance.

Second, although private sector uses of the term 'productivity' may apply to public sector contexts and, in some instances, carry the same conventional meanings of appraisal, the internal complexity of the concept and differences between the conduct and purposes of the firm and of the public organization combine to establish very different points involved in the measurement of public performance. For, as we have shown, the conventional usages or interpretations of productivity found in private sector contexts may be employed (without contradiction) in the measurement of public performance. However, there are some additional interpretations of productivity which seem only to apply to public sector contexts.

The structure of the concept helps account in part for why the applicability of the universe of terms used to characterize productivity tend to function in this fashion. In any context, the concept of productivity appears to comprise three elements of a state of affairs common to its various uses as follows:

(1) accountability for results;
(2) an acknowledged achievement of appropriate work done; and
(3) a relationship between factors used and results achieved.

Taken together these elements constitute a framework that governs the application of the concept productivity. As such, they perform two crucial functions. First, they define the limits of the interpretations of productivity by providing the conditions both necessary to establish meaning in alternative contexts and sufficient to distinguish the point of usage. Second, and more importantly, these elements can be used to explain the similarities and differences in the application of productivity to public and private contexts.

As we suggested earlier, private sector interpretations of productivity tend to be limited to internal measures of productivity (for example, technical or instrumental efficiency), while public organizational applications focus on external measures such as social effectiveness, because such purposes are dictated in part by legislative mandates. The differences in emphases suggest a way to compare private and public context in terms of the conditions enumerated above. If we were to draw comparisons between private and public sector uses of productivity with respect to the common elements of the framework above, they would exhibit the relationships shown in Table 2.2.

The comparison reveals that, although the framework is shared, the emphasis differs because of the contrasting purposes of market and political activity. The private sector focuses on profit as the ultimate indicator of all the elements common to the concept of productivity.

On the other hand, an essential purpose of politics is to strike an acceptable relationship between the distribution of power and affected

Table 2.2   Distinguishing private and public sector productivity emphases

Common elements of productivity	Private	Public
Form of accountability	profit market criterion	political representation (multiple masters with multiple goals)
Appropriateness of results	acceptability measured indirectly through long-run marketability and profit poor quality shows up as profit penalty	explicit measure of quality distribution of goods and services
Relationship between factors and results	factors of production balanced to maximize profit	democratic values (e.g., justice, equity representation) or other interest served in achievement of results

interests. Importantly, persons, groups and organizations enter the political arena much as they do a marketplace, to bargain for change or protection of their interests. But unlike the marketplace, where the consummation of exchange leaves the power status of the buyer and seller relatively unchanged in the short run (that is, at equilibrium), the results of the political conflict may both redistribute power among the participants and result in a differential distribution of burdens and benefits between the contestants. This is not to say that politics is necessarily a 'zero-sum' idea of power, for each contestant may benefit from an exchange. The fact that the initial distribution of power among the contestants may be unequal is not intractable, but may be subject to change as a *result* of compromise. Thus, the way that the burdens and benefits are actually distributed as a result of the political exchange, and what that implies about the subsequent distribution of power is what is both essential about politics and what sets it apart from market activities.[6]

The mechanism of public accountability, which public performance must serve, is also complicated by the contests over political structures and processes thought to best serve the functions of representation. For example, it is often disputed whether improvements in productivity will, in fact, enhance representation of the public interest (or at least make public organizations more accountable to public officials). What contributes to the conflict is that opponents involved in the dispute may advance different interpretations of productivity. For example, some may argue that increased organizational effectiveness will be sufficient to increase or enhance representation of affected interests while others contend that representation can be more effectively served through changes in program strategies (social effectiveness) or redefinition of recipients targeted for assistance (political allocation).

Resolution of disputes such as these cannot be achieved merely by appeal to the results of evaluation data. For not only do alternative policy and program evaluations provide ambigious if not contradictory assessments of outcomes or achievements of policy innovations, but they fail to address issues central to the governance implications of public performance in a democratic state. We shall elaborate more about this contention later.

Further, conceptual disputes are not only manifested in the language or rhetoric of public debate but help form the practices and behaviour which they characterize. There is a necessary connection between language and action for several reasons. In the sense that human action is, in part, intentional (motivated by purposes), a correct understanding of the motivations for (or intent of) given actions contributes to an understanding of the context. On the one hand, it permits the initiator to form reasonable expectations about how actions may be received or interpreted and, on the other, limits the range of judgement exercised by the respondent necessary to interpret the actual intent that the communication conveys. The stakes involved in political relations, however, increase the incentives to disguise intentions through deceit or manipulation. As a consequence, the relative power position and intentions of participants are likely to be disguised in order to gain leverage over the consequences that may result from the changes in the measurement of public performance.

In another respect shared meanings render human practices more comprehensible and predictable in institutional settings. This is so for two reasons. First, through their (non-deceptive) application, linguistic conventions produce a regularity and predictability in human inter-actions, including that of political exchanges. When such conventional foundations are modified or completely revised, the opportunities for institutional change increase, and, thus, the likelihood of political reform.[7]

Finally, because language and the conventions which govern its use constitute, in problemmatic ways, the actions and behaviour it characterizes, measures of public performance which endure over time (for reasons we shall discuss below) are reflected in structural characteristics which give an organization its unique form or configuration.

To be sure, we do not argue here that the outcomes of conceptual disputes alone account for (that is, are sufficient conditions for) programmatic or organizational change. Rather, the continuous contests over performance measures which go on over time contribute to two related phenomena we shall discuss later:

(1) they shift the burden of evidence of performance away from some interests towards others; and

(2) they help reconstitute organizational structures in ways that are compatible with the revised performance measures.

To recapitulate the argument thus far, several independant factors give the measurement of public performance a distinctively political character. Political conflicts over measurements of performance originate, in part, from contests or disputes over the interpretation of productivity in particular contexts. While such uses share some conventions, the conventions are shared *imperfectly* because of substantial political differences over the point of their usage. And, what determines the purposes of application of the term 'productivity' are importantly, the *interests* which are to be served by appraising public performance in a particular way. Thus, what distinguishes or gives public sector applications of productivity their unique character (compared with private sector usages) are differences in the interests served by various mechanisms for public accountability.

PRODUCTIVITY AND ORGANIZATIONAL STRUCTURE: THREE MODELS

Observers of organizational behaviour (Allison, 1971; Downs, 1967; Elmore, 1978) have acknowledged that organizational structures shape the perspectives and behaviour of unit members towards their external environments in ways that produce predictable responses to the policy environment. While this literature has produced many new and useful insights, for example, about the relationship between organizational structures, decision-making processes and implementation routines, or innovation processes, it has failed in most instances to provide ways to clearly distinguish organizational structure from instances of unit member behaviour (with the exception of Yin, Heald and Vogel, 1977). Further, the applicability of their typologies is limited by the policy areas from which they are drawn and the purposes of their analysis. The terms 'behaviour' and 'structure' must be defined more precisely in order to allow an empirical investigation of the relationship between productivity measures and organizational structure. Moreover, clarification of these terms also suggests that a distinction between organization and system is needed in order to advance any theory of public organization. (We use public organization to refer to any formal government agency or publicly-chartered social units.)

By organizational *structure*, we mean a framework within which a common set of expectations are established with respect to the governance, staff composition, decision-making, roles, tasks and routines involved in the execution of an organization's mission. The elements of structure and their configuration in alternative organizational models will be discussed in greater detail below (Yin, Heald and Vogel, 1977, p. 69).

In contrast, organizational behaviour captures a very different idea. We define *behaviour* or *action* to consist of the way unit members, particularly leaders, interpret/react towards and reconcile internal goals and administrative policy with external demands and interests in the exercise of discretion involved in the execution of tasks.

One implication of the distinction advanced here is that although structure and behaviour are interrelated or may interact, structural forms are likely to endure regardless of unit member behaviour. For structure exerts a strong influence on behaviour by virtue of the inclusiveness of the elements that condition the relations among unit members (see Table 2.3). Structural elements are more resistant to change because they account for the distinctiveness of a particular organizational configuration over time. Behaviour may also influence structure, but it does so largely as a result of the responses to external conflicts that arise periodically over the measurement of an organization's performance. Our theory proposes the following relationships between organizational structure, behaviour and productivity:

(1) Public organizations may be classified as one of three types or models based on their predominant structural characteristics;
(2) There is no *unique* interpretation of productivity that is most closely associated with a particular organizational structure; but certain measures are more politically rational than others for each model;

Table 2.3 Structural characteristics of organizational models

	Bureaucratic routine	Professional expertise	Collegial
typical organization	police regulatory agency public utilities	planning departments LEAA state planning agency Offices of prosecution CETA prime sponsors social service agencies	judiciary university hospital
goals			
mandate	legislative mandate	(federal) legislative mandate	general societal purpose
specificity	focused, legalistic, specific	multiple, specific	intangible
policy approach	regulatory or direct service	programmatic or client-oriented	direct service
governance			
authority	elected officials or autonomous department head	elected officials or mixed board of elected officials serving ex officio and appointed representatives	elected officials or appointed board representative of special community interests
decision and communication structure	extensive hierarchy	administrative hierarchy	administrative hierarchy
staff access to policy and administration	low staff access	moderate access regarding policy, not administration	high access regarding policy, not administration

staff composition and roles

professionalization	low (unionized or in craft or trade)	moderate to high (including nascent professionals)	high, specialists experts
occupational status	low status	moderate status	high status
management background	management from within the trade	general management, usually political appointment	mid-level management from within the discipline; high level general managers
discretion	high discretion in applying policies; roles locked within routine	high discretion, little routine	autonomy
diversity of tasks, incentives, etc.	low diversity	moderate–high diversity	high diversity
formalization of roles	high formalization	low–moderate formalization	low formalization
productivity interpretation under stable conditions	technical efficiency instrumental efficiency	instrumental efficiency social effectiveness	social effectiveness organizational effectiveness

(3) Contestants within and outside organizational settings will perceive the mandates and goals of an organization differently and thus contribute to the uncertainty of organizational responses to external pressures regarding the measurement of performance;
(4) While centrifugal pressures mount over time to expand the terms of performance appraisal to emphasize external measures, centripetel forces react to contain performance appraisals to internal measures.

At the risk of proliferating definitions, one final term needs to be introduced here – the idea of 'system'. The term 'system' is most commonly associated with a model or explanatory construct of politics advanced by David Easton (1965) to depict the way in which public demands are translated into policy decisions. Instead, we shall use 'system' to mean something quite different – that is the policy area in which an organization operates. A system is constituted by at least two or more organizations which vary along structural lines and share a common pattern of historical and institutional practices and involve a set of interdependant functional relations which are joined by a similar policy focus. The concept of system is best understood as capturing a set of dialectical relationships (or tensions) between organizations divided by dissimilar structural characteristics (which include its performance measures), but joined by a common pattern of inter-organizational relations. When these relations take on regularity or routine from repetition over time, they may form a practice. When combined with other practices around a similar policy goal, an institution is formed (for example, educational or employment and training institutions). There are two important reasons why system needs to be defined in a descriptive rather than an explanatory sense. A descriptive definition does not preclude investigation of the variety of interactions that may occur between organizations within a system, or organizations or sub-unit members and external interests or even between systems. Next, system defined in this way permits investigation of the ways in which the conceptual, dispositional and structural aspects of political conflicts influence and condition (over time) the historical patterns and institutional practices of organizational structures, as they are manifested in the politics of the measurement of public performance.[8]

An examination of public sector organizations using the definition of structure explained above, suggests three typical structures: bureaucratic routine, professional expertise, and collegial – each labelled by its most distinguishing feature (that is, task discretion, staff composition, and governance, respectively). Each of these models is described briefly below, with its main structural characteristics and the interpretations of productivity associated with it. The characteristics of each model are summarized in Table 2.3.

Bureaucratic routine refers to the kind of public organization that fits the popular stereotype of governmental agencies. Its characteristics are well known (Allison, 1971, pp. 77–8; Downs, 1967; Elmore, 1978, p. 199). Briefly, the bureaucratic routine model describes an organization whose purposes are defined in terms of providing public goods or controlling (through regulation or enforcement) externalities of private behaviour. Organization unit members are accountable to elected public officials, but usually through relatively autonomous department heads appointed from within the substantive field or agency. Employees are typically unionized and may be trained in a specific trade or craft – for example, police guilds. In addition, this organization type has a centralized or hierarchial communication and decision-making structure, a limited variety of tasks and incentives (diversity), and rigidly specified roles formalization (Yin, Heald and Vogel, 1977, p. 69). However, the key distinction of this model from a pure, mechanistic type is how discretion and routine are balanced in conducting daily activities. Discretion is dispersed among lower-level employees who tend to resist any attempts to increase control over their work or change the routines upon which their tasks are based (Elmore, 1978, pp. 200–2). Police departments and regulatory agencies in general are typical examples of bureaucratic routine organizations. State employment security services, public utilities, and public works departments also fit this model.

These organizational characteristics tend to foster interpretations of productivity in terms of technical efficiency. They do so in the sense that task outputs lend themselves to quantitative measurement – for example, number of arrests or permits issued, garbage collected, streets improved, and so forth – and thus total output provides the easiest measure of performance.

A second interpretation of productivity by which bureaucratic routine organizations may measure their performance is instrumental efficiency. For example, regulatory agencies cannot control the number of applications for permits so their productivity may appear to decline when fewer applications are filed. Interestingly, both police work and land use regulation, where an emphasis on *due process* impinges upon the way in which the work is done, require greater attention to the nature of the procedures by which output is achieved. The way that due process rights are incorporated within routines or standard operating procedures become the 'right' way to do the work, and thus may reconstitute characteristics of the bureaucratic routine model.[9]

Our second model, professional expertise, represents some characteristics of Weber's rational-legal structure but emphasize special professional staff characteristics (Etzioni, 1964, p. 76). Such organizations often trace their origins to federal legislation which established both programs and new organizations to execute them (for example, CETA prime sponsors) but also include offices of prosecution and a variety of non-profit contractors. Those organizations which are artifacts of federal programs are accountable to a representative board which, if a public agency, may include elected officials serving ex officio and appointed members (usually nominated by the executive and confirmed by the legislative body).

The professional expertise organization typically has a centralized administrative structure but overlapping task structures enable greater staff influence over how policy is made and programs develop. As indicated by the label, the staff is professionally educated, but enjoys only a moderate occupational status because they are from emerging professions like planning and public administration (Mann, 1979). Tasks are diversified but not rigidly allocated among employees, and employees have substantial discretion in how they perform their duties. Managers may have limited technical backgrounds or be politically appointed generalists. Professional expertise organizations tend to employ rational or systematic policy-making processes (Allison, 1971, pp. 32 – 3; Elmore, 1978, p. 191). Social services, prosecutors' offices, and planning agencies, including special purpose ones like LEAA and CETA, are all archetypal professional expertise agencies.

Social effectiveness is most easily identified with this model because federal mandates enunciate explicit social purposes for programs they execute. Further, this measure of productivity is consistent with the public service ethic of professionally educated staff, who often advocate social equity and redistribution of power and resources for disadvantaged groups.

The measurement of the performance of professional expertise organizations may also be construed in terms of instrumental efficiency. For example, citizen participation and staff training in community relations and small group dynamics represent an emphasis on process, whereby procedures supplant outputs as a way that planning efforts may be judged.

Collegial organizations represent our third structural model. The mission of this organizational type is dictated by broad societal purposes. The collegial organization is typically governed by either an appointed board (who represent selected community interests) or a joint decision-making body (for example, court justices) and has some kind of hierarchical administrative structure. Administrative staff may influence decisions through a formally acknowledged role or in decentralized policy-advisory bodies below the chief executive(s). Staff are specialized professionals or academics with high occupational status. Mid-level managers are appointed or elected within decentralized functional areas while top-level managers may be generalists. Staff enjoy a high level of autonomy both in how they conduct their work and in control of their schedules. Tasks, incentives, and rewards are diverse, but roles are not rigidly defined, with work groups and interdepartmental (or interjuristictional) task forces exercising responsibility for many organizational functions. Collegial organizations are typified by universities, hospitals, churches, the judiciary, and some research institutions.

Social effectiveness is also commonly associated with collegial organization because social purposes are typically involved. Broad mission statements allow individuals to adopt a variety of decisional approaches, research, and innovation strategies which may produce a variety of results.

Organizational effectiveness also has some utility as a measure of the performance of a collegial organization. Staff expect to derive not only remunerative benefits but also satisfaction from participation, public recognition, and gratitude (for example, from former students or patients) for services rendered.

There is a significant reason why none of the organizational models exhibit a relationship to allocative notions of productivity. The three models maintain their own characteristic performance measures because they are most congruent with internal structural characteristics and provide the greatest degree of internal control over appraisals of performance. Allocative efficiency or political allocation among interests surface during periods of time when an organization undergoes external political pressures aimed at levering these measures to gain important concessions or benefits from the organizations to serve some interests as opposed to others. Under these conditions, organizations are naturally uncomfortable with productivity measures which challenge their mission or independence.

Thus, where external pressures mount for external measures of organizational performance (for example, allocative efficiency or political allocation), a crisis is likely to occur in which the organization will undergo structural change. Although these external pressures may invoke utilization of 'internal' productivity measures (such as technical efficiency within a collegial organization) the new measures may not only be inappropriate to its mandated goals or purpose but may reduce the leverage the organization or its unit members may exercise over the way its performance is measured.

POLITICAL CONFLICT, BARGAINING AND ORGANIZATIONAL LIFE CYCLES

A critical barometer of when an organization is undergoing pressure to change how its performance is measured is the degree of bargaining that occurs within the organization and between it and other units. Thus, in contrast to other recent organization theory, we argue that bargaining and conflict (Elmore, 1978; or for governmental or bureaucratic politics, Allison, 1971) is not a distinct *structural* model, rather we contend that external and system pressures are necessary (although not sufficient) conditions for bargaining and conflict *behaviour* to occur within an organization.

When the public organization enters the bargaining mode, both the administrator and unit members place a premium on self-interest and survival. While in this mode, the organization is highly susceptible to 'divide and conquer' tactics utilized by external and other system interests (or some combination of these) because of the uncertainties and risks associated with the common or mutual defence of organizational mission, productivity measures, and structural configuration. However, over the short run it is likely that a strong administrator (in conjunction with other supportive alliances) will secure unit member support sufficient to present a united front against the antagonistic interests that surface, for example, during legislative reauthorization debates. Unit member support is particularly likely when the short term is clouded with doubt and the relative power position of the external interests and system rivals is uncertain.

The likelihood of success, in the short run, of a strategy intended to preserve the organizational mission, performance measure, and thus its structure is determined by the extent to which those activities under the control of the organization under pressure can be maximized (for example, budget, programmatic areas of control, and clientele) and burdens minimized. Moreover, as a corollary to the latter idea, to the extent possible and politically feasible, the organization under pressure will have greater incentives to ensure that the burdens inflicted are redistributed or deflected as much as possible towards system counter-parts or rivals. Such burdens may be minimized by, for example, weakening the relative power position or program responsibilities, undermining the productivity emphasis, or increasing co-ordination burdens of its system competitors. Thus, the short run will be characterized by adaptive-conflictual efforts to unhinge the rivals and displace the external threats.

However, over the long run if pressures mount and conflict becomes intractable, new productivity measures take hold, programmatic em-phases are shifted, and regulatory tools are diluted, shifted, or withdrawn; the unit members are more likely to be split from common conceptions of the agency mission and undertake separate and isolated bargaining strategies with external interests or system rivals in order to secure personal security and survival. Under these circumstances, the organization is more likely to undergo structural transformation, or alternatively, disintegration (for example, legislative abandonment or transfer of staff and functions to another agency).

Another characteristic of an organization propelled into a bargaining mode is that the measure of its performance or productivity is in a state of flux; both interests internal and external to the organization, including system counterparts, will each attempt to gain the maximum leverage or influence over how the organization's performance is measured. As we demonstrate below, there are multiple examples, from life cycle histories of each organizational model, of periods of organiz-ational stress punctuated by tugs-of-war over appropriate and/or acceptable measures of performance. Obviously, such conditions can reinforce organizational confusion, demoralize and drive unit members from mutual defence strategies and soften leadership to the point of premature capitulation.

The life cycle of an organization is revealed by the pattern of ways in which its productivity is measured as it alternates between periods of stability and times of crisis. Depending upon its internal structure and characteristics, such as leadership and political strength, an organiz-ation may influence how it moves from a period of crisis to a new equilibrium.[10]

The characteristics of organizational life cycles are captured by the following propositions.

(1) During periods of stability certain expected or politically rational measures of productivity may be associated with each organiz-ational model.

(2) These interpretations of performance are ones over which the organization has strong internal control.

(3) When external environmental pressures mount, they impose new interpretations of productivity (allocative efficiency and political allocation) which are external measures of performance. Environmental forces include the national political and economic climate, especially legislative mandates and executive or judicial interpretations; the immediate political and economic climate in which the organization functions; and the way in which federal–state–local intergovernmental relations are handled (Hayward and Kuper, 1978; Mann, 1980, p. 357).

(4) A second factor that creates pressure for new productivity measures is the policy system or industry in which the organization works (Yin and Yates, 1974, p. 196).

(5) The use of external productivity measures as a result of environmental and system pressures tends to disrupt an organization and leads to bargaining and conflict behaviour.

(6) As a result of political bargaining an organization may be able to maintain its structure and preferred measures of productivity or it may be transformed into a different model using the measures of performance appropriate to equilibrium conditions for that new model.

(7) Factors that help account for or explain why an organization may go in one direction or another include its political power or status within the policy system, and its leadership, age, size, past success in fulfilling goals, and the presence of 'slack' which gives it flexibility (Downs, 1967, p. 88, 193, ch. 9; Kimberly, 1980a, p. 28; Miles and Randolph, 1980. p. 50; Nelson, 1978, pp. 35–6; Yin, Heald and Vogel, 1977; and Zaltman *et al.*, 1973).

While the factors that create pressure for changing the interpretation of productivity are similar for all public organizations, each model responds differently because of its unique set of structural characteristics. Each model exhibits a life cycle which represents the usual or most likely pattern an organization will traverse when external forces move it away from equilibrium through a period of transition and crisis (when external measures of productivity are required) to a new equilibrium. The pattern for each model is illustrated in Table 2.4.

The bureaucratic routine model is the most stable and resilient under external pressures and consequently has the least complex life cycle. Typically, the cycle begins with a strong emphasis on technical efficiency

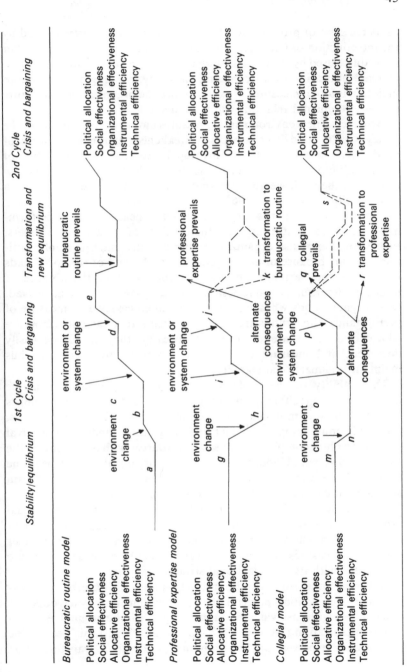

as its measure of productivity. Environmental changes precipitated by the introduction of new legislation or judicial rulings, intended to alter procedures used by the organization in meeting its mandate, will tend to increase utilization of instrumental efficiency. So long as it is able to maintain internal measures of performance the organization's structure and environmental relations will remain stable.

However, if new environmental pressures mount or the capacity of the policy system to deliver services is weakened, external measures of productivity are likely to be instituted. Because of the ability of bureaucratic routine organizations to be highly resilient to new directives, they will weather externally precipitated crises and reach a new equilibrium (Downs, 1967, p. 197).

In professional expertise organizations, the measurement of perform- ance tends to centre around the notion of social effectiveness. Professional expertise organizations periodically undergo public criti- cism, in part because of a multiplicity or ambiguity of the social ends they serve and variability of results achieved.[11] In the absence of political consensus on what desirable social goals should be achieved, these organizations will adopt instrumental efficiency as a measure of performance – how funds are expended, clients are treated, students are educated or cases are disposed of – because they can more easily document and measure the quality of service provided and thus maintain organizational stability.

The stability of the professional expertise organization may be threatened when either recipient groups or other attentive publics challenge the way in which resources are allocated. In these instances, leadership must adopt a conflict and bargaining mode as a survival strategy to blunt competition for scarce resources with other units in the same policy system. Under these conditions, organizations will be prone to maximize advantages and minimize burdens by deflecting criticism and its political consequences towards system counterparts.

Two different results may occur. One outcome is that a professional expertise organization with strong political power and effective, innova- tive leadership will bargain successfully to get a new mandate under which new measures of social effectiveness may be proposed which are compatible with its organizational structure.

However, under other conditions, the professional expertise organiz- ation may lack political power in the policy system, or may have aged so that concern with survival undermines support for the original purposes of the organization (Downs, 1967, pp. 19, 22). When this occurs, the professional expertise organization may undergo a transformation toward a bureaucratic routine organization by accepting a new definition of its goals that can be measured in terms of technical efficiency. Concurrently, if other critical structural characteristics change, it may become more hierarchical (for example, as a line department) and the role of the policy board may decline or change. Job descriptions may become more formalized and routine takes over. If changes in staff composition are thoroughgoing, the transformation from professional expertise to bureaucratic routine will be consummated. On the other hand, if the organization's political strength is quite weak, and the agency young, the organization itself may be eliminated, or some of its functions absorbed and routinized by other organizations with greater strength in the policy system.

Our final model, the collegial organization, illustrates yet a third set of interdependent relations between structure, environment, and performance. Since the goals of collegial organizations are typically characterized by intangible social purposes, its performance may be measured by social effectiveness. However, we contend that what makes a collegial organization different from the other two types is its governance structure. For, under stable conditions, the extent to which a collegial organization is successful is dependent on how effectively it is organized to make policy decisions. Collegial organizations must rely more heavily upon participative, co-operative and collaborative strategies in order to govern themselves and produce results *because* unit members have a high degree of autonomy.[12]

As with the previous two models, though, external factors may impinge upon its policy space in ways that put pressure on its external performance. As a result, collegial organizations may compete with other organizations in the policy system which are affected by the same environmental forces and bargain for continued survival within the parameters of political allocative processes.

The integrity of the structure of collegial organizations will tend to prevail and enter a new period of stability, if it is strong within the policy system and has effective leadership. However, if environmental pressures are sufficient to narrow its mandate, then the collegial organization may gravitate towards or be transformed into a professional expertise model.[13] Moreover, as the goals come to be specified externally, staff autonomy and participatory decision-making structure are likely to be modified. In these instances, professional staff become proportionately more important and a general management background is valued over promotion or hiring from within the field or discipline. Under such conditions, a new equilibrium may be realized in which performance is measured according to social effectiveness or instrumental efficiency.

APPLICATIONS

Bureaucratic Routine: Police Organizations and Productivity

Police organizations are often cited as the epitome of the bureaucratic routine model in that they exhibit a tight hierarchical structure, prescribed routines, structured but flexible discretion, and a minimum of staff participation in administrative decision-making. Herbert Packer (1968) has advanced two alternative ideologies or goals available to police; the Crime Control Model (CCM) and the Due Process Model (DPM).

Significantly, Packer's model closely parallels actual tensions precipitated in law enforcement by judicial intervention in the administration of criminal justice and thus marks a recent point of departure in the life cycle of police organizations.

The CCM approach is based on the premise that repression of criminal conduct is the most important function being performed in criminal justice. Thus, successful law enforcement depends upon high or maximum rates of apprehension, and finality of disposition (for example, sentencing), and must ensure that such activities are executed with dispatch and are both uniform and final with respect to minimizing occasions for challenge or appeal. Importantly, the pivot upon which the model turns is the 'presumption of guilt' (for example, 80 to 90 per cent of all cases are settled by plea bargaining where a lighter sentence is exchanged for a guilty plea), as the operational expression of the confidence of an efficient law enforcement system.

The CCM is closely associated with a legalistic style of policing in that it is defined by a strict interpretation of the law, centralized organization, and standards for recruitment and training of patrol officers within a common pattern. Stated in the context of the notion of technical efficiency the outputs (for example, number of cases cleared by arrest and conviction) are given priority over the means (for example, combination of inputs) to achieve a given end (see *a* in Table 2.4).

While the CCM model closely approximates an assembly line, the DPM is best characterized as an obstacle course. Each successive stage of the criminal justice process (starting with the obligatory pre-arrest and post-arrest 'Miranda Rights', rules of evidence and others) places primary emphasis on the rights of the accused over an efficient but potentially unjust disposition. Thus, there is a presumption of innocence.

Consequently, the DPM variation of bureaucratic routine can be equated with the notion of instrumental efficiency (see *b* in Table 2.4). This is so because the overriding concern of the DPM is to ensure that the standards which govern various activities of law enforcement and criminal justice are maintained, not to guarantee a guilty plea, but to ensure that the right or appropriate disposition is meted out. The means are considered to be far more significant than a given end in the sense that a person should only be deprived of liberty when there is a fairness of procedure, completeness of evidence, and exhaustion of appeals.

Two external factors help explain which approach will be paramount at a particular time. First, at the national level rulings like the *Miranda* decision or a resurgence of 'law and order' values will move policing toward the DPM or back to a CCM approach (Wasby, 1970; Milner, 1971). Secondly, to the extent that police chiefs and sheriffs are elected, candidates for the job must enunciate their views about crime and the justice process and be accountable to the community for their subsequent performance. Periodic fluctuations between harder and softer lines towards crime can be accommodated by police organizations because performance according to either set of values can be measured as technical or instrumental efficiency, either of which is compatible with the structure of a bureaucratic routine organization.

Productivity measurement for police organizations becomes more problematic when other external pressures arise. For example, passage of the Crime Control Act (1968) in response to increased crime rates has thrust police into an allocative dilemma in which pressures mount to expand more resources to apprehend 'career' criminals (*c* in Table 2.4). But 'revolving door' justice (for example, lenient sentencing practices) may undermine such goals by ensuring the almost immediate return of convicted criminals to the community through probation or suspended sentences.

The conflicting policy effects between police and courts, which originate from differences in organizational structure and goals, may be minimized when performance measures are in tandem (for instance, when police maximize apprehension of wrongdoers and the courts support swift and certain punishment for those convicted). Or, such conflicts may be exacerbated (as in the case where police arrests for possession of drugs are maximized but prosecutors refuse to bring charges). Moreover, the consequences of productivity emphases undertaken at the front end of the criminal justice process may undermine or be counterproductive to the actions taken at the back end of the system, where for example, prison populations reach critical levels of over-crowding because of increased arrests and longer prison sentences (see *d* in Table 2.4).

Under these circumstances, police organizations may be frustrated in attempts to meet an identified public need because of conflicting practices or priorities in other elements of the criminal justice system. As a consequence, such policy concerns are translated into political conflict in the legislative arenas where, for example, many states have passed determinant sentencing laws which routinize a set of expectations among police about post-arrest actions (see *e* in Table 2.4). Such policy changes may contribute to a new balance among the units in the system, and thus enable the police organization to revert to utilization of measures of technical efficiency, given a new set of more predictable standards for disposition of criminal offences (see *f*, Table 2.4).

PROFESSIONAL EXPERTISE: LEAA, CETA AND PRODUCTIVITY

Examples that we believe closely approximate to the professional expertise type are the State Planning Agencies, which were established to plan and administer law enforcement assistance (LEAA) grants under the Omnibus Crime Control and Safe Streets Act (1968), and the Prime Sponsor Organizations designed to plan and administer federal block grant funds to localities under the Comprehensive Employment Training Act (CETA, 1973).

Both CETA and LEAA programs were launched in climates of high tension (recession for CETA and a law-and-order period for LEAA) and thus, there were anxious public expectations that something immediate should be done to reduce unemployment and crime. However, monies were expended so rapidly (especially by LEAA for hardware) that serious doubt was cast upon the effectiveness of such choices for crime reduction or system improvement (see *g*, Table 2.4). Critics charged that a one-sided emphasis on law enforcement expenditures threatened civil liberties and undermined due processes (Center for National Security Studies, 1970; Navasky, 1976).

Moreover, because the CETA program was launched just at the onset of the national recession (1973–4), the Title VI 'public service jobs' program was grafted on shortly thereafter as a countercyclical subsidized jobs program. This not only escalated expenditure rates but resulted in a gross imbalance of appropriations for Title VI in subsequent years and nearly swallowed the original intent of CETA, which was meant to be a training and pre-employment assistance program for the disadvantaged (Van Horn, 1979; Mirengoff *et al.*, 1980). Following the initial glut of spending, prime sponsors became more concerned (given federal prompting) with documenting eligibility and ensuring that services were provided to clients (see *h*, Table 2.4).

Moreover, both LEAA and CETA organizations have had to face allocative crises because of an inability to demonstrate external results (for example, neither crime rates nor unemployment substantially declined). During the mid-cycle years of the LEAA program (for example, 1972–8) conservatives and liberals grew increasingly critical. Not only had crime not been reduced, but it was increasingly evident that numerous deficiencies within the criminal justice system seemed largely to account for the inability to get results (for example, prosecutorial discretion, inadequate information co-ordination, administrative standards, sentencing practices, prison overcrowding) – see *i*, Table 2.4.

LEAA and the state planning agencies responded to these pressures with innovative and experimental projects (for instance, using computer technology) designed to determine which functions of the system were most amenable to reform and thereby most promising in terms of potential improvements in output. Significantly, this was a period marked by nearly exclusive emphasis upon strategies of interorganizational co-ordination as a cure-all for the ills in the criminal justice system (Marchand, 1980; Skoler, 1977). Similarly, as the CETA program has undergone re-examination, interorganizational strategies have been attempted, such as a wide variety of demonstration projects designed to co-ordinate the employment training system (see *j*, Table 2.4).[14]

However, through the end of the mid-cycle, both the LEAA and CETA programs (for example, for LEAA 1978–80; for CETA 1979–81) and their organizational artifacts (such as SPAs and prime sponsors) have come under new political pressures which, in the case of LEAA, have resulted in the near abandonment and, in the case of CETA, have led to legislative reorganization. For example, during the time between 1977 and 1980, the LEAA and state planning agency programs came under increased scrutiny as to whether the block grant had really fulfilled pressing needs or demand for the level of expenditures provided. Of course, President Carter's order that the LEAA federal regional staff be called back to Washington, DC, in early 1977, was an important early warning of things to come. In addition, the acrimony surrounding the 1978 reauthorization of the Crime Control Act of 1968 and the intense bargaining by the courts and correction components to increase their percentage of resources relative to the other components were driving criminal justice organizations further away from strategies of mutual planning and co-ordination. Thus, disputes over allocative issues and the relative distribution of power and policy control began to dislodge and dismantle the LEAA program and its state level organizational interest structure.

Indicative of this pressure was LEAA's more desperate but somewhat limited success in its attempt to mandate state statutory recognition of SPAs and privacy regulation of criminal records information system. The idea was that if the various pieces of the program could somehow be institutionalized at the state level, then this would be insurance against the closure of LEAA (Marchand, 1980). The LEAA strategy here, had it been successful, would have transformed the LEAA structure into a model of bureaucratic routine. The extent that LEAA has failed to be successful accounts for the substantial cuts in its budget allocation, reorganization within the department of justice and the vastly scaled-down purpose and policy agenda (see *k*, Table 2.4).

In the case of CETA, a similar scenario has unfolded. The prime sponsor system has been replaced by a new organizational hybrid fashioned out of the Title VII Private Sector Initiative Program (see *l*, Table 2.4), called the Job Training Partnership Act (1982).

One impetus behind efforts to judge CETA's performance has been private sector alarm and criticism of the growth of the public service jobs (Title II and VI, CETA), which critics argue, is not the intended purpose of CETA. Moreover, it is contended that such a trend has had deleterious effects on the ability of the private sector to attract workers, substituted subsidized jobs for 'real' jobs, made government the employer of last resort, and generally undermined the foundations of private enterprise. Such criticism found its way into the centres of power and thus has led to the defunding of Title VI of CETA.

In another important respect, with the passage of the Title VII of CETA in 1978 (The Private Sector Initiative Program, or PSIP) and its emphasis on allocative efficiency, the private sector critics of CETA have driven another wedge between CETA and its legislative mandate. This is so because the PSIP program has been launched to bring about greater 'co-ordination' between CETA prime sponsors and the private sector;

heretofore, it is argued, CETA has been largely unsuccessful in matching employers needs with skilled workers – in other words, supply did not correspond with actual demand. As a consequence, business interests are more comfortable subjecting CETA to such market tests or even better, to productivity notions (technical or instrumental efficiency) that have more direct application to private sector contexts. Evidently, the private sector has not demonstrated any more aptitude in achieving better results by these same measures.[15] One result of this conflict is the resurgence of the State Employment Service in its control over employment and training programs, (see *k*, Table 2.4).

COLLEGIAL ORGANIZATIONS: UNIVERSITIES AND PRODUCTIVITY

Social effectiveness fits the classical university as its measure of productivity although, as shown in Table 2.4, it may be subject to environmental pressures that induce utilization of other efficiency measures which propel the university toward adoption of the structural characteristics of professional expertise organizations.

It is not easy to characterise exactly what higher education produces and how its results contribute to better private or public performance. One reason for this is that education has been expected to deliver not only creative and productive workers (for example, innovative and skilled) but also numerous intangible, cultural, social, and civic benefits such as well-adjusted, co-operative, helpful citizens, active in civic affairs and supportive of democratic processes, rights and values. The diversity of disciplines and course offerings makes it easier for some departments to demonstrate a more direct relationship between curriculum and social productivity (see *m*, Table 2.4). Moreover, the survival of many of the arts and humanities is dependent upon such courses being core requirements for entry level students, for various departmental majors and for undergraduate degrees.

University governance structures account for the second measure of productivity appropriate to consensus management organizations – organizational effectiveness (see *n*, Table 2.4). Faculty participation in policy-advisory roles through departmental and college committees, rank and tenure procedures, and curriculum development is long-standing. Further, faculty are recognized for many non-teaching roles, especially research and consulting work, civic contributions, and administration. Thus, the measurement of university performance is, in part, a function of how effectively diverse units can co-operate in joint government processes.

The GI bill following the Second World War precipitated an allocative crisis for higher education because it greatly expanded access, previously limited to the financially secure or those who had demonstrated ability (see *o*, Table 2.4). A college education became necessary to upward mobility and occupational success. This required an enormous expansion of plant and faculty and, of course, administration, especially in public universities. Concurrently, corporate and governmental interests found great appeal in tapping academia for research and consulting needs. Such forces produced two principal effects: (1) a departure from the priority of teaching as the basis of academic reward; and (2) a gradual transformation of university structure resulting from internal pressures for disciplinary specialization, productivity for externally-marketed research, and rationalization of administrative functions (Barzun, 1981). Federal involvement in education has been instrumental in instigating the latter two trends; the federal government is the primary source of university based research and increased intergovernmental regulation has greatly enlarged university administrative functions (Morgan, 1981) – (see *p*, Table 2.4).

In response to these external pressures, during the 1960s the university structure came under new tensions and pressures generated from within. Students wanted 'relevance' and only loose curricula, faculty and students demanded participation in university decision-making processes and some coalitions of both groups insisted that the university sever its ties with business and government. Thus, social effectiveness was elevated to the loftier heights of political responsibility. As a result of these forces many universities have undergone (during the early and mid-1970s) stages of bargaining and conflict during which two divergent paths have been followed. Traditional liberal arts schools with strong academic leadership redefined social effectiveness through adoption of 'relevant' innovative and interdisciplinary programs, and maintained organizational effectiveness by expanding faculty and student participation in decision-making (the Evergreen State College, or the University of California at Santa Cruz) – see *q* in Table 2.4. In contrast, many state universities and community colleges have adapted to external occupational demands and sponsored community service projects (for instance, through Title xx of the HEA, 1965) that are more akin to the professional expertise organization (see *r*, Table 2.4).

Since that time (late 1970s, early 1980s), external pressures have begun to reshape the universities' agenda and organizational form through a second allocative crisis. There has been a substantial drop in enrolments (which is expected to become more precipitious) as children of the baby boom after the Second World War have graduated. This drop, combined with federal funding cuts and state budget shortfalls, has forced streamlining within universities, where 'efficiency' and other similar jargon has replaced the niceties of the liberal arts education (see *s*, Table 2.4). Moreover, saturation of the labour market for those with a college education in the 1970s and continuing credentialization now creates pressure for educational institutions to either divest themselves of all but the marketable core (for example, business and engineering) or take the plunge. Thus, the professional expertise organization model would appear to hold greater promise for the survival of a university caught in the pivot of such cross pressures. Under such emergent circumstances, the university of the future may have more in common with the CETA prime sponsor, a vocational school, or a consulting firm than with the classical university of an earlier era. It is possible under these circumstances that what will be cultivated is not the ideals of creativity, self discipline, and citizenship, but career adaptation, market discipline, and civic obligation.

NOTES FOR FURTHER RESEARCH

In this chapter we have advanced a broad theoretical framework with which to understand factors that contribute to the politics of measurement of public performance. As such, the theory implies that several key relationships hypothesized between external interests, productivity measures, and system and subunit factors could be tested under empirical conditions. We suggest additional lines of inquiry for empirical investigation of the relationship of the politics of public performance to organizational reform and institutional change.

Further research would contribute to an understanding of several questions or issues implicated in current studies of policy implementation. These issues include, but are not limited to:

(1) the nature and role of federal intervention;
(2) factors significant in accounting for the likelihood and extent of adoption or implementation of these innovations;

(3) the possibilities for realizing an institutional change from adoption of policy innovations; and
(4) the implications of such changes for the prospects for representation and other values central to the governance of a democratic state.

It is commonly argued that federal initiatives are necessary to induce state and local policy innovations. Reasons for this include the necessity for federal funds to cover start-up costs and serve as an incentive to otherwise indifferent and conservative state–local interests. Until recently, federal policy innovations have been largely restricted to programmatic as opposed to structural approaches. However, the shift from categorical to block grants beginning with the 1970s marked an increased emphasis upon structural rather than program innovations. These structural emphases, like administrative reform precursors, not only seek to improve public performance, but also to advance basic changes in governance patterns, especially federal intergovernmental relations.

The theory advanced here provides a way to examine the significance of the federal role in advancing structural reform in two ways. First, the theory specifies in precise terms the reasons for and conditions (for example, when external pressures mount for allocative efficiency) under which federally induced structural innovations are likely to occur. Second, the more detailed elaboration of the characteristics that constitute an organizations's structure and policy system may enable a more careful examination of which elements of structure and thus which organizations within a system, are more or less amenable to change through federal intervention, and how such structural differences support or constrain changes in policy and governance patterns. Moreover, ancillary issues may be explored, such as the interdependent effects between programmatic structural innovations.

Students of policy implementation are concerned with identifying those factors that help explain why things happen as they do. The literature is divided as to whether policy performance can be measured as something traceable to original statutory objectives (in cause and effect terms) or, rather, to non-statutory, intervening factors which are themselves subject to contextual variations. Thus, either policy performance is considered immutable and measurable against some fixed standard (see, for example, Lowi, 1979; Sabatier and Mazmanian, 1980) or it is relative; that is, its effects are subject to variable interpretation depending upon the signficance of influences of various non-statutory factors (Elmore, 1979). Two non-statutory factors considered to be very significant by some recent observers (Dolbeare and Hammond, 1971; Stromsdorfer, 1981; Van Horn, 1979) are organizational characteristics and dispositions of implementors closest to policy execution. In this regard, our theory hypothesizes an important relationship between the language and politics of performance appraisal, organizational structure and the behaviour and dispositions of unit members. It suggests that an exploration of the way in which the measurement of performance, whether originating from federal grant conditions of aid or from other sources is *interpreted* by organizational leaders and unit members, may provide a fruitful line of inquiry of how such responses contribute to intergovernmental variations in the adoption of structural policy and performance.

An issue which is related to but goes beyond that of performance is the extent of institutional change that may occur as a result of the adoption of policy innovations. Recent studies of the effects of policy innovations in public bureaucracies (Yin, Heald and Vogel, 1977) find numerous instances in which innovations are adopted but performance fails to improve and little institutional change occurs. Moreover, as Dolbeare (1974a) argues, policy innovations are largely limited to small-scale adjustments in 'output', typically leaving untouched in most instances the contours of 'fundamental policy', which persist and endure unchanged.

Our theory suggests one avenue to confront these issues more squarely. We have contended that public organizations are more likely to adopt (under conditions of equilibrium) internal rather than external measures of performance. They do so because internal measures increase the leverage that an organization may exert over the way it delivers its goods or services and, thus, the way the results of that delivery are appraised. Federal policy innovations aimed particularly at structural change appear, according to our theory, to be linked to external measures of performance. This connection between federal intervention and particular types of performance measures raises some interesting questions for investigation. For example, how do the results of federally initiated structural interventions compare in terms of the possibilities of institutional change to those initiated by states or localities? What difference does it make for the possibilities of change, that regulatory conditions are attached to federal grants provided to stimulate state and local innovations? (See Neiman and Lovell, 1981, for data regarding the role of federal mandates, which is a good first step in this regard.) Further, how do such conditions of aid affect the politics of the external interests with which organizations must contend? Finally, what difference does it make if policy innovation originates from courts rather than legislatures in terms of the likelihood of organizational reform being achieved?

Finally, as we observed earlier, instances are rare in which the implications of effects of policy innovations, construed in quantitative terms, are drawn in terms of governance implications. To be sure, the continued obedience by some to the objectives of discovery of *neutral* mechanisms with which to advance administrative reform and appraise its results, helps account for this failure. The strategy of collective goods theorists (for example, Bish and Ostrom, 1973; Ostrom, 1971) is to provide objective, rational criteria by which to appraise the results, for example, of experiments in consolidation of local services or governmental units. Such data are used, in turn, to support judgements about the governance implications of structural reforms. What this and other research strategies miss, however, is that the criteria of appraisal they wish to advance are very much bound up with political contests over the measurement of public performance. Moreover, researchers' predispositions which favour certain dimensions of scale and boundary of political units in relation to service delivery, tend to close inquiry to the very questions that need careful, empirical examination – such as the relationship between performance measures, structural innovations to better co-ordinate service delivery, and representation of affected interests.[16]

In a polity where a plurality of democratic values is the rule rather than the exception, it is indeed premature to attempt a reduction of the measurement of public performance to reflect some values or interests to the exclusion of others. Thus, our theory invites research to examine ways that we may compare the results of policy innovations originated and initiated in a variety of institutional contexts, so that we may draw a closer connection between the promise of reform, institutional change and the goals of a democratic state.

Notes

1. Three additional factors reinforce recent concern with public sector productivity. First, as government budgets and employment have increased, the overall computation of productivity nationwide is influenced more and more by the productivity of public sector employees (Adam, 1979, p. 27; Peterson, 1972, p. 745; Rosenbloom, 1973, p. 156). Second, since the 1930s, government has become increasingly a direct provider of services as well as a

regulator of private economic activity so it must now be subject to scrutiny as a producer (Gilder, 1975, p. 8). Finally, the concentration of needy populations in central cities, aging urban physical facilities needing major repair or replacement, and inflation, have contributed to fiscal crises and taxpayer revolts (Bahl and Burkhead, 1977, p. 254).

2. Inputs may include all factors of production – for example, capital, technology, and energy as well as labour (Adam, 1979, p. 27; Hayes, 1977, p. 6; Hayward, 1976, p. 544; Mark, 1972, p. 748).

3. As a reading of the congressional hearings held in 1972, which ultimately launched the CETA program, indicates, Leon Sullivan, founder of Opportunities Industrialization Centers (OIC) of America, lobbied intensively, but unsuccessfully for OIC affiliates to administer CETA funds instead of the present CETA Prime Sponsor organizations. This defeat, according to one veteran CETA administrator for whom one of the authors worked in 1975, exacerbated bad feelings between OIC affiliates and the Employment Service, for example, that was successful in acquiring a contractual role with prime sponsors which empowered it to manage training referrals and monitor job placements of OIC and other subcontractors. More recent evidence of conflict between contractors and CETA includes a report that SER-Jobs for Progress, a major Hispanic-American contractor for CETA programs recommended that Prime Sponsors be scrapped in favor of a state run jobs program (Employment and Training Reporter, 1982a).

4. With a thoughtful metaphor, Wittengenstein in *On Certainty*, likens the durability of conventions that underly our ever-changing and open-textured concepts to that of the relation between the water's surface and riverbed:

> But I distinguished between the movement of the waters on the riverbed and the shift of the bed itself: though there is not a sharp division of the one from the other . . . . And the bank of that river consists partly of hard rock, subject to no alteration or only to an imperceptible one, partly of sand, which now in one place, now in another, gets washed away or deposited. (1969, p. 15)

5. In *The Terms of Political Discourse*, William Connolly argues that terms we use to appraise human achievement imply or embody a shared moral point of view. The point may be grasped, for example, by understanding the way we distinguish mistakes or inadvertant actions:

> There are an indefinite number of ways of making a mistake (for example, dropping a book, losing a key, mispelling a word, misconstruing a point). But in each case where we say a mistake has been made we characterize an act from a broadly normative point of view; we assert, by the use of the term, that the act has certain criteria or characteristics in the light of which we have some reason to excuse the agent, or to mitigate his responsibility for the outcome of the act . . . . If someone doubts this, we must ask: what role, then, does mistake play for us? Why does the concept have these particular contours in our language and not others? (1974, p. 24).

Thus, in our example, the use of the term 'profitable' or 'productive' creates the space in which judgements can be made about whether factors in production were combined in correct ways to secure the desired achievement. Importantly, it is the *context* in which these terms are used and the standards internal to shared institutional practices they embody, that capture the *normative* point shared by those who are located in a mutual context. (See Alasdair MacIntyre's *After Virtue* for an extremely insightful elaboration of this notion.) To support this idea, think of ways we distinguish between profit and non-profit organizations and how the features and contexts differ between these two cases; or reflect upon the ways in which what is considered within the sphere of market activity has expanded and contracted through time. It is these contextual features, in addition to normative points of view, which help us decide whether to characterize something as profitable is appropriate in terms of appraisal.

6. Surely we acknowledge that market exchanges are motivated in part to secure an advantage in terms, for example, of a share of total shares of a particular product market, and thus recognize that the present distribution of market power is inequitable. But if the point of market activity were maximization of power, it would justify monopoly, which is contrary to the principal of competitive market relations.

7. For a pertinent and incisive analysis of the relationship between 'conceptual revision and political reform', see William Connolly, 1974, pp. 179–210.

8. See Dolbeare (1974a and b) for specific ways in which political change can be construed for the purposes of empirical inquiry.

9. It is clear from the voluminous literature that documents, for example, the responses to and impacts of Supreme Court decisions intended to change criminal procedure, that many other factors (such as, attitudes, intensity of reactions) in addition to conceptual elements affect the likelihood of organizational change. Thus, the outcomes of conceptual contests are a necessary but not a sufficient condition of organization transformation and political change. (See Wasby, 1970, especially chs 1 and 5.) The definition of organizational behaviour proposed here reflects our recognition of the part that organizational structure and dispositions play in policy implementation.

10. We do not use the biological connotation of life cycle, which implies an inevitable order of development from conception to maturity to death (Kimberly, 1980b). Rather, we use cycle as a recurring sequence of conditions that organizations face. An organization's stage in a cycle at any particular time is triggered by external factors and, consequently, the duration of the stages may vary substantially.

11. Joan Jacoby, in a recent empirical study of the offices of prosecution, demonstrates the connection between their conception of mission or goals, measures of success and strategy, and allocation patterns required to achieve these goals. Significantly, she discovers that prosecution goals vary between four types: 'legal sufficiency', in which success is measured by the number of favorable dispositions; 'system efficiency', where success is measured largely by the length of time it takes to achieve any disposition; 'defendant rehabilitation', where the appropriateness of a disposition for the offense committed is a measure of success; and 'trial sufficiency', in

which success turns upon the number of convictions attained (1980, pp. 199–215). For examples of how the multiplicity and ambiguity of CETA statutory goals contribute to different findings about outcomes of the same programs, compare the conclusions drawn in Carl Van Horn's analysis of CETA programs (1979), Robert Taggart's (1981), and those found in the National Council on Employment Policy study (1981).

12. For example, surgeons must rely on the expertise and correct judgement of the anaesthetists and other medical professionals in order to perform successful surgery. And the competence and performance of all hospital physicians must be regulated by periodic peer review. Similarly, court justices must establish rules to govern working relationships and decision-making procedures that permit a majority view to emerge in any given case.

13. Examples that come closest, in our judgement, to organizations which mark the departure from collegial to professional expertise for organization structural elements are the health maintenance organizations (such as Group Health Co-operative) and both public megauniversities and specialized colleges in which curriculum offerings are limited to one or two disciplines. Health maintenance organizations share the CETA Prime Sponsors, for example an appointed or elected governing board, non-medical administrative staff, physicians who are salaried employees among whom tasks are divided along lines of medical expertise and so forth. State mega-universities are characterized by elaborate administrative hierarchies with departmental units divided by sub-specializations within disciplines. Under these conditions, governance processes reflect less the interests, needs and inputs of departmental units than those of higher units such as schools, colleges, and administrative domains of senior executive appointees. Although less elaborate in size and scale, governance patterns of colleges limited to specialized disciplines obviate mid-level departmental management independence by making lines of policy and supervision between administrators and faculty direct and immediate.

14. Three examples of such projects include the Work Equity Project in Minnesota, designed to utilize CETA Public Service jobs to employ WIN participants (Stromsdorfer, 1981); the Employment Opportunities Pilot Projects that transfers Work Equity concepts to other sites; and the Consolidated Employment and Training System project intended to consolidate CETA, Employment Service, WIN management, and delivery systems in Tacoma, Washington (Dalton, 1980; Hogan and Hogan, 1980). For more details on these and other employment and training projects, see Dalton (ed.), 1981.

15. For more details from a two-year study on which these findings were based, see Randall Ripley and Grace Franklin, *Private Sector Involvement in Public Employment and Training Programs* (*Employment and Training Reporter*, 1982b).

16. Bish and Ostrom (1973) argue that, since their empirical studies prove that informal methods of co-ordination of police services are more effective than methods which rely upon formal agreements and regulation, this somehow proves that a decentralized law enforcement system is more *representative* than a consolidated one. We suspect that what occurs here is some confusion between the separate points involved in applying technical

efficiency versus allocative efficiency or political allocation as measures of performance. If these distinctions are not made, perverse policies might be justified, for example, if police services were allocated in such a way that majority communities received the most efficient and effective law enforcement assistance although more crime occurred in minority communities.

References

Adam, E., Jr (1979), 'Quality and productivity in delivering and administering public services', *Public Productivity Review*, 3(4), pp. 26–40.

Adams, H. W. (1975), 'Solutions as problems: The case of productivity', *Public Productivity Review*, 1(1), pp. 36–43.

Allison, G. T. (1971), *Essence of decision: Explaining the Cuban missile crisis* (Boston: Little, Brown).

Argyris, C. (1964), *Integrating the individual and the organization* (New York: Wiley).

Bahl, R. W. and J. Burkhead (1977), 'Productivity and the measurement of public output', in Charles H. Levine (ed.), *Managing human resources: A challenge to urban governments* (Beverly Hills: Sage) pp. 253–69.

Balk, W. L. (1975), *Improving government productivity: Some policy perspectives* (Beverly Hills: Sage).

Barzun, J. (1981; November 5), 'The wasteland of American education', *New York Review of Books*, pp. 34–6.

Best, M. and W. E. Connolly (1976), *The politicized economy* (Lexington, MA: D.C. Heath).

Bish, R. L. and V. Ostrom (1973), *Understanding urban government: Metropolitan reform reconsidered* (Washington, DC: American Enterprise Institute for Public Policy Research).

Center for National Security Studies. (1970), *Law and disorder II* (New York: Field and New World Foundation).

Connolly, W. E. (1974), *The terms of political discourse* (Lexington, Mass: D.C. Heath).

Dalton, T. C. (1980), *An analysis of evaluation design issues for the consolidated employment and training project, Tacoma, Washington: A working paper* (Seattle University, Institute of Public Service).

Dalton, T. C. (ed.) (1981), *Coordinating the employment and training system: The implementation and evaluation of organizational innovations: Conference Proceedings* (Seattle University, Institute of Public Service).

Deniston, O. L., I. M. Rosenstock, W. Welch and V. A. Getting (1972), 'Evaluation of program effectiveness and program efficiency', in F. Lyden and E. Miller (eds), *Planning, programming, budgeting*, pp. 141–70 (Chicago: Markham).

Dolbear, K. M. (1974a), 'The impacts of public policy', *Political Science Annual*, 5, pp. 90–130.

Dolbear, K. M. (1974b), *Political change in the United States: A framework for analysis* (New York: McGraw-Hill).

Dolbear, K. M. and P. E. Hammond (1971), *The school prayer decisions: From court policy to local practice* (Chicago: University of Chicago Press).

Downs, A. (1967), *Inside bureaucracy* (Boston: Little, Brown).

Easton, D. (1965), *A framework for political analysis* (Englewood Cliffs, NJ: Prentice-Hall).

Elmore, R. F. (1978), 'Organizational models of social program implementation', *Public Policy*, 26(2), pp. 185–228.

Elmore, R. F. (1979), 'Backward mapping: Implementation research and policy decisions', *Political Science Quarterly*, 94(1), pp. 601–16.

Employment and Training Reporter (1981a; 12 December), 'Senator Quayle's proposal for employment and training', (Washington, D.C.: Bureau of National Affairs) pp. 297–9.

Employment and Training Reporter (1981b; 23 December), 'Specifications for a House Bill' (Washington, DC: Bureau of National Affairs) pp. 378–80.

Employment and Training Reporter (1982a; 6 January), 'CETA should retain current programs, boost state role, hispanic group says' (Washington, DC: Bureau of National Affairs) pp. 389–90.

Employment and Training Reporter (1982b; 20 January), 'Private sector role in CETA programs will remain limited, report asserts' (Washington, DC: Bureau of National Affairs) pp. 453–5.

Ervin, O. L. (1978), 'A conceptual niche for municipal productivity', *Public Relations Review*, 3(2), pp. 15–24.

Etzioni, A. (1964), *Modern organizations* (Englewood Cliffs, NJ: Prentice-Hall).

Gilder, G. (1975), 'Public sector productivity', *Public Productivity Review*, 1(1), pp. 4–8.

Hamilton, E. K. (1972), 'Productivity: The New York City approach', *Public Administration Review*, 32(6), pp. 784–95.

Hatry, H. P. (1980), 'Performance measurement principles and techniques: An overview for local government', *Public Productivity Review*, 4(4), pp. 312–39.

Hayes, F. O'R. (1977), *Productivity in local government* (Lexington, MA: D.C. Heath).

Hayward, N. (1976), 'The productivity challenge', *Public Administration Review*, 36(5), pp. 544–50.

Hayward, N. and G. Kuper (1978), 'The national economy and productivity in government', *Public Administration Review*, 38(1), pp. 2–5.

Hogan, J. B. and S. K. Hogan (1980), *The challenge of consolidation: The consolidated employment and training system in Tacoma, Washington: A case study* (Seattle University, Institute of Public Service).

Jacoby, J. E. (1980), *The American prosecutor: A search for identity* (Lexington, MA: D.C. Heath).

Kimberly, J. R. (1980a), 'Initiation, innovation and institutionalization in the creation process', in J. R. Kimberly and R. H. Miles (eds), *The organizational life cycle* (San Francisco: Jossey-Boss) pp. 18–43.

Kimberly, J. R. (1980b), 'The life cycle analogy and the study of organizations: Introduction', in J. R. Kimberly and R. H. Miles (eds), *The organizational life cycle* (San Francisco: Jossey-Boss) pp. 1–17.

Kimberly, J. R. and R. H. Miles (eds) (1980), *The organizational life cycle: Issues in the creation, transformation and decline of organizations* (San Francisco: Jossey-Boss).

Kull, D. C. (1978), 'Productivity programs in the federal government', *Public Administration Review*, 38(1), pp. 5–9.

Leathers, C. G. (1979), 'Language barriers in public productivity analysis: the case of efficiency and effectiveness', *Public Productivity Review*, 3(4), pp. 63–8.

Lowi, T. J. (1979), *The end of liberalism*, 2nd edn (New York: W. W. Norton Company).

MacIntyre, A. (1981), *After virtue* (Notre Dame, IN: University of Notre Dame Press).

Mann, L. D. (1979), 'Planning behavior and professional policymaking activity', in R. W. Burchell and G. Sternlieb (eds), *Planning theory in the 1980's* (New Brunswick, N.J.: Rutgers University, Center for Urban Policy Research) pp. 113–49.

Mann, S. Z. (1980), 'The politics of productivity: State and local focus', *Public Productivity Review*, 4(4), pp. 352–67.

Marchand, D. (1980), *The politics of privacy: Computers and criminal justice records* (Arlington, VA: Information Resources Press).

Mark, J. A. (1972), 'Meanings and measures of productivity', *Public Administration Review*, 32(6), pp. 747–53.

Miles, R. H. and W. A. Randolph (1980), 'Influence of organizational learning styles on early development', in J. R. Kimberly and R. H. Miles (eds), *The organizational life cycle* (San Francisco: Jossey-Boss), pp. 44–82.

Milner, N. A. (1971), *The court and local law enforcement: The impact of Miranda* (Beverly Hills: Sage).

Mirengoff, W., L. Rindler, H. Greenspan and S. Seablom (1980), *CETA: Assessment of public service employment programs* (Washington, DC: National Academy of Sciences).

Morgan, P. M. (1981), 'Academia and the federal government', *Policy Studies Journal*, 10(1), pp. 70–84.

National Council on Employment Policy (1981), *CETA's results and their implications* (Washington, DC).

Navasky, V. (1976), *Law enforcement: The federal role* (New York: McGraw-Hill).

Neiman, M. and C. Lovell (1981), 'Mandating as a policy issue: the definitional problem', *Policy Studies Journal*, 9(5), pp. 667–81.

Nelson, B. J. (1978), 'Setting the agenda: the case of child abuse', in J. V. May and A. B. Wildavsky (eds), *The Policy Cycle* (Beverly Hills: Sage) pp. 17–41.

Ostrom, E. (1971), 'Institutional arrangements and the measurement of policy consequences: Applications to evaluating police performance', *Urban Affairs Quarterly*, 6, pp. 447–75.

Packer, H. L. (1968), *The limits of the criminal sanction* (Stanford, CA: Stanford University Press).

Peterson, P. G. (1972), 'Productivity in government and the American economy, *Public Administration Review*, 32 (6), pp. 740–7.

Quinn, R. E. (1978), 'Productivity and the process of organizational improvement: Why we cannot talk to each other', *Public Administration Review*, 38(1), pp. 41–5.

Rivlin, A. M. (1971), *Systematic thinking for social action* (Washington, D.C.: The Brookings Institution).

Rosenbloom, R. (1973), 'The real productivity crisis is in government', *Harvard Business Review*, 32(6), pp. 156–64.

Sabatier, P. A. and D. A. Mazmanian (1980), The implementation of public policy: A framework of analysis', *Policy Studies Journal*, 8(4), pp. 538–59.

Salamon, L. M. (1981), 'The goals of reorganization: A framework for analysis', *Administration and Society*, 12(4), pp. 471–500.

Silverman, E. (1973), 'Productivity in government: A note of caution', *Midwest Review of Public Administration*, 7(3), pp. 143–53.

Skoler, D. T. (1977), *Organizing the non-system* (Lexington, MA: D.C. Heath).

Stromsdorfer, E. (1981), *Minnesota work-equity project: Second interim report, a summary of findings* (Cambridge, MA: Apt Associates).

Taggart, R. (1981), *A fisherman's guide: An assessment of training and remediation strategies* (Kalamazoo, MI: Upjohn).

Van de Ven, A. H. (1980), 'Early planning, implementation and performance of new organizations', in J. R. Kimberly and R. H. Miles (eds), *The organizational life cycle* (San Francisco: Jossey-Boss) pp. 83–134.

Van Horn, C. (1979). *Policy implementation in the federal system* (Lexington, MA: D.C. Heath).

Wasby, S. L. (1970), *The impact of the United States Supreme Court: Some perspectives* (Homewood, IL: Dorsey).

Whetten, D. A. (1980), 'Sources, responses and effects of organizational decline', in J. R. Kimberly and R. H. Miles (eds), *The organizational life cycle* (San Francisco: Jossey-Boss) pp. 342–74.

Williams, W. (1971), *Social policy research and analysis: The experience in federal social agencies* (New York: American Elsevier).

Wittgenstein, L. (1953), *Philosophical investigations* (New York: Macmillan).

Wittgenstein, L. (1969), *On certainty* (New York: Harper Torchbooks, originally written 1922).

Yamada, G. T. (1972), 'Improving management effectiveness in the federal government', *Public Administration Review*, 32(6), pp. 764–70.

Yin, R. K., K. A. Heald and M. E. Vogel (1977), *Tinkering with the system: Technological innovations in state and local services* (Lexington, MA: D.C. Heath).

Yin, R. K. and D. Yates (1974), *Street-level governments: Assessing decentralization and urban services* (Santa Monica: RAND Corporation, R–1527–NSF).

Zaltman, G., *et al.* (1973), *Innovations and organizations* (New York: Wiley Interscience).

Part II
Policy Environmental Factors, Program Design, and Productivity

3 Productivity Emphasis in Local Government: An Assessment of the Impact of Selected Policy Environment Factors[1]

David N. Ammons and David J. Molta

Much of the current literature on productivity in local government indicates the importance of top-level commitment for successful improvement programs. Based on an assessment of a variety of organizational and community characteristics in a nationwide sample of jurisdictions – jurisdictions whose officials claim varying levels of emphasis on productivity improvement – the authors report that such emphasis appears to be linked to certain organizational factors but that those factors account for only a moderate portion of the variation in emphasis across cities. They conclude that productivity improvement may be emphasized in a variety of policy environments.

Conventional wisdom suggests that recent cutbacks in intergovernmental financial assistance, a severe economic recession, and public pressure to expand services without increasing taxes have forced local government officials to focus on productivity improvement as an increasingly important means of stretching limited revenues (see, for example, Knight, 1980; LaBelle, 1980; Poister, 1983). Presumably, it is these stimuli that have produced a more uniformly high level of support for productivity enhancement measures.

Although top-level commitment is considered a necessary, though in itself insufficient, prerequisite for a successful productivity improvement effort (see, for example, US General Accounting Office, 1983; Barbour, 1980; Hayward, 1976; Hayes, 1978; Keane, 1980), relatively little empirical research has been conducted to confirm or challenge conventional wisdom regarding the determinants or stimuli for such commitment. Important questions about the topic have received little empirical attention. For example, what factors can be shown to contribute systematically to enthusiasm for productivity improvement in local government? Do local governments in which legislative and executive leaders express a greater emphasis on productivity improvement have a policy environment that differs markedly from those in which it receives less emphasis? These aspects of the study of productivity improvement in local government are examined in this exploratory inquiry. Attention is focused on factors such as the relative priorities assigned to other issues, characteristics of local politics such as the degree of consensus in legislative actions and tenure of the chief elected official, the nature of fundamental relationships between state and local governments, community socio-economic characteristics, and local government revenues and expenditures.

METHOD

A recent survey explored the priority assigned to productivity improvement by 298 local government administrators drawn randomly from the ranks of the International City Management Association (Ammons and King, 1983). Each respondent ranked ten local government problems or issues, including productivity improvement, in terms of perceived importance for their community.

The rankings by appointed executives in the earlier nationwide survey have been supplemented in this study by those of their chief elected counterparts in the same jurisdictions – primarily mayors of cities and towns and chairpersons of county commissions. The rankings by elected officials permit a comparison of potentialy differing perspectives and, through consolidation of the two rankings for each community, an improved sense of the overall policy environment regarding the importance of productivity improvement relative to other issues competing for local government attention. Of the 298 elected officials contacted by mail in November and December 1983, 221 returned completed questionnaires, a response rate of 74 per cent.

City and county clerks in the same 298 jurisdictions were contacted for the purpose of securing the minutes of two recent meetings of the governing body. A content analysis of each set of minutes led to the development of a scale of council harmony, a factor conceivably significant to managerial initiative on potentially controversial programs designed to increase organizational productivity. Replies were received from 245 clerks, a response rate of 82 per cent.

The choice of independent variables included in this study was based on existing literature in the areas of productivity improvement, administrative innovation, and local government performance in general. A belief, for example, that government structure, legislative infighting, and other local political factors can influence government efficiency has been prevalent at least since the reform movement at the turn of the century (Banfield and Wilson, 1963; Stillman, 1974). Thus, political variables such as government type, electoral practices, and mayoral tenure are included in the analysis.

Agency autonomy has been found to be a relevant factor in studies of innovation (Downs, 1976), prompting the inclusion of factors designed to measure the degree of local government discretion in state–local relationships. Among these variables, we include a measure of relative state fiscal dominance, a measure of local government legal autonomy, and measures of local discretionary authority related to structure, functional areas, finance, and personnel, all derived from a recent study conducted by the US Advisory Commission on Intergovernmental Relations (1981).

A third focus of this examination is based on the presumed association between innovation and the organization's environment, including its available resources, as well as various community and organizational characteristics (for a concise overview of innovation literature, see Bingham, 1976; Downs, 1976; Mushkin and Sandifer, 1979; and Yin, Heald and Vogel, 1977). To explore this relationship, we have included measures of local government finances, measures of individual wealth, measures of household characteristics, local crime rates, and a variety of other variables.

The method of statistical analysis was in two stages. First, the zero-order correlations of the variables discussed above with the average productivity ranking of elected and administrative officials were explored. Next, models for the total sample and selected subsamples were developed using variables identified through stepwise regression as being significant at the 0.05 level.

TOTAL SAMPLE FINDINGS

Local government commitment to productivity improvement is not determined solely by either executive or legislative leadership. The level of enthusiasm for productivity improvement, or lack thereof, held by each, solidifies or challenges its priority relative to other issues in a given community. Therefore, in examining variables for their contribution to the productivity environment, it is important to consider both perspectives on the importance of productivity improvement.

A wide range of perceptions was found among appointed officials, with some ranking productivity improvement first among the ten local government issues examined, while others ranked it last (Ammons and King, 1983). As a group, executives ranked productivity improvement fourth, assigning higher average priority to three other issues. Similarly, chief elected officials exhibited great differences in their assessments, with some rating productivity improvement first while others rated it last. On average, the chief elected officials ranked productivity improvement seventh among the ten issues.[2]

Not only was a wide range of difference found for productivity improvement rankings within the two groups across jurisdictions, considerable variation was found between the appointed and elected officials' rankings within the same jurisdictions – pointing out the importance of the use of a combined measure of the productivity improvement environment. The officials of some jurisdictions were in agreement or virtual agreement on ranking; others differed dramatically. The Spearman rank-order correlation for the productivity improvement rankings of elected and administrative officials, in fact, is a rather meagre 0.16. A mean of the two rankings was calculated for each jurisdiction, and serves as the dependent variable for all statistical analyses. The Pearson product-moment correlation of the average rankings with the rankings of elected and administrative officials was 0.76 and 0.77, respectively.[3]

Table 3.1 shows the correlations of the mayor-manager average productivity rankings with the average ranking of each of the other nine local government issues or problems that officials were asked to prioritize. The only item that was related positively to productivity improvement emphasis was staff development. Five of the nine items were found to have statistically significant inverse relationships with productivity improvement, ranging from -0.12 to -0.26.

As shown in Table 3.2, none of the policy environment factors examined was found to have a strong relationship to the jurisdictional average productivity improvement rankings for the total sample. Although some are statistically significant at the 0.05 level, the highest correlation is only 0.30. The relationships displayed in Table 3.2 suggest a tendency for productivity improvement to be emphasized in communities with harmonious local legislative bodies, relatively little local government legal autonomy, a substantial state role in local fiscal

Table 3.1 Relationship between mayor-manager average productivity improvement ranking and average ranking for nine other local government issues

Issue	Pearson product-moment correlation (r)†
Quality of life	-0.26*
Economic development	-0.24*
Staff development	0.23*
Public safety	-0.19*
Community relations	-0.14*
Intergovernmental relations	-0.12*
Capital improvements	-0.11
Labour relations	-0.06
The 'fiscal crisis'	-0.03
$n = 199$	

* significant at $p < 0.05$

† A Spearman's rank-order correlation of 0.16 has been reported for the correlation between the productivity improvement rankings of the mayor/chairpersons and manager/administrators. This table, however, compares average jurisdictional rankings – the mean of the mayor/chairperson and the manager/administrator rankings – and reports the Pearson product-moment correlations for these more nearly continuous variables. See O'Brien (1979).

matters but relatively little reliance on intergovernmental revenues, substantial public utility operations but low expenditures for welfare, housing, and urban renewal, and a high ratio of income to median housing value.

The correlations presented thus far indicate that several policy environment factors are significantly related to local government emphasis on productivity improvement. Simple, zero-order correlations, however, tend to be somewhat misleading in this instance, since many of the apparent relationships with productivity emphasis are in fact attributable to relationships among the explanatory variables themselves. This condition becomes evident through the application of stepwise regression.

As shown in Table 3.3, only three variables were found to have statistically significant regression coefficients ($p < 0.05$) in the stepwise regression procedure.[4] These three variables – percentage of owner-occupied housing, utility revenue per capita, and per capita expenditures for housing and urban renewal – account for a mere 19 per cent of the variance in the average jurisdictional rankings for productivity improvement. Thus, our total sample model has a very low predictive capacity.

Table 3.2   Relationship between average productivity improvement ranking and selected policy environment factors (n = 199)

Local political factors	Pearson product-moment correlation (r)
Unanimous council votes (as % of all votes)	0.014
Degree of council/commission harmony, as assessed by mayor/chairperson on five-point scale	0.151*
% of vote received by mayor/chairperson in most recent election	0.037
Tenure of mayor/chairperson (in months)	0.039
Degree of reformism [a]	0.076
'Liberalism' of the congressional district in which the jurisdiction is located [b]	−0.034
State—local relationship [c]	
Degree of state dominance of fiscal partnership	0.126*
Degree of local government legal autonomy	−0.124*
Degree of local discretionary authority regarding	
—structure	−0.040
—functional areas	0.049
—finance	0.073
—personnel	0.024
Community characteristics [d]	
1980 population	−0.007
Median age of population	0.061
Per capita income (1979)	0.023
Unemployment rate	−0.030
% of population below poverty line (1979)	0.050
% of occupied housing	0.081
% of occupied housing that is owner-occupied	0.102
Persons per household	0.066
% of year-round housing units built in 1939 or earlier	0.061
Median value of owner-occupied housing as % of per capita income	−0.170*
Crime rate	−0.133
Local government revenues and expenditures [e]	
Property tax revenue per capita	0.061
Sales tax revenue per capita	0.022
Utility revenue per capita	0.302*
Property tax revenue as % of general revenues	0.083
Per capita tax revenues as % of per capita income	0.097
Property tax and sales tax revenues as % of general revenues	0.128
Intergovernmental revenues as % of general revenues	−0.219*
Per capita general expenditures	0.013

Table 3.2 (*contd.*)

Local political factors	Pearson product-moment correlation (r)
Per capita expenditures for	
—education	0.055
—library	−0.049
—welfare	−0.165*
—police	−0.012
—fire services	0.108
—parks and recreation	−0.039
—housing and urban renewal	−0.194*
—financial administration	0.091
—general control	0.067
Expenditures for financial administration and general control, as % of general expenditures	0.150

* significant at $p < 0.05$
[a] Adapted from H. T. Sanders, 'Government Structure in American Cities', in *The Municipal Yearbook: 1979* (ICMA).
[b] Based upon AFL–CIO assessment of congressional voting records in *The People's Lobby* (AFl–CIO, 1983).
[c] Source of data: ACIR, *Measuring Local Discretionary Authority* (1981).
[d] Data sources: Census Bureau, 1980 *Census of Population and Housing* and FBI, *Crime in the United States: 1982*.
[e] Data sources: Census Bureau, *1977 Census of Governments* and Office of Revenue Sharing, *Initial State and Local Data Elements: GRS Entitlement Period 13* (GPO, 1981).

SUBSAMPLE FINDINGS

Three subsamples were analysed to determine whether the relationships discovered for the sample as a whole held for other groupings as well. The three subsamples are:

(1) all jurisdictions except county governments;
(2) all jurisdictions with populations over 10 000;
(3) all jurisdictions in which the chief elected and appointed officials are in substantial agreement regarding the relative importance of productivity improvement.

The third subsample is operationalized as consisting of all jurisdictions in which the elected and appointed officials' productivity improvement rankings are no more than two ranks apart. The justification for analysing this subsample is that in these jurisdictions the salience of

Table 3.3 Policy environment variables identified through stepwise regression as having strongest independent association with average productivity improvement ranking

Variable	Total sample		beta	Cumulative R-Square	Cumulative adjusted R-Square
	r	b			
% of occupied housing that is owner-occupied	0.102 (n = 198)	3.610* (n = 78)	0.302	0.109	0.097
Utility revenues per capita	0.302* (n = 92)	5.568* (n = 78)	0.257	0.175	0.153
Per capita local government expenditures for housing and urban renewal	−0.194* (n = 91)	−35.885* (n = 78)	−0.216	0.221	0.289
Intercept: 3.513					

* significant at p < 0.05

productivity improvement or lack thereof is least ambiguous – thereby offering a presumably purer basis on which to judge the explanatory value of different variables.

Excluding counties from the sample produces no substantial changes in zero-order correlations. Only two correlations greater than 0.2 were reported in Table 3.2 for the entire sample. With counties excluded, only utility revenue per capita has a correlation exceeding that figure (Table 3.4).

As can be seen in Table 3.4, excluding jurisdictions of less than 10 000 population yields several new correlations in excess of 0.2, but all correlations remain relatively low. The third subsample, however, produces notably different results. Among jurisdictions in which elected and appointed officials were in virtual agreement on productivity ranking, four factors were found to have correlations of 0.28 or greater. Especially strong correlations, compared to others in this study, were found for utility revenue per capita (0.34), property tax and sales tax revenues as a percentage of general revenue (0.29), per capita housing and urban renewal expenditures (−0.29), and intergovernmental revenue as a percentage of general revenue (−0.28).

Table 3.4 Relationship between average productivity improvement ranking and selected policy environment factors

Factors	Pearson product-moment correlation (r)			
	Total sample (n = 199)	Excluding counties (n = 189)	Population 10 000+ (n = 89)	Mayor–manager Productivity Agreement (n = 99)
Utility revenue per capita	0.30*	0.30*	0.26*	0.34*
Intergovernmental revenues as % of general revenues	−0.22*	−0.18*	−0.20*	−0.28*
Degree of local government legal autonomy	−0.12*	−0.15*	−0.16	−0.13
Median age of population	0.06	0.10	0.20*	0.04
Persons per housing unit	0.07	0.07	0.23*	0.12
Property tax and sales tax revenues as % of general revenue	0.13	0.11	0.19*	0.29*
Expenditures for financial administration and general control as % of general expenditures	0.15	0.17	0.20*	0.24*
% of housing occupied	0.08	0.07	0.18*	0.17*
% of occupied housing that is owner-occupied	0.10	0.12	0.26*	0.19*
Median value of owner-occupied housing as % of per capita income	−0.17*	−0.18*	−0.18*	−0.17*
Per capita expenditures for general control	0.07	0.14	0.20*	0.18
Per capita housing and urban renewal expenditures	−0.19*	−0.19*	−0.25*	−0.29*
Per capita welfare expenditures	−0.17*	0.09	0.08	−0.19
Degree of council/commission harmony, as assessed by mayor/chairperson	0.15*	0.15*	0.21*	0.19*
Degree of state dominance of fiscal partnership	0.13*	0.14*	0.11	0.13

* significant at $p < 0.05$

Stepwise regression using the first two subsamples produced model with the same explanatory variables and virtually the same R-square values as the model for the total sample reported in Table 3.3. The third subsample, however, including only those jurisdictions in which there was substantial agreement between chief elected and appointed officials regarding the productivity improvement ranking, produced considerably different results (Table 3.5). In this model, four variables were found to have statistically significant regression coefficients at the 0.0; level. Property tax and sales tax revenues (as a percentage of general revenue), utility revenue per capita, expenditures for financial administration and general control (as a percentage of general expenditures) and the degree of state dominance of the state–local fiscal partnership were all positively related to average productivity improvement rankings. Although still failing to explain even half of the variation in the dependent variable, this model performs much better than the others accounting for 47 per cent of the variation.

Table 3.5 Policy environment variables identified through stepwise regression as having strongest independent association with average productivity improvement ranking

| *Variable* | Jurisdictions in which elected and appointed officials were in virtual agreement on productivity improvement ranking† | | | | |
	r	*b*	*beta*	*Cumulative R-square*	*Cumulative adjusted R-square*
Property tax and sales tax revenues as % of general revenues	0.288* (n = 56)	7.447* (n = 38)	0.628	0.283	0.263
Utility revenues per capita	0.343* (n = 49)	6.455* (n = 38)	0.310	0.396	0.361
Expenditures for financial administration and general control as % of general expenditures	0.244* (n = 56)	14.410* (n = 38)	0.288	0.468	0.421
Degree of state dominance of fiscal partnership	0.133 (n = 99)	1.009* (n = 38)	0.270	0.528	0.471
Intercept: −0.005					

* significant at p < 0.05
† Excluded from the sample were all jurisdictions in which the appointed official's productivity improvement ranking differed by more than two steps from that of the chief elected official.

DISCUSSION

Care must be exercised in interpreting the results of this inquiry. The absence of major explanatory power for a relatively sizeable set of policy environment factors suggests that the development of a productivity emphasis may not be tied to any single type of policy environment.

To the extent that productivity improvement emphasis and actual productivity improvement are related, this study suggests several areas of exploration with potential relevance to local government performance. An emphasis on productivity improvement was found to be negatively related to an emphasis on eight of the nine other issues ranked by chief elected and appointed officials. Particularly strong negative relationships were found with emphasis on economic development ($r = -0.24$) and quality of life ($r = -0.26$). It seems ironic that communities intent on economic development, presumably in order to strengthen their tax bases as well as the local economy in general, would overlook productivity improvement as another important means of balancing resources and demands.

Utility revenue per capita was found to be positively related to productivity improvement ranking in each of the models. Perhaps the most notable distinction between public utilities and other services offered by local governments involves the more tangible, more measurable nature of the former. This distinction – that is, the circumstance that finds some governing bodies responsible for large utility operations with more easily measured products and problems, and others responsible for a different set of services where performance assessment may be more subjective – may influence perceptions regarding the relevance of productivity improvement strategies generally, even beyond the confines of the utility departments. Still another explanation for the relationship may lie in the high-profile nature of consumer charges for utility services and the readily apparent advantages of cost containment measures. Governments responsible for major utility operations may simply be more sensitive to citizen concerns regarding demands of the local government on personal resources than are those governments that are responsible for a more limited, and less costly, array of services.

The percentage of owner-occupied housing in a jurisdiction was found to be positively related to productivity emphasis in the total sample and in the first two subsamples. It should not be surprising to find a more cost-conscious citizenry in communities with relatively less absentee ownership.

An inverse relationship between per capita local government expenditures for housing and urban renewal and productivity emphasis was found to be significant at the 0.05 level for the total sample and the first two subsamples. Under similar conditions of owner-occupancy and local government utility operation magnitude, local governments with substantial housing and urban renewal programs tend to de-emphasize productivity improvement among other major issues.

A different set of explanatory variables was found to be relevant for the third subsample, comprised of jurisdictions in which the chief elected and appointed officials were in virtual agreement on the ranking of productivity improvement. Only utility revenues per capita was repeated as a relevant explanatory variable from the total-sample model.

The variable with the greatest explanatory power in the third subsample is property tax and sales tax revenues as a percentage of general revenues. As in earlier studies of local government expenditures, the matter of whose money is being spent appears to be an important factor. The source of local government funds – that is, own-source or intergovernmental revenues – has been shown to be an important determinant of local policies and expenditure patterns (Dye, 1975; Sacks and Harris, 1964). The source of funds has also been found to be relevant to relative productivity levels among municipalities offering highest-quality services (Ammons, 1984). In this study, the relevance of revenue source for productivity emphasis appears in a variety of the zero-order correlations. Perhaps most notably, a significant negative correlation was found between intergovernmental revenues and productivity emphasis (that is, as reliance on intergovernmental revenues goes up, a jurisdiction's emphasis on productivity improvement tends to decrease). The model for the third subsample exhibited a positive relationship between productivity improvement emphasis and property tax and sales tax revenues as a percentage of general revenue. Those jurisdictions that rely most heavily on these very high-profile forms of own-source revenue also tend to emphasize the importance of productivity improvement.

In the model for the third subsample, a positive relationship was also found between productivity improvement emphasis and the percentage of general expenditures devoted to financial administration and general control. Research indicates that productivity improvement efforts are most likely to flourish in governments with 'a tradition of professionalism and good management' (Hayes, 1978, p. 17). Professionalism and good management have often involved a commitment to strong central staff offices – a commitment that would be reflected in expenditures for financial administration and general control.

The final factor included in the model for the third subsample, the degree of state dominance of the state–local fiscal partnership, was not found to have a significant zero-order correlation with productivity improvement emphasis, but nevertheless did have a significant relationship with the dependent variable when other relevant explanatory variables were controlled. This finding suggests that among jurisdictions relying heavily on own-source revenues, having substantial utility operations, and devoting greater-than-average resources to financial administration and general control, those with relatively less fiscal autonomy and, presumably, less flexibility in such matters as revenue generation and local debt are more likely to emphasize productivity improvement for its resource-stretching properties.

CONCLUSIONS

What can be concluded from this exploratory analysis? Two points seem especially pertinent. First, the impetus to express an interest in, or a commitment to, productivity improvement may come from several stimuli. A rather wide array of factors potentially relevant to such commitment were examined here – yet the models constructed could account for no more than 47 per cent of the variance in the dependent variable. Second, the recurrence of factors such as the source of local government revenues and the degree of involvement of the jurisdictions in the provision of public utilities as significant influences on productivity commitment indicate the possible existence of fundamental relationships warranting further attention.

Notes

1. The research for this chapter was supported by a Faculty Research Grant from North Texas State University.
2. The order of average priority ranking of the ten issues among appointed officials (from highest priority to lowest) was as follows: the 'fiscal crisis', capital improvements, economic development, productivity improvement, public safety, community relations, staff development, quality of life, labour relations, and intergovernmental relations. Among elected officials, the order was as follows: economic development, capital improvements, the 'fiscal crisis', quality of life, public safety, community relations, productivity

improvement, intergovernmental relations, staff development, and labour relations.

3. Pearson's product-moment correlations were used in the analysis of this study's data, much of which was interval level but some of which was ordinal. The principal dependent variable in the analysis was the average jurisdictional ranking of productivity improvement – frequently a fractional mean of two ordinal rankings. For a defence of the use of Pearson's product-moment correlations with ordinal data, see O'Brien (1979).

4. Listwise deletion of missing data was used in the stepwise regression procedure. Zero-order correlations, based on pairwise comparisons and in most cases having larger *n*s, are also reported in all tables.

References

Advisory Commission on Intergovernmental Relations (1981), *Measuring local discretionary authority* (Washington, DC: US Government Printing Office).

Ammons, D. N. (1984), *Municipal productivity: a comparison of fourteen high-quality-service cities* (New York: Praeger).

Ammons, D. N. and J. C. King (1983), 'Productivity improvement in local government: its place among competing priorities', *Public Administration Review*, 43, pp. 113–20.

Banfield, E. C. and J. Q. Wilson (1963), *City politics* (New York: Vintage Books).

Barbour, G. P., Jr (1980), 'Key factors influencing productivity of state and local government activities', *Public Productivity Review*, 4, pp. 273–82.

Bingham, R. D. (1976), *The adoption of innovation by local government* (Lexington, MA: Lexington Books).

Downs, G. W., Jr (1976), *Bureaucracy, innovation, and public policy* (Lexington, MA: Lexington Books).

Dye, T. R. (1975), *Understanding public policy* (Englewood Cliffs, NJ: Prentice-Hall).

Hayes, F. O'R. (1978), 'City and county productivity programs', *Public Administration Review*, 38, pp. 15–18.

Hayward, N. S. (1976), 'The productivity challenge', *Public Administration Review*, 36, pp. 544–50.

Keane, M. E. (1980), 'Why productivity improvement?', in G. J. Washnis (ed.), *Productivity improvement handbook for state and local government* (New York: John Wiley and Sons) pp. 7–15.

Knight, F. (1980), 'The productivity improvement puzzle', *Public Management*, 62, pp. 5–6.

La Belle, D. J. (1980), 'Managing for productivity', *Public Management*, 62, pp. 10–11.

Mushkin, S. J. and F. H. Sandifer (1979), *Personnel management and productivity in city government* (Lexington, MA: Lexington Books).

O'Brien, R. M. (1979), 'The use of Pearson's r with ordinal data', *American Sociological Review*, 44, pp. 851–7.

Poister, T. H. (1983), 'Monitoring the productivity of a state highway maintenance program', *Public Productivity Review*, 7, pp. 324–43.

Sacks, S. and R. Harris (1964), 'The determinants of state and local government expenditures and intergovernmental flows of funds', *National Tax Journal*, 17, pp. 75–85.

Stillman, R. J., II (1974), *The rise of the city manager: a public professional in local government* (Albuquerque, NM: University of New Mexico Press).

US General Accounting Office (1983), *Increased use of productivity management can help control government costs* (Washington, DC: G.A.O).

Yin, R. K., K. A. Heald and M. E. Vogel (1977), *Tinkering with the system: technological innovations in state and local services* (Lexington, MA: Lexington Books).

4 Assessing the Relationships between Program Design and Productivity: A Framework for Analysis

Patricia W. Ingraham and
Stephen H. Anderson

Though public productivity is most often discussed and measured in terms of service delivery or output measures, the authors argue that process, or institutional change, measures are also important. The State Small Cities Community Development Block Grant Program is examined to determine who participates in program design and choice of performance criteria. The analysis asks whether the nature of that participation is linked to the adoption of specific performance criteria and whether it is possible to determine, early in the life of a program, what kinds of performance criteria are dictated by participation and design considerations.

The findings of this study indicate that even though output measures are considered important by participants in the Small Cities effort, process and procedural changes are also given high priority. This suggests the need to reconsider current definitions of public productivity and to incorporate additional questions into future research on the subject.

INTRODUCTION

The issues surrounding public program productivity are many and complex. A major issue concerns the need for achieving both efficiency and effectiveness in public programs (see Balk, 1978). Another issue involves the problems in measuring productivity (see Hatry, 1976). In this paper we discuss both issue areas, but from a perspective that emphasizes the impact political policy processes have upon program performance and productivity. We suggest that certain elements of policy design and implementation may be related to the criteria selected to judge program performance and, thus, to efforts to assess program productivity. We suggest further that, because those relationships are a natural outgrowth of the policy process, they are a valid component of any consideration of public productivity. Finally, we note that, because we are dealing with public programs, efforts to conceptualize and measure productivity must include the uniquely public notion that programs often strive to change institutions and processes, as well as to deliver services. If programs do succeed in effecting institutional change, they have achieved their objective and been productive, though that type of productivity is difficult to measure.

EFFICIENCY AND EFFECTIVENESS IN PUBLIC SETTINGS

In a 1978 *Public Administration Review* symposium on public productivity, Burkhead and Hennigan discussed the concepts of effectiveness and efficiency and noted that, 'part of the difficulty with productivity measurement resides in the effort to combine these two concepts – whether one emphasizes technological efficiency or consumer efficiency, the public sector has certain characteristics that make either approach difficult to apply' (p. 34). One of the recurring difficulties is, obviously, the difficulty of measuring public program output with any degree of accuracy. Part of the problem may be, however, that output is too narrowly defined and that, in our search for concrete and quantifiable measures, we have overlooked important aspects of government activity.

Students of public administration have long recognized that normal bureaucratic activities encompass a range that goes far beyond service delivery. Similarly, analysis of various public policies, especially those associated with social programs, notes that those programs have institutional change, in addition to service delivery, as part of their overall objectives. Keevey, for example, in analysing productivity improvements at the state level, notes that procedural and structural improvements are often considered to be as important as improvements in actual service output though the two are closely linked (1980). More recently, Ammons and King, surveying efforts at productivity in local governments note, 'Few see productivity improvement as a single dimensional concept, most avoiding definitions which simply equate productivity with automation or procedural improvement' (1983, p. 115). In a similar vein, many efforts to operationalize productivity measures such as those at the Urban Institute, have utilized multidimensional measures and tools (see Greiner *et al.*, 1981).

We carry these definitions of productivity one step further and suggest that not only do many in the public sector view institutional change as one kind of bureaucratic productivity, but that performance criteria related to procedural/institutional changes emerge from design and implementation processes whose characteristics are different from programs more stringently orientated toward a 'unit of delivery' approach. To do so, we propose a simple model that specifies some elements in the environments of policy design, examines potential links between design and choice of implementation strategy, and analyses the relationship of both design environment and implementation strategy to probable program output. In the second part of the analysis, we use data from the federally funded State Small Cities Community Development Block Grant Program (SCCDBGP) to test simple associations between design environments, implementation strategies, and potential for program productivity.[1]

A FRAMEWORK FOR LINKING DESIGN, IMPLEMENTATION, AND POTENTIAL PRODUCTIVITY

Public policy and public management literature describe the variety of settings in which policy may be designed (see Jones, 1977; Bullock, Anderson and Brady, 1983, ch. 1 and epilogue; Mayntz, 1983; Henry, 1975, chs 1, 6 and 12; Lynn, 1981; Nakamura and Smallwood, 1980). For example, design can occur primarily in a legislative setting and be influenced most strongly by elected officials and professional legislative staff. Alternatively, policies can be designed primarily in a bureaucratic setting and be most strongly influenced by career civil servants. Major design activities might also occur outside both the legislative and the administrative arenas and be very strongly influenced by key interest groups. Each of these variants will have a special imprint on the policy being designed, simply because each represents a different primary interest and set of objectives.

Various implementation strategies may also have differing impacts. Implementation plans and strategies for any particular program may be centralized or decentralized, or they may resemble a revenue sharing strategy. The expertise, training, and orientation of program staff will vary from program to program and from setting to setting. The extent to which elected leaders continue to play a role in the program during the implementation process may vary. The implementation plan may be long-term, perhaps estimating several years for achievement of program goals, or short-term in its focus.

In recent years, implementation activities have been the subject of numerous analyses, most of which emphasize the problematic nature of the endeavour. The underlying assumption in much of the implementation literature is that the process very clearly does affect performance and productivity, but most often in an adverse way. This is so because, as a program is implemented, deficiencies in design become obvious, obstacles to further implementation are encountered, resources are diverted, and original goals and objectives are redefined (see Nakamura and Smallwood, 1980; and Bardach, 1977). The appropriate means for ameliorating these problems are open to some debate.

Some argue that a highly decentralized design and implementation strategy is most likely to yield productive results (Elmore, 1982). Others discuss a centralized incentive or penalty system to ensure that program resources are directed toward the desired objectives (Brigham and Brown, 1980). Still others argue that political 'fixers' must frequently reassert their goals and priorities during implementation if implementation is to be effective (Bardach, 1977, ch. 11).

For the purpose of the preliminary model and analysis presented here, the following points about design and implementation are important.

(1) The broadly defined purposes of many programs, most notably delegated programs, leaves enormous discretion to the administrative entity that must operate the programs both in terms of design and implementation strategy.

(2) In a setting with broadly defined goals and objectives and consciously decentralized intergovernmental controls, ability to specify where and for what purpose program resources are to be allocated is very limited.

(3) The values inherent in such an overall policy design move the choice to appropriate performance criterion or measures for program productivity away from straightforward service delivery, or output measures, toward more complex process, or institutional, measures. Such design assumes that if the process is changed and if there are different (and more knowledgeable) participants in the process, the eventual outcome will be changed as well, presumably for the better. As this discussion indicates, design and implementation strategy for a program strongly influence the manner in which program performance or productivity will be judged.

Given the diversity in policy design and implementation strategy, great potential variation in measures of performance exists. At one end of the continuum, proposed standards for evaluation could be very specific service delivery and impact-orientated measures. One such measure for the Small Cities Program, for example, could be total number of new jobs created with program funds. At the other end of the continuum, proposed criteria could be process, or procedure, orientated. In this sense, emphasis would not be on the extent to which actual services were delivered, but on the extent to which changes occurred in the institutions and processes that would ultimately deliver these services. Examples of performance criteria at this end of the continuum would be 'more open participation' in policy processes or 'more flexible' design and delivery mechanisms.

In summary, then, we suggest that variations in policy design and implementation strategy are associated with varying expectations for program performance and with various criteria for judging productivity. In fact, the nature of productivity also varies from setting to setting.

METHODOLOGY AND RESEARCH QUESTIONS

The focus of this research is on the state-administered SCCDBDP. The state administered part of the program was created in 1981, as part of the Reagan administration's New Federalism initiatives (Bleakly *et al.*, 1983). Operating with very broad and somewhat controversial national objectives, the program provides state governments that opt to administer their own programs with virtually unlimited discretion in program design and delivery strategy. This freedom has created a natural experiment and an opportunity to observe policy design and implementation in a number of settings.

In the spring of 1983, the 42 states that had chosen to administer the Small Cities Program were surveyed by mail.[2] Thirty-four state program directors responded. The returns reported here are not skewed toward any region of the country or toward any specific program choices. Based on other available information, they appear to be representative of the entire group of state programs. The findings from the survey are supplemented with individual state data gathered by the Small Cities staff at HUD in Washington and by reports to HUD from private contractors who studied the program.

The following research questions guided the survey and the analysis of the data:

(1) *Design environment*   Who participated in the design of the programs in the states? What kinds of programs were designed? Will the goals and objectives adopted permit, or enhance, analysis of performance and productivity?

(2) *Implementation strategy*   What types of implementation strategies were adopted? Does·there appear to be a relationship between program goals, proposed implementation strategy, and proposed performance criteria?

(3) *Performance criteria and program productivity*   Is it possible to discern a relationship between components of design, implementation, and performance? What are those identifiable characteristics that lead to enhanced productivity?

Design Environment

There were essentially three arenas in which states could significantly influence the design of their Small Cities Program. The first arena concerned that set of decisions in which states chose the agency that would have the most responsibility for administering and setting in motion the process of goal formation and program design. In relation to these decisions, two basic patterns of participation and influence existed. In the first, the governor and gubernatorial staff were prominent in choosing the lead agency and in determining overall program emphasis. This pattern occurred in approximately one-half of the states responding to the survey. In the remaining states, similar decisions were strongly influenced by career professional staff or by local elected officials who preferred state administration to that of HUD in Washington. About one-third of the states responding indicated that, although there had been little direct legislative involvement, the legislature's oversight function had been a prominent part of early design activities.

The second arena in which design of the Small Cities Program could be influenced involved that set of decisions leading to the formation and adoption of a set of specific state objectives for the program. Only two of the states responding to the survey had chosen to adopt the federal objectives rather than develop their own. In the remaining states, a concerted effort was often made to expand participation as widely as possible. This was achieved through the use of advisory committees, through a series of public hearings throughout the state, and through the use of selected intragovernmental 'experts', such as COGs, Regional Planning Agencies, and local planning officials.

The third and final way in which preliminary design of the program could be influenced concerned the adoption of specific project selection criteria. As would be expected, professional staff played a major role in this regulation writing function. In about one-half of the responding states, however, citizen advisory groups and local elected officials continued to play a role.

The overriding finding in relation to participation in the design environment is its very diffuse nature. Indeed, in only four of the states responding to the survey was there essentially the same group of participants in all three design decision arenas. Even more notable, in nine of the states it appears that there were three separate sets of actors for each of the three design activities. (To the extent that there was common participation in these cases, it was that of the professional staff.) In twenty of the states, there was common participation in two of the design activities, usually choice of state objectives and choice of selection criteria, but a different group of actors for the third activity.

Implementation Strategy

States also displayed considerable variation in relation to the implementation strategies they adopted. In only one of the states, Ohio, was the strategy of pure revenue sharing adopted. Other states varied primarily in the extent to which they decentralized the administrative function between central state staff and regional offices or groups. In some cases, program monitoring and technical assistance functions were reserved for central staff, while program funding decisions were reserved for regional offices or advisory groups. In other cases, funding responsibility was retained by central state staffs but a separate staff was responsible for monitoring. Finally, states varied in the extent to which the governor's office and the state legislature stayed involved in implementation activities. In four of the states, the governor either retained the program in his own executive offices or continued to play a major role in funding decisions. In eight of the states, members of the state legislature supplemented their oversight function by also serving as members of program advisory committees.

The nature of the goals adopted prior to implementation and project selection criteria also varied by state. The most frequently adopted state objectives fell into three broad categories:

(1) to enhance economic development – this objective was often associated with gubernatorial support for the program and included such activities as job creation, industrial development, and improvement of public facilities;

(2) to benefit low income residents of the state – this goal included such emphases as improving housing, decreasing blight, and targeting funds for low income areas and groups; and

(3) to increase openness and flexibility in program administration. Many states noted that they had opted for state administration because there was greater understanding of local needs and a greater willingness to work with local officials at the state level than there was among federal officials. This goal reflects the belief that state administration would change both the procedures related to the program and the nature of participation in the program. Such a goal is an excellent example of the 'process' priorities noted earlier.

The most frequently adopted project selection criterion was demonstrated need, while the second most frequently cited criterion was potential for leveraging funds, that is, for utilizing Small Cities monies to obtain additional funds from other sources. Finally, about one-third of the states indicated that the 'potential impact' of project activities was a selection criterion, but did not define the term further.

In sum, the data indicate the following:

(1) the number of participants in the design activities of Small Cities was large;

(2) the states adopted a variety of implementation strategies to administer the program; and

(3) a large number of program activities could be eligible for funding under the goals and selection criteria adopted.

Given this diversity, how would program success be judged? In the survey instrument, we asked respondents to name three potential performance criteria for their programs. To supplement these data we also examined HUD records to determine the number of applications received and grants awarded during the 1982–3 fiscal year.

Performance Criteria

Thirty-two of the thirty-four states had given some consideration to potential performance criteria. Despite the fact that many states had cited output-orientated or numbers-orientated selection criteria early in the survey instrument, at a later point in the same instrument, a large majority of respondents listed process or procedure-orientated performance criteria. In only nine of the states could performance criteria be accurately categorized as output-orientated. Many states combined output criteria with procedural concerns. In such cases, performance criteria included 'percent of funds directly benefiting low and moderate income persons' as well as 'acceptance by knowledgeable local officials' (Ingraham, 1982). In those fifteen states, which included at least one output criterion in their list, only six noted that these measures should be compatible with the selection criteria used to choose the programs. Four showed no relationship between the two sets of criteria, while the remaining five demonstrated at least passing awareness of the relationship.

The Relationship between Design and Outcome

The data cited above indicate that, though there may be some associations between design and implementation environments and activities, links between those levels of policy development and performance assessment are somewhat tenuous. Because our analysis demonstrated no relationship between type of implementation strategy and suggested performance criteria, we tested further for simple associations between elements of participation in design, nature, and size of administrative staff and the nature of the proposed performance criteria. As the tables indicate, the associations also provide little evidence of continuous linkages. They do, however, begin to clarify relationships between certain characteristics of participation and design priorities to administration and performance criteria.

As Table 4.1 indicates, some patterns of design participation are associated with the nature of state objectives adopted. The most interesting finding in this regard is the significant, but negative,

Table 4.1 Participation, design, and staff association

Level of influence	Staff size	State objectives Improved access	Flexibility
Governmental	− 0.27*	− 0.31*	− 0.01
Local	0.00	0.42*	0.35*

* Kendall Tau B significant at 0.05

association between gubernatorial (or gubernatorial staff) participation in program design and choice of objectives that emphasize more open and accessible program processes. Of equal importance, extensive local participation in early program design is associated rather strongly with emphasis on flexibility and accessibility of the program. Neither of these participation characteristics, however, is significantly associated with any performance criteria. That association is provided by certain staff characteristics (see Table 4.2).

As Table 4.2 indicates, modest association relationships exist between the professional background of the administrative staff and the nature of the proposed performance criteria. Perhaps the most interesting of these statistics are those demonstrating the relationship between professional planners and an emphasis on timeliness and on openness/flexibility. The significant negative relationships between openness/flexibility and staff background in budget or in general management are also of interest and suggest topics for future research on implementation.

Finally, in an effort to make a simple assessment of early program productivity, we analysed the associations between elements of design and implementation and total number of applications received and grants awarded, two performance criteria pertinent to organizational productivity. We used these preliminary measures of productivity rather than actual services delivered because of the relative youth of the program.

Table 4.3 shows some significant associations between design environment, design priorities, and preliminary measures of program performance. The fairly strong associations between staff size and number of applications and grants reaffirm common sense, but affirm-

Table 4.2   Association between background of professional staff and performance criteria

| | Performance criteria | | |
Staff	Timeliness	Flexibility	Quality
Size	−0.08	0.13	0.04
Planners	0.37*	0.27*	−0.04
Budget Analysts	0.21	−0.31*	—
Program Specialists	0.10	−0.22	0.10
General Managers	−0.24	−0.30*	0.26*

* Kendall Tau B significant at 0.05

Table 4.3 Association between elements of design and preliminary performance

| | Fiscal year 1982–3 | |
	Applications	Grants awarded
Gubernatorial involvement	0.42*	−0.08
Local participation	−0.02	0.05
Size of staff	0.57*	0.56*
Development objectives	0.41*	0.51*
Accessibility objectives	0.29	0.10
Flexibility objectives	0.20	0.34*

* Kendall Tau B significant at 0.05

ation of the association is, none the less, reassuring. Finally, the lack of a significant association between program objectives that emphasize openness and accessibility and preliminary program performance lends some credence to our hypothesis that programs that emphasize process objectives must be evaluated in terms other than quantitative performance measures.

SUMMARY AND CONCLUSIONS

Our analysis of the State Small Cities Program has demonstrated that attempts to judge productivity in the program are difficult. Important findings are discussed in the following paragraphs.

Given the freedom to choose program direction and design, states displayed considerable independence in their choice of program goals, in the manner in which they chose to implement the program, and in the criteria by which they selected specific programs for funding. This diversity demonstrates the natural diffusion that exists in the policy process and highlights the difficulties such programs present for evaluation. The nature of productivity varies; so too does our ability to recognize it.

Though the number and characteristics of the actors in the design environment varied from state to state, there do appear to be some associations between the nature of that participation and the nature of expectations for program performance. Gubernatorial participation was negatively associated with early emphasis on procedural or structural change; decentralized participation by local officials or other representatives was associated fairly strongly, and positively, with such change.

Similarly, some associations appear to exist between the background and size of the professional staff assigned to the program and the performance criteria that are suggested as measures of program performance. In addition, our analysis revealed a fairly strong association between some characteristics of professional staff and simple measures of program productivity. (We would note with these associations, as with others, that the level of aggregation may have distorted some relationships.) Our study made clear, for example, that in at least two cases, new staff looked at existing program operations, determined they were not productive, and immediately began lobbying for changes in both overall program goals and method of administration.

It is also important to note, however, that our analysis revealed significant discontinuities in the policy processes related to the Small Cities Program. The nature of participation varied for the decision to choose the lead agency, for selection of program goals, and for choice of selection criteria. Not surprisingly, then, there were also discontinuities between the priorities established by each of these decision-making processes. In some cases, the criteria suggested for program performance showed little relation to either program goals or selection criteria. Those discontinuities very clearly demonstrate the difficulties of judging productivity in such programs: the analysts' imposition of another set of performance criteria may or may not be related to what occurred before.

Again we restate our earlier point that different participation and different expectations for program performance mandate different definitions and measures of productivity. Those programs that consciously emphasize procedural change or 'flexibility' require different analyses than those programs that emphasize number of applications, number of jobs created, or number of dollars generated throughout the program development process. Further, it is important to note that the view of performance and productivity as procedural or institutional change is deeply rooted in the 'publicness' of public sector activities and sets them apart from private efforts. Though such qualities of public policies are not easily amenable to specific measurement of output, or perhaps even to measurement of eventual impact, they are an integral part of the contribution of public program efforts to the public good and to improvements in the quality of life. Programs that manage to achieve such changes are, in a very real sense, productive.

Finally, we note that when federal and state governments move to create more delegated, open-ended programs such as the State Small

Cities Program, there is always, at the beginning, a de-emphasis on concrete performance or productivity measures. Inevitably, however, the pendulum swings, and a demand to know what the program has accomplished arises. The data presented in this paper demonstrate the problems posed for evaluation and productivity assessment by variations in design and implementation and by the absence of linkages from either one to adequate performance criteria. Recognizing broader definitions of productivity would be a partial solution. Attempts to measure structural and procedural changes, as well as the satisfaction of citizens and elected officials with them, should rank high on our research agenda.

Notes

1. The SCCDBG was created in 1981 by the Omnibus Budget Reconciliation Act. It gave states the option to administer the Program and, if they chose to do so, provided them with very flexible funding opportunities. Though there were national objectives attached to SCCDBG, they were broad and permitted states to define their own priorities and programs. The natural experiment created by this flexibility and freedom, and the authors' familiarity with the parent Community Development Block Grant Program, caused us to choose the State Small Cities Program for study.
2. Since that time, approximately six additional states have chosen to participate in the state-administred Small Cities Program. No attempt was made to include those states in this analysis.

References

Ammons, D. N. and J. C. King (1983), 'Productivity improvement in local Governments: its place among competing priorities', *Public Administration Review*, (March/April) vol. 45, pp. 113–20.

Balk, W. L. (ed.) (1978), Symposium on 'Productivity in Government', *Public Administration Review* (Jan/Feb), vol. 38, pp. 1–52.

Bardach, E. (1977), *The Implementation Game* (Cambridge, MA: MIT Press).

Bleakley, K., C. Ferguson, C. Pendone, M. Millman and E. Small (1983; May), *The State Community Development Block Grant Program: The first year's experience*, Unpublished final report (Washington, DC: US Department of Housing and Urban Development).

Brigham, J. and D. Brown (eds) (1983), *Policy implementation: Penalties or incentives?* (Beverly Hills, CA: Sage).

Bullock, C. S., J. E. Anderson and D. W. Brady (1983), *Public Policy in the Eighties* (Monterey, CA: Brooks/Cole).

Burkhead, J. and P. J. Hennigan (1978), 'Productivity Analysis: A search for Definition and Order', *Public Administration Review* (Jan/Feb), vol. 38, pp. 34–40.

Elmore, R. L. (1982), 'Backward mapping: Implementation research and policy Decisions', in W. Williams (ed.), *Studying implementation: methodological and administrative issues* (Chatham, NJ: Chatham House), pp. 18–35.

Greiner, J. M., H. P. Hatry, M. Kass, A. P. Miller and J. P. Woodward (1981), *Productivity and Motivation: A Review of State and Local Government Initiatives* (Washington, DC: Urban Institute Press).

Hatry, H. P. (1976), 'Issues in Productivity Measurement for Local Government', in Holzer, M. (ed.), *Productivity in Public Organizations* (Port Washington, NY: Kennikat Press) pp. 89–105.

Henry, N. (1975), *Public Administration and Public Affairs* (Englewood Cliffs, NJ: Prentice-Hall).

Ingraham, P. (1982, March) Unpublished raw data (SUNY Survey, Center for Social Analysis).

Jones, C. O. (1977), *An Introduction to the Study of Public Policy* (North Scituate, MA: Duxbury).

Keevey, R. (1980), 'State productivity inprovements: Building on existing Strengths', *Public Administration Review* (Sept/Oct), vol. 40, pp. 451–8.

Lynn, L. E. (1981), *Managing the Public's Business* (New York: Basic Books).

Mayntz, R. (1983), 'The conditions of Effective Public policy: A new challenge for policy analysis', *Policy and Politics*, vol. 11, no. 2, pp. 123–43.

Nakamura, R. and F. Smallwood (1980), *The Politics of Policy Implementation* (New York: St. Martin's).

5 Workfare in New Jersey: A Five-Year Assessment[1]

Valerie Englander and Fred Englander

The initiatives of the Reagan Administration in the area of welfare reform have been orientated toward strengthening work requirements. This paper reviews the debate on the relative virtues of such 'workfare' and examines how successful these early workfare programs have been. Most evaluations of these programs have concluded that they were not successful in producing lasting changes in the labour market experience of participants or in reducing welfare rolls sufficiently to justify the resource costs of administering the programs.

The focus of this paper is on the New Jersey General Assistance Employability Program (GAEP), a workfare program imposed on New Jersey's General Assistance (GA) recipients in mid-1978. A general description of the mechanics of GAEP and the services offered by the program will be provided. Also included will be comparisons between GAEP and previous workfare programs, as well as comparisons between GAEP and the current Reagan Administration's emphasis on work requirements. An interrupted time series regression model will be presented to measure the impact of GAEP on the enrolment in the GA program. Results from this model will allow an assessment of what Bradley Schiller has called the 'taxpayer cost-effectiveness' of GAEP. That is, does the reduction in transfer payments generated by the program exceed its operating costs?

The regression model relates monthly total enrolment in GA, from 1970 through most of 1983, to a binary policy intervention variable and to variables that standardize for cyclical movements, population changes, the generosity of grants relative to average wages in the New Jersey manufacturing sector, and seasonal variations. Preliminary regression results suggest that GAEP has been successful in generating a tax saving in excess of the programs cost.

The concluding section addresses the limitations of the analysis and reviews the impact that GAEP, with its implicit effort to screen out less deserving recipients, has had on the adequacy of GA grants.

Despite the questionable success of incorporating work requirements into many welfare programs, the popularity of this concept persists. President Carter's proposed Program for Better Jobs and Income placed a strong emphasis on work requirements. Welfare recipients were to be given search assistance leading to private sector jobs. However, if such a placement did not occur, recipients would have to face acceptance of a public service job or the termination of their welfare status (Congressional Budget Office, 1978).

The principle initiative of the Reagan Administration in the area of welfare reform is contained in several of the provisions of the Omnibus Budget Reconciliation Act (OBRA), effective October 1981. A key feature of the Reagan program is to allow states greater flexibility in the development of work requirements. States are now permitted to establish a 'Community Work Experience Program' (CWEP) whereby a recipient must work in public service jobs to 'earn' his or her Aid to Families with Dependent Children (AFDC). They earn the minimum wage (Rein, 1982a). Recipients who do not co-operate with this provision are deleted from AFDC rolls. These features of a CWEP are directly parallel to the workfare program imposed on New Jersey's General Assistance (GA) recipients. Under the Reagan program, states may otherwise promote work requirements by designing work incentive demonstration projects (Rein, 1982a).

There are also parallels between New Jersey's workfare program and recent initiatives taken to stiffen the work test applied to participants in the Food Stamp program. As of January 1981, employable recipients are required to engage in an intensive job search over an eight-week period, including mandated contacts with a minimum number of potential employers and visits to public employment service offices (Rodgers, 1981).

Given the similarities between New Jersey's workfare program and the current directions in welfare reform, and also considering the greater discretion allowed states to meet the work requirement objectives mandated by OBRA, a consideration of the New Jersey experience may prove beneficial.

Taxpayers may view workfare as a means of reinforcing the work ethic among those receiving public assistance. Taxpayers may also expect workfare to produce meaningful financial dividends by strengthening the integrity of the eligibility review process and by increasing the quantity or quality of public services. If these dividends exceed the costs of operating the program, then workfare may be assessed as a productive mechanism of expressing society's policy of strengthening the work ethic among the poor. The central issue of this study is whether efforts to subject New Jersey's GA population to work requirements have generated sufficient reductions in transfer payments to justify the resources necessary to administer this reform. The methodology section develops a multiple regression based model to explain changes in the size of the GA population based on economic and labour market conditions, seasonal variations, secular trends, the relative generosity of GA payments, and the presence of workfare.

THE WORKFARE DEBATE

Those who have studied the concept of workfare – the imposition of work requirements on 'able-bodied' welfare recipients – soon become impressed with its popularity with the American public. For example, Blanche Bernstein, former administrator of the New York City Human Resources Administration, notes that 80 per cent of those surveyed in several national polls agreed that the people who can work should take public service jobs if private employment cannot be obtained (Bernstein, 1978).

To the extent that welfare reform proposals place greater emphasis on work requirements, they move a greater distance away from the idealized negative income tax plans that have received considerable attention over the past two decades. Negative income tax plans offer the advantage of a more limited administrative structure. Advocates hope that prudently established income guarantees and tax rates on labour effort would leave the recipients with greater work incentive than they have under current procedures. Though the results of the New Jersey and Gary Income Maintenance Experiments are consistent with this view, the more recently performed Rural Income Maintenance Experiment and the Seattle–Denver Income Maintenance Experiment found greater reductions in work effort (Masters and Garfinkel, 1977). Although such reductions in work effort may be moderated by imposing lower, more liberal, tax rates on earned income, additional evidence indicates that these lower tax rates would make more families eligible for program benefits by raising the break-even income level. This would induce a more than offsetting reduction in work effort among this latter group (Levy, 1979). This may be partially responsible for the strong interest in work requirements in the above-mentioned Reagan plan.

Workfare schemes can offer several advantages to recipients. They provide the client with work experience, on-the-job training, and often training in independent job search. The work effort may also be psychologically fulfilling. It is likely, however, that a major source of public support of such programs stems from the belief that imposing such a program will discourage actual or potential welfare recipients with less legitimate claims to society's largess. In other words, workfare is seen as a mechanism to relieve the burden placed on taxpayers (Bernstein, 1978).

It is on this latter point that such workfare critics as Leonard Goodwin have focused a major part of their attention. Goodwin (1978, p. 41) quotes a 1961 Department of HEW review of workfare in 27 states that had implemented workfare schemes: 'As currently administered work relief by itself is not significantly reducing the assistance rolls. . . . Work relief costs more in public funds than an assistance program without work relief'. Goodwin goes on to report similar findings from more recent workfare experiments such as California's Community Work Experience Program, New York City's Work Relief Employment Project, the Welfare Demonstration Project that emerged from the Emergency Employment Act of 1971 (initiated at twelve sites in four states), and the WIN program.

Tracing the evolution of work requirements under the WIN program into 1981, Mildred Rein has argued that these work requirements have been ineffective in promoting work effort, reducing caseloads, or moderating the growth of welfare costs. She argues that inadequate funding, congressional ambivalence, and the ideological opposition of the social service professionals entrusted with implementation have consistently frustrated the operation of the work requirements concept (Rein, 1982b).

Rein's negative conclusions as to the ability of work requirements to reduce enrolments in public assistance programs is shared by Charles Rodgers. Rodgers reviews the application of work requirements in the WIN Program, the Minnesota Work Equity Project that served AFDC, Food Stamp, and GA recipients, and the Massachusetts Work Experience Program serving male WIN recipients. The latter two programs were undertaken in the late 1970s. Rodgers attributes the inability of these efforts to reduce welfare enrolments to the same factors enumerated by Rein, but he particularly stresses the resistance of the staff of the welfare agencies comprehensively to impose and enforce work requirements. Given these difficulties, Rodgers (1981, p. 16) concludes, 'In the current welfare system, it is all too easy for the costs of effectively monitoring and enforcing these requirements to outstrip the potential benefits'.[2]

In his 1981 article reviewing the welfare directions of the 1960s and 1970s, Bradley Schiller has remarked on the variety of attempted strategies that have failed to achieve the stated goal of reducing caseloads:

These various welfare reforms would seem to have provided welfare recipients with every social and manpower service they might need to become productive workers. In its various manifestations, WIN alone has provided the following services: child-care assistance and financial aid; family planning; home and financial management; housing improvements; literacy training; basic education; high-school-equivalency training; vocational counseling; vocational training; training stipends; employer tax credits; vouchers for training and education services; work-orientation-and-experience positions; personal counselling; transportation assistance and subsidies; job search, referral and placement assistance, medical examinations and care; on-the-job training; and subsidized public employment. Indeed, most of these services have been available simultaneously, and financial incentives and sanctions have been used to help speed the actual movement of recipients off the rolls and into the jobs. Perhaps we haven't tried everything or all combinations of services, but no one can fault WIN's record of experimentation. The failure of previous welfare programs and reforms cannot be attributed to a lack of ingenuity.   (p. 58)

Schiller argues that the disappointing results may be caused by the unrealistic objectives by which we judge these programs. That is, moving these individuals from welfare rolls to employment rolls may not be feasible or productive strategy. Hence, the welfare system, he argues, should focus its energies on improving the provision of various support services to welfare clients.

NEW JERSEY'S GENERAL ASSISTANCE EMPLOYABILITY PROGRAM

The impetus for welfare reform in New Jersey can be traced to the proclamation made by former Governor Byrne (1977, p. 41) in his annual message in January 1977: 'As long as there is honest work to be done, nobody who is capable of doing it should be able to sit on his duff and draw welfare checks.' The governor's plea apparently struck a responsive chord among New Jersey taxpayers and led to the legislation passed and signed in November 1977 that mandated workfare for the state's then 26 000 GA recipients. The legislation (New Jersey Public Law, 1977, p. 3) requires the recipients, 'except when good cause exists, to perform public work as shall be assigned to them by the New Jersey Employment Service'.

GA recipients are persons who are not eligible for other types of assistance that provide greater financial support, such as AFDC, AFDC-Unemployed Parent, or Supplemental Security Income. The maximum monthly grant for GA recipients categorized as employable was $119 per month for the year prior to the introduction of the workfare program. These recipients do not qualify for more generous programs as they do not have children. They are nearly all single, and are predominantly males, non-high school graduates, and black or Hispanic. The determination as to whether a GA recipient is employable is made by the municipal welfare offices under guidelines established by the New Jersey Division of Public Welfare.

The New Jersey Department of Labor, Division of Employment Services was designated by law to implement and administer this program, generally referred to as the General Assistance Employability Program (GAEP). During this planning stage of the program, the New Jersey Department of Labor decided that rather than just assigning 'employable' GA recipients to municipal worksites, the Division of Employment Services' GAEP staff would make every effort to find unsubsidized employment for able-bodied recipients. It was hoped that by assisting people on welfare in getting real jobs, the Employment Service could demonstrate a greater saving to the taxpayers and at the same time give those GA recipients who were able to work an opportunity to attain a degree of economic self sufficiency.

The Employment Service assigned approximately 60 people to this project. The project included teams of counsellors, job developers (who would work with applicants and local firms to match job vacancies with potential employees), and clerks.

GA recipients deemed employable by the municipal welfare offices are referred to interviews with the nearby GAEP teams. At this interview, a determination is made (1) to refer someone with marketable skills directly to an appropriate private sector job; (2) to refer the applicant to another agency (for example, CETA or vocational rehabilitation) where needed supportive services are currently available; (3) to assign the individual to the orientation component of the program; (4) to assign the person directly to an appropriate municipal worksite; or (5) to call the person in at some later point in time if for some reason he or she cannot participate at present.

Those individuals who are assigned to orientation are considered worksite participants in order to meet the provisions of the law. As such, they are required to attend semi-weekly, half-day sessions in order to 'earn' their welfare grant. The purpose of orientation is to enable participants to obtain and be retained in appropriate unsubsidized employment. Emphasis is placed on teaching participants job-seeking skills, including how to fill out an application, how to handle a job interview, how to organize and conduct a job search, and, finally, job survival. Following this classroom module, orientation participants are assigned to monitored job search. In this component, clients must provide the names and addresses of employers with whom they have sought employment. These employers are contacted by GAEP staff on a random basis to verify this information. Participants may remain in orientation for no longer than three months. If, at the end of that time, they have been unable to find employment, they could be assigned to a municipal worksite. Municipal worksite participants work as many hours as necessary to 'earn' their monthly grants and are paid the wage rate that prevails for the assigned activity. GA recipients not complying with any one of these activities or procedures described above would be subject to termination from GA rolls.

METHODOLOGY

In the following interrupted time series regression equation, monthly data from October 1971 through June 1983 are used to estimate the impact of the GAEP on the number of GA cases in New Jersey. The model also standardizes for seasonal variations, the relative generosity of GA payments, cyclical changes and trends.

Equation 1

$$LNGA_t = B_o + \sum_{i=1}^{11} B_i M_i + B_{12} \, GADUM_t +$$
$$B_{13} \, TIME_t + \sum_{k=1}^{12} B_{14,k} \, LNGAREPL_{t-k} +$$
$$\sum_{j=1}^{18} B_{15,j} \, URATE_{t-j} + e_t$$

where:

$LNGA_t$ = the natural log of GA caseload in month t.
M_i = a set of monthly dummy variables for each month except September.

GADUM$_t$ = a policy intervention dummy variable; valued at 1 in those months (post June 1978) when GAEP was imposed on the employable GA population, 0 otherwise.

TIME$_t$ = 1 for January 1971; 2 for February 1971; 3 for March 1971, etc.

LNGAREPL$_t$ = the natural log of the ratio of average GA payments per case to the average wave in New Jersey manufacturing industries, in month t.

URATE$_t$ = the New Jersey unemployment rate in month t.

e_t = a stochastic error term.

The key variable for the purposes of this study is GADUM. It is hypothesized that the coefficient of this variable is negative, indicating that GAEP had a negative impact on GA caseloads.

The monthly dummy variables are included in the regression equation in order to determine if there are any seasonal patterns in the number of GA cases.

The trend variable is included to capture the effect of any variables changing over time that are not explicitly accounted for in the model. Examples of such factors may be population growth over the sample period or the perception of stigma associated with receiving GA.[3]

The state unemployment rate is a measure of general economic, and particularly labour market, conditions. Increases in this variable may be expected to increase the flow of applicants to GA and decrease the flow of terminations out of GA. Substantial lags in this process may be expected, given that potential applicants who have become unemployed may be able to collect Unemployment Insurance and/or draw on past savings and other assets before they apply for GA. Once they apply, further processing lags are possible. These considerations are formalized in the 18-month distributed lag specification of the unemployment rate variable presented in Equation 1. A positive relationship between the lagged unemployment rate and the level of GA caseloads is expected.[4]

The log of the ratio of average GA payments to average manufacturing wages, is a relative measure of the adequacy of GA payments. If, as C. T. Brehm and T. R. Saving (1964) suggested, the potential GA recipient may be likened to a rational consumer who weighs the costs and returns of applying for GA payments, a higher payment makes the program more attractive and would thus increase enrolment. The denominator of the ratio provides a measure of the opportunity costs of GA enrolment. The denominator, strongly influenced by changes in the cost of living, also serves to transform the level of GA payments from a nominal to a real measure. Applications for GA are a function of the current or recent adequacy of GA benefits, but, the dependent variable, the level of GA enrolment, is itself a function of applications in prior months. Thus, it appears reasonable to relate the level of GA applications to lagged values of the variable measuring the adequacy of GA benefits. A 12-month polynomial lag structure is utilized. A positive coefficient is expected for this variable.

THE FINDINGS

Equation 1 was estimated over the 141 monthly observations from October 1971 through June 1983, using the Cochrane–Orcutt maximum likelihood estimation technique to correct for autocorrelation. The results are presented in Table 5.1.

Table 5.1 Regression equation explaining the natural log of monthly GA cases in New Jersey

Explanatory variable	Estimated coefficient	t statistic
Constant	9.0914	26.990*
M1	0.0427	4.405*
M2	0.0452	4.487*
M3	0.0674	6.357*
M4	0.0404	4.049*
M5	0.0135	1.408
M6	−0.0043	−0.472
M7	−0.0052	−0.646
M8	0.0140	2.396*
M10	0.0021	0.363
M11	−0.0086	−1.118
M12	0.0302	3.365*
GADUM	−0.0411	−1.962*
TIME	0.0067	4.540*
LNGAREPL		
t–1	0.0024	0.087
t–2	0.0035	0.140
t–3	0.0046	0.201
t–4	0.0058	0.268
t–5	0.0069	0.338
t–6	0.0080	0.405
t–7	0.0092	0.462

Table 5.1   (*contd.*)

Explanatory variable	Estimated coefficient	t statistic
t–8	0.0103	0.503
t–9	0.0114	0.529
t–10	0.0126	0.541
t–11	0.0137	0.544
t–12	0.0148	0.540
URATE		
t–1	0.0016	0.841
t–2	0.0017	1.011
t–3	0.0018	1.217
t–4	0.0020	1.468
t–5	0.0021	1.776*
t–6	0.0022	2.146*
t–7	0.0024	2.576*
t–8	0.0025	3.026*
t–9	0.0026	3.407*
t–10	0.0028	3.610*
t–11	0.0029	3.590*
t–12	0.0031	3.407*
t–13	0.0032	3.155*
t–14	0.0033	2.898*
t–15	0.0035	2.666*
t–16	0.0036	2.464*
t–17	0.0037	2.292*
t–18	0.0039	2.146*

Notes:
Sum of lag coefficients for LNGAREPL = 0.1031; standard error = 0.2369
Sum of lag coefficients for URATE = 0.0489; standard error = 0.0138
R^2 (adjusted for degrees of freedom) = 0.9865
Durbin–Watson statistic = 2.094
* indicates significance at 0.05 level

The coefficient of the GADUM term is negative and statistically significant, indicating that the GAEP did have an impact on reducing GA caseloads. When this coefficient is transformed, it generates an estimated 4.194 per cent decrease in GA caseloads as a result of GAEP. Further computation demonstrates that GAEP resulted in an estimated drop in monthly GA caseloads of 1095. Note that this reduction in GA caseloads may have resulted from (i) a shorter average duration on the welfare roll as some participants succeeded in getting jobs as a result of services received in the program; (ii) a reluctance of some potential recipients to apply for GA benefits, given that they do not have the desire or ability (that is, they may have jobs 'off the books') to be burdened by GAEP obligations; or (iii) an administrative purging from the rolls of those clients who have not complied with program responsibilities.

The coefficients of the lagged values of the LNGAREPL variable are positive, as predicted by the view that higher GA payments attract more recipients. However, these coefficients are not statistically significant. GA rolls are increasing over time, holding everything else constant, according to the result for the trend variable. With respect to seasonal patterns, GA rolls appear to rise significantly over the January to April period, again in August, but fall in November at a rate which approaches statistical significance.

The expected positive relationship between GA caseloads and the lagged values of the unemployment rate is also observed. Although the relationship between GA caseloads and the lagged unemployment rate is insignificant for lag periods $t-1$ to $t-4$, this relationship is statistically significant for lag periods $t-5$ to $t-18$.

While a full cost-benefit evaluation of GAEP is beyond the scope of this chapter, the data are clear enough to allow us to develop estimates of the program's benefits (that is, the reductions in GA expenditures) and to compare these with the program costs. The average monthly enrolment reduction of 1095 computed from Table 5.1 translates into a total reduction of 65 700 recipient months over the 60-month post-implementation period. Given an average monthly benefit of $110 for non-employable recipients over this period, a total dollar savings of $7 227 000 is estimated. This measure of program benefits is considerably above the accumulated program costs of $4 666 233 over the five-year post-implementation period.

Of course, this comparison ignores some measures of program benefits, both tangible and intangible. The value of the extra output of GAEP participants placed in private or public sector jobs and possible reductions in the demand for other public service programs are not included. Hence, these figures provide a conservative measure of the cost-effectiveness of the program.

CONCLUSION

It seems clear that New Jersey's General Assistance Employability Program reduced state GA rolls substantially and significantly below what they would have been in its absence. This resulted in a tax saving substantially in excess of the program's costs, unlike the case in many

other such programs. Therefore, Schiller's conclusion that work requirements are unworkable appears premature. Although it will take
time for the current workfare policy initiatives to be evaluated, the New
Jersey experience raises the distinct possibility that workfare is a cost-
effective strategy for effecting society's preferences that able-bodied
welfare recipients should work for their welfare grant.

Yet there are several important issues that this study does not address.
Given the nature of the data available, it is impossible to determine how
many of the individuals who found unsubsidized employment would
have done so in the absence of GAEP. It is also impossible to determine
how many individuals deterred from GA rolls by GAEP did indeed have
a legitimate claim to benefits. In fact, some may argue that it amounts to
harassment of those most vulnerable members of society who are least
able to defend themselves. On the other hand, the somewhat more lax
enforcement of eligibility requirements, which preceded the imposition
of GAEP, probably allowed many recipients to receive GA without a
legitimate claim to such benefits. The significant public perception that
the size of GA rolls may be swelled by the presence of many recipients
with a dubious claim to these benefits may have contributed to the
substantial reduction in the real value of GA grants that has been
observed over the five years preceding GAEP. To the extent that the
GAEP program has succeeded in purging GA rolls of recipients without
legitimate claim to benefits, public resources could have been concentrated on those remaining recipients, presumably with greater need,
and the public and its elected representatives may have felt more
comfortable in increasing the purchasing power of GA grants. However,
this has not been the case. The purchasing power of GA grants has
continued to fall over the five year post-GAEP period.

Notes

1. The authors wish to express their gratitude to Lester Barenbaum, Steven
   Director and Neil Sheflin for their helpful comments on an earlier draft of this
   paper.
2. Note that this theme is also stressed in a recent review of work requirements
   in New York City's eight WIN offices (see Lawrence Mead, 1983). Although
   Mead focuses on the narrower performance measure of client job placement
   rather than impact, overall caseloads, or cost-effectiveness, he finds higher
   performance in those WIN offices where the staff took a more active roll in
   clarifying and reinforcing the obligations imposed on the client by the work
   requirement program. Mead concludes that the overall success of the
   program is hampered by regulations that provide insufficient sanctions to
   those clients who do not meet their obligations.

3. For an interesting, recent discussion of this issue, see R. Moffit (1983). Note that although monthly population figures are available, the variable was very highly correlated with the trend variable and thus was not included in the model.
4. For a discussion of the first degree polynomial lag approach, followed for the URATE and LNGAREPL variables, see R. S. Pindyck and D. L. Rubinfeld (1981). Note that other lag lengths and second and third degree polynomial lag structures were attempted. In all of these specifications altering the lag lengths for the LNGAREPL and URATE variables, the lag length of the URATE variable was six months longer than the lag length of the LNGAREPL variable. This follows from the assumption that it takes approximately that long for many potential GA applicants to exhaust their Unemployment Insurance benefits. The results were not substantially different with these other specifications. The specification provided in Equation 1 was selected as it provided the best fit of the data.

References

Bernstein, B. (1978), 'Do work requirements accomplish anything? – The case for work requirements', *Public Welfare*, 16, pp. 36–9.

Brehm, C. T. and T. R. Saving (1964), 'The demand for general assistance', *American Economic Review*, 54, pp. 1002–18.

Byrne, B. (1977), 'Third annual message delivered to the state legislature, January 1977' (Trenton, NJ: Office of the Governor).

Congressional Budget Office (1978), *The administration's welfare reform proposal: An analysis of the program for better jobs and income* (Washington, DC: US Government Printing Office).

Goodwin, L. (1978), 'Do work requirements accomplish anything? – The case against work requirements', *Public Welfare*, 16, pp. 39–45.

Levy, F. (1979), 'The labor supply of female household heads, or AFDC work incentives don't work too well', *Journal of Human Resources*, 14, pp. 76–97.

Masters, S. and I. Garfinkel (1977), *Estimating labor supply effects of income maintenance alternatives* (New York: Academic Press).

Mead, L. (1983), 'Expectations and welfare work: WIN in New York City', *Policy Studies Review*, 2, pp. 648–62.

Moffit, R. (1983), 'An economic model of welfare stigma', *American Economic Review*, 73, 1023–35.

New Jersey Public Law (1977), Chapter 286, Approved 30 November 1977 (Trenton, NJ: New Jersey State Legislature, 1–4).

Pindyck, R. S. and D. L. Rubinfeld (1981; 2nd edn), *Econo-Metric models and economic forecasts* (New York: McGraw-Hill).

Rein, M. (1982a), 'Work in welfare', *Social Science Review*, 57, pp. 211–29.

Rein, M. (1982b), *The dilemmas of welfare policy* (New York: Praeger Publishers).

Rodgers, C. (1981), 'Work tests for welfare recipients', *Journal of Policy Analysis and Management*, 1, pp. 5–17.

Schiller, B. (1981), 'Welfare: Reforming our expectations', *Public Interest*, 60, pp. 55–65.

6 Indirect Provision of Government Services: Contracts and Productivity

James Latimore

The effect on productivity of 'contracting out' public services, such as manpower and health care, is examined. This is done by comparing the concept of productivity and the requirements for achieving productivity gains with some of the essential features of the contract. In general, the contract, as presently used, is seen to impede productivity in the public sector. This is explained in part on the basis of the structured relations of government, relations that lead to a greater interest in contract compliance and accountability than productivity. A case study of a manpower program and an analysis of recent changes in the Medicare program are offered as examples of the 'productivity brake' applied by the federal government. The material is then used to derive some recommendations for increasing productivity in contracted work.

Much of the work of the federal government is actually performed by contractors and vouchering agents – that is, organizations such as hospitals that are reimbursed for services performed. When work is contracted out in the public sector, this appears to affect the productivity gains possible, in some instances at least, making an increase in productivity more difficult to achieve. To understand why this is so, it is necessary to consider briefly what is involved in measuring productivity and achieving productivity gains, to discuss certain essential features of contracts, and to relate these to the structured relations of the federal government. Then the results obtained from the study of a contracted manpower program will be summarized, and some implications for the Medicare program will be discussed.

PRODUCTIVITY

Space does not permit a thorough review of the concept of productivity and the problems involved in measuring it. It will be sufficient, however, to identify a few of the most important features of the concept.

(1) Productivity is measured by means of a ratio of outputs and inputs (0/1). Total factor productivity involves identifying all the relevant outputs and inputs and incorporating them into the ratio so as to assess the net savings achieved in production (Kendrick, 1977, pp. 1, 3, 6).

(2) Productivity is a relative and comparative measure rather than an absolute one: gains or losses can be gauged only by means of comparisons with earlier time periods or with other organizations (Kendrick, 1977, p. 13). As a corollary, we might add that in the absence of such comparisons, the necessary steps to achieve productivity gains will not be taken.

(3) The factors that affect productivity are interactive: changing (or fixing) one affects the others (Greenberg, 1973, p. 2). A corollary is that unplanned changes stemming from the environment require internal adjustments to maintain productivity.

(4) Productivity gains require an investment of some kind. Machinery represents one kind of investment. However, intangible investments, in research and development, education and training, even safety and health, are usually required (Kendrick, 1977, p. 9).

(5) In the services sector, productivity is not increased by decreasing the service (Heaton, 1977, pp. 47, 58–9). In other words, productivity, in the quantitative sense, that is gained at the expense of quality is a spurious gain.

(6) The measurements of productivity employed, whether single factor or total factor, have an ideological and social-control dimension (Heaton, 1977, p. 13; Macarov, 1982, p. 14)

CONTRACTS

The contract is a basic instrument in a market economy, so familiar that we tend to take it for granted. Yet contracts require making certain assumptions, and the contract form takes on certain typical features that have some bearing on productivity.

Assumptions are usually deceptively simple, and these are no exception. They are:

(a) that there is sufficient knowledge of the matter at hand to make rational judgements and enter into a contract;

(b) that acts and events are discrete, and thus there are no contingent effects of the contract nor is the contract affected by other factors;

(c) that the world is static for all practical purposes; and

(d) that the parties have conflicting, even opposite, interests at stake and are not to be trusted in principle.

At least partly for these reasons, the form of the contract usually takes on the following characteristics:

(1) it is written;
(2) it contains specified objectives or quotas to be achieved;
(3) it is present-orientated and situational in almost every respect – for example, negotiated on the basis of strength or need, without reference to the performance of any other organization;
(4) the terms of the contract are fixed, irrevocable, and binding;
(5) performance under the contract is verifiable, involving monitoring provisions, but not subject to any direct control;
(6) the contract is ultimately coercive (rather than consultative or co-operative);
(7) the capital inputs are fixed and limited to protect the 'investor'.

Given these features, it seems evident that when government work is performed indirectly, through contracts, productivity gains are harder to come by. No direct control over inputs exists; no productivity-enhancing adjustments are possible. The inputs are fixed and specified (as are the throughputs often). Investment is not directly provided for or contemplated and is, in the short run, actively discouraged. Output will be focused on specified objectives or quotas ('single-factor output') with a resultant decline in overall output or 'quality'. Even if all these should be reversed, there is no 'productivity clause' in the typical contract – that is, no comparisons or base performances to gauge productivity, and no rewards for doing so. Productivity involves a target in motion: past gains are incorporated in the base, which must then be surpassed. Investment and innovation are crucial. Contract compliance involves stationary targets. Budget-like items, monitoring, and enforcement of standards are crucial.

These considerations would, for the most part, apply to contracted work in any setting, private or public. The difference is that in the public sector, it is somewhat more difficult for officials to escape the constraints if they should desire to do so.

STRUCTURE

Government is essentially a power structure, not a production mechanism, and survival of the 'organization' does not really depend on its productivity in a market. Thus, productivity is seldom a central concern, compared with gaining office. This is also reflected in the particularistic staffing of appointed positions: one's friends and supporters are more qualified for the positions than others (even though strong ideological differences are notably lacking in American politics). Productivity is also a peripheral matter in government operations when it requires compromising the interests of some constituency, as it often does. What should be a simple matter of closing down an unneeded military base is not a simple matter.

Not only is any incentive for productivity in government negated by other more powerful forces, the use of productivity measures (when this occurs) tends to be based more on the desire for accountability within the structure than on the net saving of resource inputs – a prime consideration when productivity is concerned. The 1973 report of the Joint Federal Productivity Project attempted to clarify 'what productivity measures are and what they *are not*', and concluded that they are 'techniques to make managers explain past trends in resources expended per unit of final output', and are 'means of reporting productivity change to the Congress'. That is, they are significant in terms of accountability.

Linder (1978) has argued that the structure of American government, with its separation of powers, along with judicial interpretations of the Constitution regarding the delegation of congressional discretion and authority, lead to formal controls over executive agencies – controls involving terms and standards of accountability. On the one hand, separation of power requires that the legislature impose formal controls on executive agencies to enforce responsiveness and accountability, while on the other, extensive administrative discretion 'is taken as an abuse of popular sovereignty' by the courts. Restricted delegations of authority to administrative agencies are not precluded, but they must be clearly specified and delimited to certain purposes. Thus, for constitutional and structural reasons, federal administrative agencies are required to be responsive and accountable to Congress in terms that can be operationalized, involving delimited delegation of discretion. Legislative intent specifies areas of concern; these provide cues for the agencies in the development of more precise indicators so that quantitative reports of progress can be made when seeking further funding. In principle, this does not exclude productivity, though it does make the necessary delegation of authority and discretion more problematic. From this standpoint, we can also see why contracted work in the public sector is focused more on accountability than on productivity.

PRODUCTIVITY IN A MANPOWER PROGRAM

Productivity is a ratio of outputs and inputs. While there is no 'absolute productivity', since it is a comparative measure, the concept itself would necessarily mean effective utilization of the resources available. Resources (representing investments) sitting idle or not needed for the task at hand are for that reason wasted and thus reduce the productivity of the organization in terms of the measured output.

In the author's study of a contracted manpower program, the non-profit agency providing the service grew in a four-year period from a rather small organization funded largely by private contributions supplemented by 'best effort' contracts with local government units to a moderate-sized organization funded to a great extent by CETA money accompanied by production-orientated contracts. 'Best-effort contracts' were those in which the general objectives of the relationship were specified – in this case, it was counselling and job placement for disadvantaged youth – but without further specifications of 'production quotas' (an agreed number of placements required for contract compliance), or the technology for accomplishing the task. The agency was to make its 'best effort' to obtain the desired results. The subsequent 'production-orientated contracts', by contrast, contained measured outputs (number of job placements to be effected in total, and by the month), detailed characteristics of the clients to be served (material input), and the throughputs required, such as the use of a job-preparation workshop and the number of job-site visits once a client was employed. In addition, the reported placements were verified by government representatives, and the contract had provisions for penalizing the manpower agency should the placement quotas not be met. The intent of these provisions was to maximize 'productivity' by getting the most output (placements) for the given input (contract cost). The effect of this was all the greater since the agency grew increasingly dependent on such contracts.

One consequence of these changes was to decrease the effectiveness in the agency program. Under the earlier best-effort contracts, counsellors in the agency accepted the responsibility for placing those clients who were the hardest to place: the youngest ones, especially those with the least education and work skills or experience. It was not easy to get such clients to return to the agency several times, which was necessary to secure them a job. Many clients were 'correctional cases', suspicious of institutional services and they were often under pressure from parole or probation officers. These clients were very time-consuming in terms of the results (placements) achieved, but this was defined as one of the major purposes of the agency, and the effort was made, even knowing in advance that it would not pay off quickly. Under the new contracts, however, these clients were systematically 'weeded out' by requiring them to keep in touch with the counsellors by phone or in person at the agency. This requirement was aimed at weeding out the clients who were not ready for placement. The change was measured by going through the agency files and counting the number of clients who did not return after the initial interview in the two time periods. These one-interview clients increased from 17 per cent of the agency's intake to about 44 per cent in the later period. The practice of weeding out clients was also confirmed by interviews with the agency's counsellors.

The clients who were weeded out were, however, the very ones for whom the contract programs were designed. The funded 'resource inputs' included remedial education, a job-preparation workshop to improve attitudes towards employment and interview skills, video equipment for the job-preparation workshops and other purposes, tuition allowances for training in private trade schools, and training stipends.

In order to meet the production quotas and unit costs specified in the contracts, agency counsellors recruited clients from neighbourhood centres – clients who were older and in other ways more easily placed on jobs. One result was that while the placement quotas were met, the resources were not needed and, in fact, were not really used to achieve the output as it was defined in the contracts: job placements. In other words, *productivity* would have been higher if these resources had never been funded in the first place.

Productivity did, in fact, decline during the period of study. The productivity decrease in the agency can be summarized as shown in Table 6.1.

In Table 6.1, year 2 is the year immediately preceding the first of the large, new production-orientated contracts, and year 4 is the one immediately following. Whether we use man-hours or agency budget (as

Table 6.1

Year	Agency budget ($)	No. of clients seen	No. of clients placed	Staff size	Man-hours
1	389 787	2737	2213	24	40 320
2	423 498	2866	2191	24	40 320
4	709 118	3210	1333	46	77 280

a crude indicator of all factors) in assessing productivity, if the number of placements is the measure of output, as it was, then productivity declined between year 2 and year 4. A shortage of unskilled jobs at the time undoubtedly contributed to a decrease in the number of job placements. However, the main point is that the contracts neither measured nor stimulated productivity in dealing with a given clientele. Contract accountability took precedence over productivity. In the case of this manpower program, the measurements of production used were probably effective controls in that they 'got the attention' of the personnel and made some accountability possible, but not effective in so far as they encouraged subterfuges to obtain acceptable results. And, of course, they were not effective in promoting greater productivity, which, as we noted earlier, is usually obtained through *investment* rather than coercion, and requires keeping an eye on the *ratio*, not output alone.

MEDICARE AND PRODUCTIVITY

The federal government's most recent major intervention in the economy, with implications for productivity, involves changes in Medicare reimbursements. Reimbursements will be standardized for a specific 'diagnosis related grouping' (DRG). The intent or the hope is to stimulate productivity gains in the health-services sector by eliminating the *carte blanche* formula previously used and by putting a cap on reimbursements for specified diagnoses (and thus treatment). Hospitals and doctors will have to work out ways to provide their services in a more efficient and less costly manner. Presumably, this will take the form of greater productivity: fewer inputs for the same output.

This will not be an easy task. Besides the familiar problem of defining and measuring output, including quality, there is no direct control by the federal government over all inputs – including investments – which we have suggested is essential for the achievement of productivity gains.

In the health-care sector, investments are largely controlled by the 'high-tech' industrial firms, with their productivity being stimulated by (and reflected in) their profit margins and stock prices. But for the hospital, productivity requires accepting the investments of others (suppliers) that are directed to the market of doctors – then trying to make 'productive' use of them in a labour-intensive industry. The government, of course, has even less control over these forces at present than the hospital does. Given these conditions, we might not expect much in the way of productivity increases – keeping in mind that production gains or cost reductions accompanied by service reductions do not represent an increase in productivity. However, this analysis, while on the whole probably correct, obscures some interesting and important features of the situation. Two points seem particularly important in this connection. The first is that voluntary hospitals are somewhat limited in their ability to invest in productivity-enhancing technologies. Aside from local bond issues these hospitals rely on accumulated reserves to finance investments. These reserves are set aside from income which, of course, includes income from Medicare.

The second point is that there are two rather different kinds of technology observable in the hospital field. The first might be described as 'quality-enhancing technology' and would include CAT scanners, digital radiography equipment, ultrasound machines, and the like, the main effect of which is to increase the quality of health services, where quality is defined as including fewer invasions of the body, improved diagnostic capabilities, and more effective treatment. There are, however, 'cost-reducing technologies' also: autoanalysers in the laboratory, computers, disposables, waste-disposal systems, the layout of nursing stations and rooms, outpatient surgery centres, to name but a few.

The capital for investment in both technologies comes from accumulated reserves, revenue bonds, or local bond issues. Construction of new facilities or renovations of existing ones, one of the most costly items in the health-care field (and not the most productive one by any means, since it often reflects aesthetic concerns and protection of territory) will continue to be financed by local bond issues will not be directly responsive to the Medicare caps. However, investment in technology may well be affected. The risk is that investment in either quality-enhancing or cost-reducing technology (or both) will be reduced. The result would be that the technological advance, which is said by all to be the most important single stimulus to productivity gains, is here curbed. Of course, this technological advance on the whole has in the recent past been purchased at an ever-increasing cost. But it will not help to achieve greater productivity if services are reduced, or, more to the point, if the cost-reducing technologies are restrained by the same mechanism that curbs the quality-enhancing technologies. It is too early to say whether this will occur or not, but there seems to be the distinct possibility, inherent in the changed regulations, that the cost caps alone may have a negative impact on productivity. Some events may be predicted with a little more certainty however: layoffs (already occurring) and a decline in services, for example. This is not necessarily bad (unless, of course, you are a hospital patient). From a productivity standpoint, however, a decline in services is not a productivity gain. Other somewhat more likely projections would include the 'weeding out' of costly patients by sending them to government-run hospitals whenever possible, or discharging them at the financially-optimal time. That such tactics are being actively considered is evident in a recent issue of *The Wall Street Journal*:

> The real problem with the prospective payment system, others fear, is that hospitals will become adept at getting around it. One possible tactic: arbitrarily assigning patients to DRGs that pay more than their ailments would warrant. . . . Another: shifting costs to non-Medicare patients. Some software companies are peddling computer programs they claim will show hospitals how to do just that. (Phillips, 1984)

This does not mean that the new system will have no effect on costs. On the contrary, there is a decided shift in the operation of hospitals already, with an increased emphasis on ambulatory surgery and free-standing 'minor medical centres'. Some hospitals are going into the home-health-care business while others are experimenting with 'self-care wards' in which certain patients take care of their own routine needs. And there appears to be more and more sharing of costly equipment, such as CAT scanners, among smaller hospitals, by means of contractual arrangements with mobile scanner services. The cost of diagnosing and treating certain ailments (for certain people) will probably be affected by these trends (none of which began with the prospective payment system, but all have been impelled forward by it). However, the productivity of the hospital will not necessarily be increased thereby. For one thing, the minor medical centres, ambulatory surgery facilities, and so on, have to be built, requiring an investment — that is, increased capital input. In the short run, competition from HMOs or from some other source may reduce output by limiting the input of 'material', or patients, and thus, reducing output. From a productivity standpoint the output of a hospital is, in the simplest terms, *former patients* (or whatever we choose to call them). If output declines, because of fewer admissions stemming from the diversion of patients elsewhere, and there is no significant reduction in other material inputs (embodied in the high-tech diagnostic and therapeutic technologies), the result may be a decline in productivity also.

There is no indication that Congress really wants to face up to the quality question in health care, preferring in this case to limit financial inputs and hoping thereby to encourage or force others to decide how much to invest in new life-saving technology and who shall have access to it. But quality is crucial. Whether the output of hospitals ('former patients') are living or dead makes a difference.

The DRG seems to be designed essentially to measure work rather than increase productivity. In any event, two things seem clear at present. The first is that for the most part doctors will continue to practise medicine as they have been trained to do (until they are trained otherwise) and will anticipate the same rewards. At first glance, it would seem that hospitals (and other service industries) are unique in that their raw materials (patients) cost them nothing. But in reality, the patients are 'sold' by their doctors who expect, in return, extensive and up-to-date facilities and other privileges. The second is that hospitals are caught in the middle between doctors and the health-care industry which must market its products and will not hesitate to discontinue services on existing models so as to build sales for new ones. Efforts to promote productivity in this case should focus on the doctors and on the private industries, rather than the hospital.

SUMMARY

The effort to promote greater productivity in the public sector, where the work is contracted, faces several obstacles. One has to do with the contract itself, as it is presently used. In a word, the contract makes the wrong assumptions about the world – for example, that it is unchanging and made up of discrete elements – and then further limits the search for productivity gains by focusing exclusively on the specific production quotas, and so on, required for contract compliance. Another obstacle derives from the government's lack of control over resource inputs. Productivity is measured by the ratio between outputs and inputs. To increase productivity requires ongoing control over and surveillance of inputs. Where services are contracted, the contracting organization represents all major inputs except a portion of capital, and government has little or no control over changing the mix of inputs. Thus, it is in no position to increase productivity. A government agency can control or negotiate price (through bids, for example) but heretofore has made little attempt to negotiate productivity. The best it can do (or does do) is to accept low bids, fix unit costs and terms of accountability, and engage in work measurements. However, these may encourage subterfuges such as the substitution of 'material' (clients) in the manpower program studied and in general may inhibit productivity gains rather than the contrary.

Finally, in an elective political system, the more fundamental interests of political officials take precedence over production. The federal government is primarily a power structure rather than a production entity. Its activities as a whole and those of its incumbents are designed to secure and maintain power and control – over the populace, over contenders, over foreign threats, and others. Productivity, and the measures of it as well as the programs to achieve it, are subordinated to power. Internally, it has no competitors, no 'market test' of productive efficiency. The major incentive to 'do better', in terms of a ratio between outputs and inputs, is to maintain power thereby. Power is maintained by focusing on short-term goals consistent with the interests and outlooks of powerful supporters.

OUTLOOK

These tendencies, important though they are, need not prevent the federal government from having a beneficial effect on productivity in the organizations with which it contracts for the performance of government services. Some ways in which this might be brought about are suggested below.

(1) Productivity gains may be negotiated, in addition to (if not instead of) cost.
(2) Productivity gains may be rewarded. Sharing the savings is never a bad idea. We must remember, however, that reducing services does not by itself represent a productivity gain.
(3) Greater attention should be paid to the 'material' processed in human services than to production quotas. The material specified should be the actual material input.
(4) A readiness to increase investment (in labour or equipment) during the life of a contract may yield productivity gains more readily than fixing investment at the outset of the contract.
(5) A break-in period to test the technology, the adequacy of the labour input, and so on, may make it possible to then formulate productivity gains to be sought during the contract period.
(6) If there is to be 'accountability', it should be in terms of material, quality, and productivity, rather than quotas and simple unit costs.

(7) Productivity gains can only be ascertained by comparisons with earlier time periods. Thus, one-shot contracts cannot provide this. Longer, multi-stage contracts, contingent on productivity gains might be appropriate.

References

Greenberg, L. (1973), *A Practical Guide to Productivity Measurement* (Washington DC: Bureau of National Affairs, Inc.).

Heaton, H. (1977), *Productivity in Service Organizations: Organizing for People* New York: McGraw-Hill).

Joint Federal Productivity Project (1973), *Measuring and Enhancing Productivity in the Federal Government, Summary Report*, in M. Holzer (ed.), *Productivity in Public Organizations* (Port Washington, NY: Kennikat Press, 1976) pp. 87–8.

Kendrick, J. W. (1977), *Understanding Productivity: An Introduction to the Dynamics of Productivity Change* (Baltimore: Johns Hopkins University Press).

Linder, S. H. (1978), 'Administrative Accountability: Administrative Discretion, Accountability, and External Controls, in Green, S., R. D. Hedlund, and J. L. Gibson (eds), *Accountability in Urban Society Public Agencies Under Fire* (Beverly Hills: Sage Publications) pp. 181–95.

Macarov, D. (1982), *Worker Productivity: Myths and Reality* (Beverly Hills: Sage Publications).

Phillips, C. (1984), 'Medicare's New Limits on Hospital Payments Force Wide Cost Cuts', *Wall Street Journal*, 2 May.

Part III
Cost Containment Strategies and Productivity

7 Obstacles to Doing More with Less: Illustrations from the Kansas Experience

Kim S. Hunt

State budgeting reforms are often instituted with a strong desire to improve the productivity of state government. This article examines the connections between productivity and budgeting reforms. A decision-making framework is developed with which to suggest potential obstacles to successful implementation of budget reforms. Using examples from the Kansas experience, these obstacles are systematically examined.

The rallying cry for state and local government during the 1980s is 'Doing more with less'. This pronouncement holds great appeal to elected officials who must attempt to manage the high expectations of citizens for services during a climate of citizen resentment of taxation. 'Doing more with less' is also appealing to students of budgetary politics who perceive that changing conditions herald new demands on the budget process (Caiden, 1981, 1984; Bozeman and Straussman, 1982). On the heels of Proposition 13 and other tax reduction movements, states throughout the nation faced the most severe recession in over forty years. The recession led to budget retrenchment challenges brought on by revenue shortfalls. Loath to cut services, many states sought temporary or permanent tax increases in addition to budget cuts.[1] However, it is not likely that state leaders have forgotten the popularity of tax reduction movements and must expect to do more with less by demonstrating the efficiency and effectiveness of state expenditures.

Productivity improvements tied to budget processes are one way to demonstrate a commitment to fiscal 'belt-tightening'. This paper seeks first to clarify the concepts of productivity as it relates to budgeting, then to briefly describe the Kansas budget innovation within this context, and

127

finally to present the obstacles to productivity and budgeting innovations using a decision-making framework, with illustrations from the Kansas experience. The fiscal climate in Kansas during the period of study was not unlike the climate prevailing in most states. Kansas state government faced declining budget balances during fiscal years 1982 and 1983 and responded with expenditure cuts, expenditure delays, and advanced tax dates during FY 1983 (National Governors' Association, 1983). In short, the Kansas setting was one of fiscal stress; conditions in which 'doing more with less' through budgeting and productivity innovation had become important.

PRODUCTIVITY AND THE BUDGETARY PROCESS

The emphasis on improved productivity, on doing more with less, has been heightened by the fiscal crisis that many state and local governments have recently experienced. In this sense, these concerns may seem temporary and merely fashionable, particularly if state and local governments look back on this period as a short-range crisis. After all, some states are now reporting budget surpluses where only recently alarms were sounding over record deficits. However, the concern with productivity is deeply ingrained in American politics, dating back at least as far as Woodrow Wilson (1887), who promised a higher standard of efficiency to accompany governmental activism. American government at all levels has pursued higher standards of productivity through the mechanism of the budget process, dating back to the emphasis on expenditure control evident in the Budget and Accounting Act of 1921. The pinnacle was reached in Luther Gulick's seminal contribution, in which he stated that 'efficiency' was 'axiom number one in the value scale of administration' (Gulick and Urwick, 1937, p. 192).

The concept of productivity is not limited to efficiency. James Harkin (1982) coined the term 'effectiveness budgeting', a term intended to include a variety of budget reforms attempting to link activities with intended outcomes so that the desired results would be produced during the budget cycle (p. 112). Among these techniques are Program Planning and Budgeting Systems, Management by Objective, Zero Base Budgeting, and the many hybrids that have been adopted nationwide (Schick and Harry, 1982). These techniques seek to hold government to a higher standard of productivity, through a systems approach linking the use of resources to consequent outcomes. In contrast, measures of simple efficiency tend to emphasize only one portion of the system.

Bahl and Burkhead (1977) conceive a system consisting of five vectors: environment, input, activities, output, and consequences. Environment describes conditions leading to a need for government intervention; inputs are labour and capital employed by the public sector; activities concern the deployment of inputs in certain patterns; outputs reflect decisions made during the activities stage and consist of the quantity and quality of the public good or service; and finally, consequences concern the effect of the output upon the environment relative to some standard (pp. 258–61).

Measures of productivity tend to focus upon only one or two of these vectors at a time. A relatively narrow measure of productivity is expenditure control, which treats inputs in relative isolation. A somewhat more ambitious standard of productivity, one much stressed in management literature, relates inputs to activity patterns. Both of these productivity measures are well within the purview of traditional line-item budgeting which tracks spending by category. A more ambitious standard of productivity is efficiency, which relates inputs to outputs. It is at this level that decision-makers begin to encounter serious problems regarding conceptualization and measurement. There are few discrete units of public output, and no price tags can be regularly attached to units of output (p. 256). As the public finance literature informs us, these problems are particularly acute for public goods not intended to be divisible. Bahl and Burkhead (1978) conclude that 'any attempt to establish a simplistic relationship between inputs and outputs is conceptually flawed' (p. 258) for the public sector.

Effectiveness Budgeting techniques, including the Balanced Base Budgeting System in Kansas that this paper describes, use a still more ambitious standard for productivity. They attempt to link inputs and activities to outcomes (Harkin, 1982). Outcomes, and the standards by which outcomes are measured, are commonly held to be ambiguous, ambivalent, and multiple. Outcomes are difficult to isolate (Greenberg *et al.*, 1977). Productivity, conceptualized as effectiveness, is difficult to conceptualize and measure on paper; it is even more difficult to implement into an annual budgeting process. However, these difficulties do not seem to have stemmed the tide of budget reform directed at enhancing increasingly more ambitious notions of productivity, nor does failure to meet these lofty standards suggest that much might not be accomplished in the attempt. Research into the implementation of these techniques is needed.

DECISION-MAKING OBSTACLES TO PRODUCTIVITY INNOVATION

Balanced Base Budgeting and other Effectiveness Budgeting systems face significant but not insurmountable conceptual and measurement problems. The conventional wisdom of the budgeting literature suggests additional and perhaps even more substantial decision-making obstacles (Wildavsky, 1975, 1979). Simple application of optimization techniques, along the lines of the rational comprehensive model (Lindblom, 1959), may yield a productivity algorithm to be developed and implemented with optimum results. This rational comprehensive model rests on several assumptions; that individuals are utility-maximizing, economically rational actors; that information is abundant and readily available; that groups and organizations may be treated as single actors (Allison, 1971). Implementation of Effectiveness Budgeting techniques is assumed to proceed in clearcut fashion. That is, fiscal stress will yield political pressure to do more with less, which in turn will stimulate decision-making innovation and productivity enhancement, yielding optimum levels of productivity.

APPROACH TO THIS CASE STUDY

Using well-known models of decision-making processes as summarized by John Forester (1984), obstacles to the rational-comprehensive model of budget and productivity reform are examined using illustrations from the Kansas experience. Kansas adopted a balanced base budgeting system in 1981. The obstacles are collapsed into four broad categories of bounded rationality (March and Simon, 1958). These boundaries represent cognitive limits, factored problems, pluralism, and structural distortions. These categories are used to structure the case study presented below.

The case study material results from interviews conducted during the spring and summer of 1982, after approximately one year's experience with the new system. The primary focus of the study was state agencies and bureaus, represented in this study by the Department of Corrections, the Department of Health and Environment, and the Kansas Board of Regents. Also studied was the role of the legislative branch, legislators and legislative budget staff members, and the Division of the Budget, including the director and budget analysts.

BALANCED BASE BUDGETING IN KANSAS

Kansas Governor John Carlin appointed a new Director of the Budget in February 1981, replacing a director with over twenty years' experience. The new director instituted the new Balanced Base Budget System (BBBS), a 'hybrid' of previous budget reforms, drawing liberally on Program Budgeting, Zero Base Budgeting, Management by Objectives (MBO), and other executive budgeting structures.

The new budget system rested on three concepts. The first is a program format, which requires agencies to integrate activities under a program. To be useful for planning purposes, the program must be defined in such a manner as to include *coherent activities*, must be directed toward a *defined purpose*, must be managed by a single *identifiable authority*, and must have impacts or effects that can be *measured*. Through this mechanism, activities may be compared as to their cost and effectiveness, and planning advanced accordingly. The second concept, *base budget*, communicates the general range of revenue targeted to that issue area by the Governor in advance of final budget submissions. The amount is based on estimated revenues for that fiscal year and 'issue papers' devoted to an analysis of service needs as previously submitted by agencies. The base budget establishes a mechanism for involving the Governor more directly in fiscal control as well as communicating state goals with dollar signs attached. The third concept, *alternative service levels*, involves the agencies in detailing not only how they would spend their base funds, but also how their activities and programs would be affected by a budget reduction and a budget increase. This represents, at least in part, another tool to make gubernatorial choices more clearcut at an earlier stage in the process. In short, BBBS holds out the promise that the budget process will help rest state policy choices on a firmer analytical foundation than has previously been the case, and combat fragmentation by bringing the Governor in at an earlier stage in the process.

Budget informational meetings were held with state agency personnel having budget authority in March 1981, and implementation began. A survey of state agency middle management conducted in November 1981 registered the surprise these officials felt at the rapid introduction of the new system. As implementation proceeded, however, decision-making obstacles arose as March and Simon's description of bounded rationality suggested they would.

BOUNDARY I – BOUNDED RATIONALITY DUE TO COGNITIVE LIMITS

Herbert Simon (1975), both alone and in his collaboration with James March (1958), demonstrates that comprehensive rationality is qualified by the cognitive limits of the actor. Information is not perfectly available, and actors operate under time and resource constraints that force them to adopt satisfying strategies, dropping expectations of optimal solutions to productivity questions for satisfactory ones. Under traditional line-item budgeting systems, productivity is measured by expenditure control. The focus of decision-making is inputs, treated in relative isolation. Comprehensive rationality may not be strained so long as this standard of productivity dominates.

The Kansas BBBS strained comprehensive rationality; it tested the cognitive limits of budget-makers by imposing a standard of productivity substantially more sophisticated than simple expenditure controls and involving more procedural complexity. The increased cognitive demands under BBBS may be divided into three categories: the budget unit, information requirements, and planning requirements.

The fundamental budget unit under the Kansas BBBS is the program, 'usually defined as a coherent and interdependent set of activities undertaken in pursuit of a defined goal or objective' (Muchmore and Duncan, 1982, p. 13). The program-based structure was developed to align numerous individual expenditure decisions with the purposes that government activities are supposed to serve. However, as Wildavsky (1966) notes:

> Programs are not made in heaven. There is nothing out there that is just waiting to be found. Programs are not natural to the world; they must be imposed on it by men. . . . There are as many ways to conceive of programs as there are of organizing activities.　(p. 386)

While a form of program budgeting was already in place in Kansas, BBBS integrated the program design more completely in planning and spending limits, further straining the cognitive limits of budget-makers.

BBBS inserted information and planning requirements substantially more ambitious than simple input or workload information. Budget-makers in Kansas state government were directed to include productivity information which measured the *efficiency* and *effectiveness* of activities to which inputs were applied. An example of the three measures for a hypothetical program is as follows:

Workload: The number of parents of handicapped children provided with training on home therapy techniques, a measure of activities only.

Efficiency: The average cost of home therapy seminars provided to parents of handicapped children, a measure of the ratio of inputs to activities.

Effectiveness: The number of handicapped children enabled to live in a non-institutional setting because of training for parents, a measure of consequences.

Operations planning data was also required in conjunction with budget submission, overtly linking expenditures with operations for long-term program direction.

Many middle-level and lower-level managers in the bureaus studied expressed confusion over the cognitive requirements of BBBS. A psychologist in Vocational Rehabilitation and Training questioned how to measure the performance and effectiveness of counselling programs. No confidence was held in the measures and plans submitted. A maintenance supervisor at a corrections facility questioned the applicability of the Budget's requirements to typical maintenance activities: 'Fixing things when they broke'.

BOUNDARY II – BOUNDED RATIONALITY DUE TO FACTORED PROBLEMS

Comprehensive rationality is also bounded by the factoring of problems, by the fact that organizations are not single actors but socially differentiated units which use division of labour to factor complex problems into manageable pieces (Simon, 1975). Boundary II adds another set of obstacles to comprehensive rationality, and therefore to the most ambitious productivity improvement techniques. The organization is disaggregated into groups and individuals who treat only one aspect of broad objectives and problems. Problems are complex, therefore only a limited number of aspects may be addressed at one time. Problems are divided into independent parts which various units of the organization treat separately. As a result, organizations develop search procedures and standard operating procedures which work along both formal and informal lines to gather information. Social networks are cultivated, and decision-making is not only cognitively bound but socially differentiated (Braybrooke and Lindblom, 1963; Cyert and March, 1963; Forester, 1984).

Productivity improvement through budget reform must confront objectives and policies that have been parcelled out among a number of actors. Comprehensive rationality must ideally recombine and reintegrate what has been scattered (Rein, 1976). The program concept, as noted under Boundary I, integrates interdependent activities undertaken in pursuit of a common, defined goal. Legislative decisions and governmental agencies are not typically organized under this rational, comprehensive system of goals, but develop incrementally in response to varied political forces, diverse clienteles, and a complex intergovernmental system.

The director of the Bureau of Maternal and Child Health explained that all of the diverse programs incorporated in the bureau, whether nutrition programs, preventive medicine, or treatment programs, pursued the common goal of better prenatal and postnatal care over a period of years. There were several separate programs within the agency established for budgetary purposes. However, previously the bureau director had some latitude to shift funds and activities within and between programs as conditions arose which threatened the broad goal of maternal and child care. This informal co-ordination between factored problems has largely been eliminated by the reporting requirements and procedural changes of BBBS. In short, the factoring of problems that is fostered by BBBS presents obstacles to its acceptance among program personnel and may even present obstacles to the very program effectiveness which BBBS is intended to promote.

BOUNDARY III – BOUNDED RATIONALITY DUE TO PLURALIST CONFLICT

As Graham Allison (1971) notes, the reality of public decision making also includes governmental or pluralist conflict. In addition to the constraints already presented to comprehensive rationality, actors are not only socially differentiated but form competing interest groups or coalitions to advance selected interests (Cyert and March, 1963). As E. E. Schattschneider (1960) explains, problem definition becomes a critical element of pluralist conflict. Effectiveness Budgeting, emphasizing clarifications of problems and objectives, opens up a new dimension of complex bargaining and mutual adjustment strategies. In addition, the high premium placed on information concerning all aspects of the system's operation from inputs to outcomes serves to underline the importance of information as a political resource; to be contested, withheld, manipulated, and distorted (Forester, 1984, p. 27). Pluralist conflict may be expected to shape implementation strategies of budget-makers in ways which compromise the comprehensive rationality. Legislative decisions and governmental agencies are not typically organized under this rational, comprehensive system of Effectiveness Budgeting. BBBS was developed in part to confront the expansionary incentives of incremental budgeting. It was recognized that individual agency managers will inevitably submit expenditures plans which sum to a total outlay exceeding revenues. Without prior restraint, such behaviour is rational. Recognition of the mass of data and the decentralization inherent in budget preparation led to the development of BBBS. BBBS redistributes the responsibility for rationing expenditures to the Governor through fixed-ceiling allocations. These allocations are designed to hold agencies to expenditures which, taken in aggregate, meet projected state revenues. In turn, the agency is granted substantial responsibility to map out the details throughout the budget preparation stage. The system, while recognizing decentralization, 'front-loads' the decision-making in favour of fiscal responsibility.

Further, agency budget preparation in the Kansas BBBS includes requirements for a tri-level expenditure plan. Agencies are asked to prepare, in addition to the expenditure plan set at the initial allocation, a plan under conditions of fiscal deprivation and a plan under conditions of fiscal munificence. Comprehensive rationality is fostered by prioritization of activities and expenditures under incrementally different fiscal conditions.

Many programs in the Kansas Department of Health and Environment have experienced federal and state expenditure cuts. Agency personnel revealed a keen awareness of fiscal stress. Further, in many agencies there was a prevailing feeling of competition with other state programs over scarce state expenditures, a climate comparable to a zero-sum game. BBBS was criticized with regard to both the initial allocation system and the tri-level budget preparation. Several managers were sceptical that initial allocations were made on a rational rather than political basis. Agency budget preparers questioned the wisdom of an honest appraisal of priorities through the tri-level reporting system, fearing that they would be left suffering cuts while less honest and forthcoming agencies benefited. In short, BBBS seems to have heightened the sense of pluralist conflict in Kansas government. This development threatens comprehensive rationality because information becomes a clearcut political resource, and agency personnel recognize their rivalry with other units.

BOUNDARY IV – BOUNDED RATIONALITY DUE TO STRUCTURAL DISTORTIONS

John Forester further argues that comprehensive rationality is compromised by inequalities of power which shape the context of decision making, a point familiar to students of state and local politics and community power studies (Bachrach and Baratz, 1970). Budget-making is a heavily structured process which sets the terms of resource commitments for the coming fiscal year, guaranteeing that the stakes will be high. There are at least two important ways in which inequalities of power present obstacles to the implementation of productivity improvement techniques through budget reform. First, organizations and groups may have enough structural power to avoid the budget practices which would open their unit to scrutiny similar to that which other units receive. During a period in which a subgovernment maintains exceptionally strong ties to legislative and executive branches, that agency may ignore important elements of performance monitoring and evaluation with which other agencies must comply. In Kansas government, one corrections institution in particular was able largely to circumvent all but a cursory implementation of BBBS due to political clout within the department and in the legislature, a situation one member of top departmental management found particularly bothersome.

Second, budget reforms of the type found in most Effectiveness Budgeting techniques contains the seeds for substantial power shifts within and between organizations and even branches of government. James Swiss makes this point recently with respect to MBO:

> Management systems are not centralizing devices in the classical sense; they entail sharing power between top administrators and subordinate line managers. But in most large government bureaucracies, where most of the power lies below the top, such power sharing means a substantial shift in power up to the top officials. (1983, p. 244)

Many line managers with program responsibility in the agencies studied began their service while their agencies were still under the control of boards and commissions, before the installation of cabinet departments under gubernatorial control. Some of these managers saw **BBBS** as a device to further consolidate the Governor's control of their agencies through cabinet-level administrators. The intra-agency allocation powers given these top administrators lends credence to this perspective. Line managers and even bureau directors could be expected to resist such potentially redistributive changes, either overtly or covertly. No overt resistance was evidenced. However, the director of the Bureau of Maternal and Child Health recognized the structural changes inherent in **BBBS** and, rather than resist, simply removed herself from her central role in budget preparation.

Conversations with legislative staff and the chairman of the House Ways and Means Committee revealed the impression that legislative spending perogatives were being circumvented by the allocation and tri-level expenditure process. The Director of the Budget, an important member of the executive branch, does not deny the expanded policy-making role of the Governor in **BBBS**, although he stops short of suggesting that this power comes at the expense of the legislative branch. Potentially important structural change is under way, though the implications of this change are not yet clear, particularly if the legislative branch responds to this change with increased budget control of its own. However, structural power inherent in entrenched political influence and in the constitutional separation of powers presents obstacles to the implementation of **BBBS**, and to its comprehensive rationality.

SUMMARY AND CONCLUSION

This case study of the Kansas BBBS has examined the nature of productivity improvement techniques and the obstacles to their adoption in the budgeting arena. During periods of fiscal stress, doing more with less is difficult to dispute in general. Further, improved productivity is a continuous theme of American public administration. However, it is important to clarify just what is meant by productivity, of 'doing more with less'. Using a general systems framework, it is clear that productivity may mean many things. Recent budget reforms and Effectiveness Budgeting techniques reflect ambitious concepts of productivity, ones which are difficult to apply in the public sector.[2]

The obstacles to implementation of these techniques stem from several aspects of the limitations of the comprehensively rational model of decision-making. The examination of these bounded rationalities in the Kansas setting serves as a warning, one which has been made consistently by critics of Effectiveness Budgeting. None the less, we are left with the fact that these techniques and the concern with governmental productivity continue to flourish. Perhaps this trend simply reflects a bias in our society for rationalistic approaches and for the value of efficiency. Perhaps executives and legislatures institute these practices for political gain, satisfying public desires at a symbolic level while maintaining substantial power, shaping reforms to meet institutional aggrandisement schemes behind the scenes. It is also possible that the prevailing wisdom of incrementalism, that marginal adjustments rather than comprehensive productivity systems best serve public policy, no longer holds sway among practitioners or academics. Further study is needed to uncover the motivations behind productivity reforms, their implementation, and the power shifts that are promoted by such changes.

Notes

1. Figures published by the National Governors' Association and the National Association of State Budget Officers indicated that in fiscal 1983, 47 states used some type of budget balancing measure. Most frequently used were hiring limits (42 states), selective program cuts (37), restricted out-of-state travel (32), and temporary or permanent revenue increases (33). This research concentrates on one technique focusing on permanent procedural change for budget retrenchment or stabilization.
2. These comments should not be misconstrued as discouraging the design and application of more ambitious and sophisticated measures of productivity. For a useful discussion, see Nagel, 1984.

References

Allison, G. T. (1971), *Essence of decision* (Boston: Little, Brown).
Bachrach, P. and M. S. Baratz (1970), *Power and poverty: Theory and practice* (New York: Oxford University Press).
Bahl, R. W. and J. Burkhead (1977), 'Productivity and the measurement of public output', in C. Levine (ed.) *Managing Human Resources: A Challenge to Urban Government* (Beverly Hills, California: Sage), pp. 253–69.
Bozeman, B. and J. D. Straussman (1982), 'Shrinking budgets and shrinkage of budgetary theory', *Public Administration Review*, 42, pp. 509–15.
Braybrooke, D. and C. E. Lindblom (1963), *A strategy of decision* (Glencoe, IL: The Free Press).
Caiden, N. (1981), 'Public budgeting amidst uncertainty and instability', *Public Budgeting and Finance*, 1, pp. 6–19.
Caiden, N. (1984), 'The new rules of the federal budget game', *Public Administration Review*, 44, pp. 109–17.

Cyert, R. and J. March (1963), *A behavioral theory of the firm* (Énglewood Cliffs, NJ: Prentice-Hall).

Forester, J. (1984), 'Bounded rationality and the politics of muddling through', *Public Administration Review*, 44, pp. 23–31.

Greenberg, G. D., J. S. Miller, L. B. Mohr and B. C. Vladeck (1977), 'Developing public policy theory: Perspectives from empirical research', *American Political Science Review*, 71, pp. 1532–43.

Gulick, L. and L. Urwick (eds) (1937), *Papers on the science of administration* (New York: Institute of Public Administration).

Harkin, J. M. (1982), 'Effectiveness budgeting: The limits of budget reform', *Policy Studies Review*, 2, pp. 112–26.

Lindblom, C. (1959), 'The science of muddling through', *Public Administration Review*, 19, pp. 79–88.

March, J. G. and and H. A. Simon (1958), *Organizations* (New York: J. Wiley).

Muchmore, L. and H. Duncan (1982), *The Kansas budget process: Concept and practice* (Topeka, Kansas: Capital Complex Center).

Nagel, S. S. (1984), *Public policy: Goals, means, and methods* (New York: St. Martin's Press).

National Governors' Association, Office of Research and Development (1983; June), *Fiscal survey of the states 1983* (Washington, DC: National Governors' Association).

Rein, M. (1976), *Social science and public policy* (New York: Penguin Books).

Schattschneider, E. E. (1960), *The semisovereign people* (Hinsdale, IL: The Dryden Press).

Schick, A. and H. Harry (1982), 'Zero base budgeting: The manager's budget', *Public Budgeting and Finance*, 2, pp. 72–87.

Simon, H. A. (1975), *Administrative behaviour* (New York: Macmillan).

Swiss, J. E. (1983), 'Establishing a management system: The interaction of power shifts and personality under federal MBO', *Public Administration Review*, 43, pp. 238–45.

Wildavsky, A. (1966), 'The political economy of efficiency: Cost-benefit analysis, systems analysis, and program budgeting', *Public Administration Review*, 26, pp. 292–310.

Wildavsky, A. (1975), *The politics of the budgetary process* (Boston: Little, Brown).

Wildavsky, A. (1979), *Speaking truth to power: The art and craft of policy analysis* (Boston: Little, Brown).

Wilson, W. (1887), 'The study of administration', *Political Science Quarterly*, 2, pp. 197–222.

8 Why Government Cannot Contain Health Care Costs: An Interpretation of the US Health Care System[1]

William P. Brandon

This chapter explores why cost-containment is stressed in health care rather than productivity. An interpretation of the political economy of the US health care system is presented and the hegemony over the analysis of public policy analysis by the dominant school of economic theory is discussed.

> *122. A main source of our failure to understand is that we do not command a clear view of the use of our words. . . . A perspicuous representation produces just that understanding which consists in 'seeing connections'.*

> (Wittgenstein, 1968)

This chapter begins by noting that for all its prominence in most discussions of economics, the concept 'productivity' plays a rather limited role in discussions of health care. The health care arena, in contrast, reverberates with talk of 'cost-containment', especially as concern increases about the resources absorbed by health care.

The observation that 'productivity' gives way to 'cost-containment' in discussions of health care and its costs leads in two directions. First, it provokes a discussion of why transactions involved in the provision of health care should be different from other familiar arenas that have easily lent themselves to conceptualization according to the family of concepts that comprise liberal market economics. The peculiarities of health care delivery in the USA provide yet more evidence – if any is needed – that the sector should be regarded as an independent system rather than as another industry in the domestic economy.

A brief survey of some features of the health care system is necessary for an explanation of government's difficulty in containing health care costs. The next section of this chapter begins with a short account of the growth of federal involvement in the health care system. Then a brief description of health care financing provides a foundation for the main achievement of the chapter: an explanation of government's inability to stop health care increases despite the extraordinary array of powers it has gained.

Secondly, a sensitivity to the distinctiveness of the health care system can lead back to questions about the general adequacy of the fundamental conceptual framework of classical economics with its emphasis on efficiency as the supreme value. (Productivity, of course, is a particular form of efficiency.) If an adequate model of the political economy of health care requires the inclusion of values in addition to efficiency and its family of concepts, perhaps other areas of public policy have been mismodelled and therefore misunderstood by the seemingly successful economizing of public policy. Although such broader considerations are relevant to the themes of this book, they cannot become the focus of this chapter, which must concentrate on the political economy of health care.

This chapter is composed of a section on concepts and another on context, but no distinction between 'ideas' or 'theory' and 'reality' is intended. The analysis rests on the assumption that the 'empirical' world is only known through concepts. At the same time we only 'know' our concepts in the judgements formed as they model or represent some passage in our extraordinarily complex form of life. The first section makes some largely logical observations about the relevant concepts; the second develops an interpretation of the political economy of the US health care system. Although the latter could perhaps stand alone, its wider implications for questions about the hegemony exercised over the analysis of public policy by the dominant school of economic theory would remain obscure without the first section.

CONCEPTS: 'COST CONTAINMENT', 'PRODUCTIVITY', AND 'HEALTH'

Productivity in its strict economic sense, as J. Joel May points out, is the relation between outputs and inputs. 'If outputs can be increased with no corresponding increase in inputs, or if inputs can be reduced without adversely affecting outputs, a 'gain in productivity' is said to have been realized' (May, 1977). Productivity, then, is but a particular form of efficiency, the central value in liberal economics.

In ordinary contexts 'productivity' – even in its strict economic sense – is a normative concept. Higher productivity is assumed to be better, even if greater production is in practice recognized to be undesirable. (Thus farmers are encouraged to lower the ratio of inputs to outputs despite the fact that we wish to limit total production of certain crops.) The dominant school of theoretical economics is able to ignore its normative component – and thereby to pretend to be value-free – because market assumptions equate efficient satisfaction of desires for goods and services with social and individual benefit. It is outside of the sphere of economics to ask whether the desire for 'widgets' or cabbage patch dolls ought to occupy any particular place in an individual's preference schedule (see Anderson, 1978 and 1979; Baier, 1982; Brandon, 1984).[2]

Discussions of health care, unlike debates about industrial policy, contain much talk about 'cost-containment', but surprisingly few references to the economic notion of 'productivity'.[3] The term 'cost-containment' reflects the realization that in an inflationary era, aggregate costs will not decrease for a basic social good like health care. This bureaucratic jargon implies that the aim is to reduce the size of further cost increases. This goal is broader than the concern for productivity, for it can be accomplished through productivity gains, by reducing the volume of health services (that is, outputs) provided, or by reducing the costs of both inputs and outputs (which need not decrease the ratio of outputs to inputs).

Policy-making in the health sector must take account of the benefits of health services, a factor that is independent of efficiency. Whereas market economics need not be concerned with the benefits of outputs in its traditional consideration of XYZ corporation's 'widgets', the concept of productivity is problematic in health care if the non-economic worth of the services produced is not considered. No one wishes to have cost-containment if the price is significant impairment of a population's health.

For the allocation of health services, as for other scarce resources, the intellectual allure of the economic model with its libertarian insistence on the sovereignty of each individual consumer and its lovely simplicity is very great. Those heeding the siren song of a market that maximizes satisfaction in balancing supply and demand sometimes seek to excuse the obvious failure of the market model in the health care sector on the grounds that it is an 'imperfect' market, one which somehow tries but falls short of achieving the assumptions of the smoothly functioning ideal market of the textbooks. They point to such considerations as the imbalance in information between consumers and providers of health services and to the anti-competitive behaviour of large provider groups like medical associations, which suppress information and competition regarding prices and services.

Activists of this persuasion work to change the empirical conditions that seem to invalidate the market assumptions; they fail to realize that the fundamental problem is conceptual. (None the less, in practice this 'market reform strategy' sometimes leads to useful cost-containment policies.) The economics developed in the Western liberal tradition has only the criterion of efficiency by which to judge the satisfaction of preferences; it lacks a standpoint for judging the preferences themselves (Anderson, 1978 and 1979; Baier, 1982). Yet when it comes to health services we *do* judge individual preferences: for example, the extreme form of seeking satisfaction by consuming health services has been dubbed the Munchausen syndrome, which is a severe, though rare, pathology.[4] Similarly, our society is unwilling to countenance the use of powerful medicines to satisfy individual preferences for enhanced athletic strength or mental stimulation. Health care is peculiar because there is a significant gap between the health service rendered and the end – health – to be served. With the emergence of this gap the simple economic tautology that recognizes preferences as the ends of human action falls apart. Thus an important part of an initiation into health policy analysis involves destroying the popular belief in a simple means – ends relation between health care services and a healthy state. In the last decade a number of notable books (for example, Cochrane, 1972; Illich, 1976; Knowles, 1977; McKeown, 1979; but see Hadley, 1982) have successfully debunked the belief that medicine is an empirically-based science in which any widely-practised treatment can routinely be expected to foster cures or other relief benefiting patients.

Whereas a policy analyst interested in industrial policy will not question the benefit of cabbage patch dolls, the health policy analyst must ask about the health impacts of new services or productivity changes in the delivery of current services. The gap between what is done and its effect appears in evaluation studies in the form of different and largely incommensurable measures, depending on whether attention is focused on the individual or the group. Impacts that are conceived and measured in terms of individual patients usually fall under the rubric 'quality of care'; health in total populations is usually measured by health status indicators. Both areas of study are very far from providing definitive answers to the question of what makes one healthy (see Donabedian, 1980 and 1982, on the difficulties of assessing the quality of health care provided to patients). Of the two, the population-based inquiries may have made the greatest contribution to date, by showing that it is very difficult to relate the health status of a population directly to the consumption of health services, because health is influenced by a host of factors in addition to health care services. At least since the conquest of widespread communicable diseases, improvements in treatments for specific diseases have rarely had a noticeable effect on the morbidity or mortality of entire populations (Fuchs, 1979; McKeown, 1979; McKinlay and McKinlay, 1977).

The argument has established that a gap exists between treatments and the healthy state that is the goal. This gap justifies questioning the single-minded application of the established model of economics which posits the efficient supply of goods and services desired by an individual at a particular time as the highest end. The development of non-economic criteria for judging the provision of medical services means that a policy of health care cost-containment can involve a number of strategies in addition to the economic effort to realize gains in productivity. The range of options for cost-containment and their relation to productivity gains can be summarized in a two-by-two table (Figure 8.1). Changes in productivity and in health benefits both provide avenues for containing costs. One major strategy for achieving cost-containment is by eliminating non-beneficial services (quadrants I and IV) however efficiently they may be produced (Havighurst and Blumstein, 1975). Of course, we also want to improve efficiency in providing the useful services that fall into the third category.

Figure 8.1   Cost-containment alternatives

Health

		Service beneficial	Service not beneficial *
Productivity	Service efficient	II	I
	Service not efficient	III	IV

* Services that are not beneficial can be further subdivided into harmless and harmful (or 'iatrogenic') services.

Yet because of the continued escalation of national health care expenditures – which finally broke the psychologically important barrier of 10 per cent of total gross national product (GNP) in 1982 (Gibson, Waldo and Levit, 1983), care in quadrant I must also come under scrutiny. This category raises difficult questions about the value of care in terms of expected health benefits *relative* to the cost of care. Individual preferences and cost-benefit analysis are important but not determinative in deciding such difficult collective issues as making coronary bypass surgery or heart transplants available or launching public campaigns for vaccinations that provide lifetime immunity from some forms of hepatitis. Faced with choices between alternatives in this category, the health policy analyst can no longer eschew judgements about the value and distribution of health benefits. The magnitude of the investments and the collective nature of the value-laden choices preclude leaving such questions to individual preferences registered in a market. Cost itself should ideally become a measure to aid in deciding among alternative beneficial health expenditures, but it cannot just be incorporated into a simplistic calculus based on such assumptions as 'willingness-to-pay' (Self, 1981, pp. 228–9).

The US has not heretofore faced the difficult questions of choosing between potential health benefits, although recent developments in federal hospital reimbursement under Medicare are intended to squeeze out beneficial care that is unlikely to make much difference to the health of the patient. The financing and delivery of health care is organized in a manner that systematically avoids the issue of limiting resources allocated for health care. The second section explains why the peculiar organization and financing of US health care allows most health care consumers to escape the discipline of normal markets for goods and services and renders government's fiscal and monetary controls impotent.

CONTEXT: COST-CONTAINMENT AND THE ORGANIZATION OF THE US HEALTH CARE SYSTEM

One difference between the health system and other domestic economic sectors is the relative willingness of government to intervene in health care. Federal and state governments have become involved in situations ranging from the threatened bankruptcy of urban hospitals to regulating the acquisition of CAT scanners and Nuclear Magnetic Resonating devices by private physicians. In contrast, the federal government has been unwilling to take action to avoid the threatened bankruptcy of the Public Broadcasting System or to interfere with a 'market' choice that has made computer video games widely available but has not vigorously developed the educational potential of computers. Even the Chrysler bail-out depended on the indirect device of guarantees for loans obtained in the private market.

Federal involvement in the health care system, which at first was indirect, began in an era when health care delivery was much simpler.[5] In the period immediate after the Second World War, the federal government initiated national policies to ensure the *availability* of adequate health resources. The three most significant such policies were the Hill–Burton program to foster hospital construction, massive biomedical research funding that changed the nature of medical schools, and an interpretation qualifying residency training for educational benefits under veterans programs. In the 1960s, this concern about the availability of health resources was augmented by measures to ensure the *accessibility* of health services through programs like Medicare, which provided the elderly with social insurance for health care, Medicaid, the federal-state means-tested welfare program that reimburses providers caring for low-income persons who qualify under certain categories, and a host of health service programs designed to help disadvantaged and minority populations secure adequate health services.

Serious federal efforts to *regulate* the health care system to promote equity and cost-containment had begun by the end of the 1960s. Regulation of the health care system under federal auspices has included health planning (Comprehensive Health Planning Agencies and Health Systems Agencies), quality assurance (Professional Standards Review Organizations and now Professional Review Organizations), capital investment regulation (certificate-of-need and section 1122 authority), and wage and price controls (Economic Stabilization Program). In terms of the alternatives outlined in Figure 8.1, planning and capital investment regulation were intended to attack inefficient and unnecessary expenditures in quadrants I, III, and IV; quality assurance before the recent federal adoption of a prospective payment scheme was largely intended to discourage the unnecessary expenditures in quadrants I and IV; and wage-price controls were an emergency measure initiated by President Nixon to secure productivity gains in all quadrants by holding down increases in the charges for outputs and the cost of some inputs. State control of the insurance industry (including health insurers) and the public aspects of professional and institutional licensure has long been established. Such regulation has not generally been used to pursue cost-containment policies. In recent years many states have begun to regulate the rates of reimbursement paid to institutional providers of health care. Such regulation puts a variety of pressures on hospitals and nursing homes. While much of this regulation is intended to increase the efficiency of services falling into quadrants III and IV, penalties for low occupancy and the widespread use of a cost-plus approach has promoted the growth of services falling into quadrants I, III, and IV. Despite the extraordinary level of intervention in the health care system as regulator, reimburser, and provider of health services and health resources, government at all levels has been singularly unsuccessful in controlling costs or changing the system's emphasis on high technology solutions to acute medical crisis, as both the national health accounts (for example, Gibson, Waldo and Levit, 1983) and voluminous scholarship (see Brandon and Lee, 1984; Salkever and Bice, 1979; Schwartz, 1981; Sloan and Steinwald, 1980; and so on) show.

Part of government's concern about health care costs is explained by its widescale financial involvement: together all levels of government have directly paid about 40 per cent of personal health care expenditure during the last decade (Gibson, Waldo and Levit, 1983). Federal and state concern about health care costs, however, extends far beyond an interest in capping governments' own financial obligations. The allocation of an increasing proportion of GNP to health care contributes to inflation in the general economy, even when those additional resources come from putatively 'private' pockets and go to purchase additional or higher quality services that are efficiently provided. Health policy analysts question whether adequate benefits are provided to society to justify the large increments in resources that the health care system absorbs each year. Their discomfort with increasing allocations to health care is more than a concern on the macro level about 'productivity'. Instead of focusing on narrow questions of efficiency, the problem is how to cut health care costs without denying effective and needed care to those who would not receive it without 'third-party reimbursement' (the generic term for payment by government or some other reimbursement source).

A more profound understanding of the health care system and its financing requires knowledge of how government also 'finances' health care that appears to be entirely private. Health insurance in the US has become widespread since 1954, when amendments to the tax law guaranteed that health insurance purchased by employers as a fringe benefit would not constitute taxable personal income to the employee (Starr, 1982, p. 333). In 1977 89 per cent of the US population under 65 was covered with varying degrees of adequacy by 'voluntary' insurance purchased through employment-related group plans (Farley and Wilensky, 1983); almost 85 per cent of all non-government health insurance was employment related (Wilensky and Taylor, 1982).

Because of the progressive income tax, the benefits of avoiding federal and any state and local income tax through a fringe benefit package accrue disproportionately to those with higher incomes.[6] In addition, employer-purchased health insurance escapes both employer and employee Social Security payroll taxes. The federal government (and other governments with income taxes) are foregoing ever larger amounts of revenue as the cost of premiums paid for increasingly expensive and more comprehensive health insurance escalates, as payroll tax rates rise, and as the wage-base on which Social Security must be paid increases dramatically (Brandon, 1982; Congressional Budget Office, 1982; President's Commission for the Study of Ethical Problems, 1983, pp. 160–9; Taylor and Wilensky, 1983). Consequently, if an upper-income family consumes the average value of health care for its plan (say services that cost $1000), the employer's premium for health insurance completely covering those services will cost much less than a thousand dollar raise and the taxes due on it (Brandon, 1982; Davis, 1975, pp. 14–17; Wilensky and Taylor, 1982; but also see Witte, 1983):

(Health Insurance Premiums for $ 1000 of services) <
($ 1000) + (Taxes Due on a $ 1000 Raise)

Of course, the family rather than the employer would pay most of the added taxes on such a raise.

The belief that the working middle and upper class pays its own way cannot be maintained in light of the fact that the federal income tax subsidy on employer-purchased 'private' health insurance, which is only one of the sources of tax subsidy, is greater than the federal expenditures from general revenues either for Medicare or Medicaid (Brandon, 1982; Gibson, Waldo and Levit, 1983; Office of Management and the Budget, 1984; President's Commission, 1983, pp. 160–9; Taylor and Wilensky, 1983). Total federal and state revenues lost from forgone income tax and FICA contributions are estimated to be more than $ 30 billion in 1983 (Taylor and Wilensky, 1983).

Although these tax subsidies constitute a mammoth government health care program for the middle and upper classes, the beneficiaries remain largely unaware of them. Forgone government revenue or 'tax expenditures' do not undergo an annual appropriation process; it is even very difficult to count what is never collected or enumerated on government computers. Moreover, public attention is focused on cutting the 'entitlement' health programs, Medicaid and Medicare, and the smaller categorical and block-grant service programs (Brandon, 1982; Wing, 1984).[7]

This invisible subsidy for the purchase of health insurance makes health insurance different from traditional forms of insurance against risk. The costs of home owner's hazard or auto insurance, for example, are not normally tax deductible and do not enjoy any hidden subsidy. Because of administrative costs and profits, the benefits paid per policy by a fire or auto insurance company for each actuarial class will be much less than the total premiums received from policyholders in the class Since unsubsidized insurance costs more than the average benefit, it is used solely to protect against risks of rare but costly events. Thus there is an incentive to reduce the cost, for example, of automobile collision insurance by self-insuring for small claims through the purchase of a policy with a high deductible. The only factors driving up the cost of such insurance (and the value of subsequent claims) if administrative costs and profits are held constant, are an increase in the risks, or an increase in either the value of what is insured or the cost of fixing any damage sustained.

In contrast, the purchase of health insurance as part of a fringe benefit package becomes a means by which many upper middle-class families *finance* ordinary day-to-day health care with tax-free income. Even though premiums still cost (the employer) more than the average value of benefits per family, the average upper-income family usually benefits by having these premiums paid instead of paying out-of-pocket for health care and receiving a commensurately higher salary. Families have little reason to refrain from consuming care that is covered, for any particular claim on the benefit pool will have a negligible effect on future premiums that the employer will pay for the family's coverage. (Insurance constitutes a pure case of the problem of concentrated benefits and dispersed costs.) Incentives to economize are particularly lacking when 'first-dollar' coverage relieves the burden of significant deductibles. Especially under plans with broad or 'comprehensive' benefits, health care approaches the status of a 'free good' for the family covered. This situation can easily lead to the consumption of care that would be omitted if the family had to pay the full price. Delivery of relatively unimportant and often inexpensive increments of care at the margin of usefulness — care in the grey zones between quadrants II and I or III and IV in Figure 8.1 – is particularly encouraged by this sort of insurance. Such health insurance benefits are like the kinds of claims that those with auto collision insurance give up in choosing to reduce premiums (typically paid by drivers themselves) by accepting higher deductibles. Under widespread first-dollar collision insurance, for example, one could expect cars with bent fenders virtually to disappear from the roads – a prospect which will warm the hearts and pockets of the owners of garages specializing in auto body work. The comparison illustrates how we have come to accept health insurance as a means of financing ordinary health care, whereas the notion sounds silly when suggested in connection with other kinds of insurance, which are purchased to protect one against the risk of a catastrophic event. This divergence can be entirely explained in terms of the generous tax subsidies for health insurance, which induce rational families to use health insurance as a financing mechanism.

The negative consequences of widespread third-party reimbursement, whether through private health insurance, Medicare or Medicaid, have been widely noted (Feldstein, 1971; Feldstein and Taylor, 1977; Havighurst and Blumstein, 1975). Inpatient hospitalization, which is associated with higher cost and more sophisticated technology, is more completely covered than outpatient episodes of care, thereby creating an incentive favouring the use of more expensive services. To the degree that individuals enjoy comprehensive health insurance that covers most forms of health care, restraints imposed on the use of health care by considerations of its cost are eliminated (Wilensky and Rossiter, 1983, p. 271). Sometimes employers or unions have achieved comprehensive coverage of common but inexpensive health problems of their constituency at the price of failing to protect adequately against truly catastrophic but rare sicknesses or injuries. Moreover, the practical arrangements for third-party reimbursement in the US create perverse incentives. Providers have faced little resistance to price rises, because traditionally health insurance in the US has simply accepted the prices that hospitals or doctors charged, although reimbursement might be fixed at less than 100 per cent of a patient's bill (Goldberg and Greenberg, 1977). Public programs paid 'reasonable' costs until recently; this practice, which is similar to public attempts to control prices in regulated utilities, increases the market for clever accountants and encourages cost escalation. Thus both public and 'private' third party reimbursement have tended to pass increases automatically through to the Social Security Trust Fund, employers, or tax-payers. Ultimately, of course, the consumer bears much of the burden in the form of higher prices. Rising health care costs produce pressure to upgrade insurance protection, thereby encouraging further cost increases.

This combination of health insurance subsidized by tax expenditures and large entitlement programs allows funding for the health care system to evade the government's two most powerful means of domestic economic control. In contrast to the direct regulatory interventions and service programs in the health system, federal policy in other sectors largely depends on its powerful monetary and fiscal levers. Power over monetary policy, which is exercised chiefly by the Federal Reserve Board, involves control over the money supply and credit; fiscal policy is the conscious use of federal spending and taxing power by the administration and Congress to stimulate or depress activity in a sector or across the general economy. Activity in an industry like construction, for example, is extraordinarily responsive to interest rates and to general economic conditions (which themselves are governed to some extent by decisions regarding the money supply). In contrast, even capital investment in health care is relatively immune from the influence of interest rates and general economic conditions. If interest rates rise, health care institutions can simply add the increased costs of capital investment – an allowable cost – to patients' bills. (In addition, much of the financing of capital investment in health care institutions involves state and local government bonds, whose tax-free features become increasingly popular as yields rise). Until the 1960s, when philanthropy ceased to be a major source of capital for the voluntary hospitals, the state of the economy was closely related to hospital construction projects.

The construction industry is also a good example of the way that fiscal policy can be used in a recession. Special appropriations for public works or for mortgage subsidies are often passed in the hope that direct or indirect stimulation of construction will ramify throughout the economy, increasing jobs, disposable incomes, demand, and economic activity in general. It might be argued that making employment-related health insurance tax-free and instituting programs to develop health resources and deliver services are pure examples of government fiscal policy, but such a view overlooks an important distinction between policy and unintended consequences. Government taxing and spending are clearly part of the fundamental reason why the health system is able to attract funding whenever it is needed, but such consequences are not a part of anyone's intended policy. (It may be true that in the 1950s the tax expenditures for health insurance were intended to promote the growth of health insurance, but the continuation of this arrangement is antagonistic to current policy goals.) Just as the tax subsidy is at cross purposes with current policy, so the *point* of making Medicare and Medicaid entitlement programs is to constitute a right to reimbursement for necessary services without regard to temporary policies favouring expansion or contraction of activity in the health care system. This fundamental truth is liable to be obscured by efforts at the margin to trim government costs or promote efficiency in the health care system through such measures as increasing patient cost-sharing and Part B Medicare Premiums or changing reimbursement methods.

In theory the federal government could embark on a sector-specific fiscal policy to reduce new funding flowing into health care (as distinct from its current efforts to lower its own bills), but it has shown itself extremely reluctant to do so. For example, even the Reagan Administration, which has cut federal Medicaid commitments and trimmed the federal Medicare bill, has not attempted to reduce biomedical research funding significantly. Although federal research funds only amounted to 5 per cent of federal health expenditures in 1982 (Gibson, Waldo and Levit, 1983), federal funding for research is an important instrument of fiscal policy determining future health care costs. The federal government, after all, is the source of most of the support that eventuates in the development of such costly items as the artificial implantable heart (Gibson, Waldo and Levit, 1983).[8] It is true that much of the federal support for the training of health professionals has been phased out, but only after it has created a surplus in many categories of health professionals. Despite the current constrictive manpower policies, this surplus of highly trained professionals, who will receive a decent, secure living through third-party reimbursements, will cause cost problems for at least a generation. Moreover, many states have continued their harmful policies of supporting the training of health professionals (see Bernstein and Ensminger, 1983; Lee, 1984). Perhaps the Health Maintenance Organization Act of 1973 and its subsequent modifications constitute the only clear example of federal use of the spending power to promote cost-containment in the health care system.[9]

The failure of fiscal and monetary control in the health sector helps to explain why cost-containment is so important for public officials and why government has intervened in health matters so often with such little positive effect. The use of health insurance by the broad middle class to finance health care (along with the sizeable entitlement programs) allows the health care system automatically to siphon off the resources it needs from other economic sectors. Not only is no *decision* involved in allocating an increased share of the GNP to health care each year, but there is not even an effective way to implement a decision *not* to increase the health care share of national income. The highly visible government intervention in the health care system, which contrasts so vividly with its relatively hands-off policy towards basic investment, cost and pricing questions in other economic sectors, then, is a *consequence* of its impotence rather than a sign of omnipotence. It regulates the use of resources in the health care system because it cannot determine the amount or destination of funds; it promotes a fifteen-month freeze on the fees that physicians can charge Medicare (Brazda, 1984b), because it cannot effectively cap its own costs or capitate payments to health care providers.

CONCLUSION: ENTER DRGs

The preceding section covered a great deal of material in a very brief compass. A comparison between arrangements for the provision of health care in the US and other economic sectors suggests that health care financing and delivery should be conceptualized as a distinct system rather than as just another industry. Without substantial modifications, market economics does not fare very well in explaining the health care system. An alternative account began by sketching the background and growth of federal involvement in the health care system and ended with an interpretation that explains both the remarkable degree of government intervention in the health care system and its impotence. Because the US health care system is organized on a putatively 'private' basis with major population groups entitled to federal or state reimbursement or covered by health insurance that is heavily subsidized by largely invisible tax expenditures, the health sector is largely impervious to federal fiscal and monetary policy. Health care is unlike any other sector due to its power to siphon added resources from industry, consumers and all levels of government.

Government regulation is generally thought to have failed to control costs and to achieve its other public health goals (Brandon and Lee, 1984; Salkever and Bice, 1979; Schwartz, 1981; Sloan and Steinwald, 1980). However, some policy analysts who accept the failure of other regulatory efforts, claim that rate regulation *can* succeed (Biles, Schramm, and Atkinson, 1980; Schwartz, 1981; Sloan, 1983). Currently the federal government is changing the way Medicare pays hospitals by instituting 'prospective payment'. This new system, which replaces retrospective cost-based reimbursement, allows an institution to retain the savings if it can provide care for a patient for less than a prospectively fixed sum – essentially a complex average calculated for each of 467 'diagnosis-related groups' (DRGs). (Of course, the institution must also swallow any loss, if its costs exceed the fee set for the appropriate DRG category.) Although currently limited to bills for inpatient Medicare patients, the new reimbursement method is forcing major changes in the daily operations of acute care hospitals in areas where the prospective payment regulations are in effect. Both the administration and Congress agreed to initiate this massive federal intervention with the hope that it will restructure the health care system by creating incentives favouring less care and less expensive care (all quadrants in Figure 8.1). This new scheme has generated so much enthusiasm in Washington that planning is under way to cover physician reimbursement and capital costs under similar arrangements. Support could, of course, wane when experience with DRGs in hospitals makes their inevitable shortcomings apparent.

The new prospective payment method is not the 'pro-competition' legislation that the Reagan Administration promised when it first assumed office but in September 1984 had yet to propose. None the less the changed incentives under prospective payment are intended to allow government to contain costs without direct regulation – a principal goal of the 'pro-competition' strategy. The new Medicare reimbursement method aims to leave hospitals free to sort out among themselves the types of patients that they can treat most efficiently. The irony is that a conservative administration which wants to return control over domestic social services to state government and the private sector is embarked on a breath-taking centralization that promises to replace the great diversity and decentralization across the US with a national system for reimbursing institutions.

Even in the unlikely event that a new day has dawned for health policy, the concepts and problems outlined in this chapter will be part of it. Telling proof lies in the fact that along with their talk of deregulation and altered incentives, proponents of reimbursement by DRGs have had to establish new institutions called Professional Review Organizations across the nation to ensure that cost containment is not purchased by forgoing important amounts of genuinely beneficial health care (see Frabotta, 1984). No one wishes to slice too deeply into the care in quadrant II (of Figure 8.1).

Notes

1. The author wishes to thank Jeffrey Wasserman, Vice President for Research, Health Research and Educational Trust of New Jersey, for his thoughtful comments in connection with this project. Of course he bears no responsibility for the final product.
2. Western market economics in reality, of course, embodies a particular view of values. As an institutionalization of utilitarianism, economics incorporates an individualistic form of psychological hedonism in its assumptions (see, for example, Northrop, 1946, pp. 66–164; Tribe, 1972).
3. The exception to this claim is found in the hospital management literature where the benefits of services are not generally considered (for example, Coyne, 1982; Elnicki, 1974; Jeffers and Siebert, 1974; Kidder and Sullivan, 1982; Kimbell and Lorant, 1977; Ruchlin and Leveson, 1974). Health policy consistently transcends the narrow focus of this microeconomic literature.
4. Individuals suffering from the Munchausen syndrome desire medical care (including surgery), which leads them to fabricate 'clinically convincing simulations of disease' (Stedman, 1982). A different and more widespread phenomenon, which is also judged inappropriate by health professionals, is the use by socially isolated individuals of the offices and waiting rooms of health care providers as a place to come for social interaction.
5. This discussion, of course, does not apply to the health care of some small populations such as Indians, the military and merchant seamen that have long been regarded as a special responsibility of the federal government.
6. The following analysis depends on the common assumption that total employee remuneration, the sum of wages and the employer's contribution for fringe benefits and payroll taxes, is the important figure in determining labour costs. Although it makes no economic difference to an employer whether a raise consists of taxable wages or a proportional addition to untaxed fringe benefits, the employee will rarely be indifferent about this choice. In the 'real' world where employers are currently demanding concessions or 'givebacks' from employees, however, employers often target the generous fringe benefits established in earlier years for rollback.
7. In its proposed budget for the fiscal year 1985 the administration wanted to levy personal income tax on employer payments for employee health insurance above $175 per month for family coverage ($70 for individual policies). Such a levy would raise $2.3 billion in additional federal revenue in fiscal year 1985. However, Congress rejected a similar proposal in 1983 (Brazda, 1984, p. 6). Senator Robert Dole, powerful Chairman of the Senate Finance Committee, was recently forced to admit that he could not secure the passage of his plan to cap tax-free health benefits at a higher level (Brazda, 1984a, p. 1).
8. If the artificial heart and similar costly technologies are not intended to be widely available and hence not very expensive, there is no reason to perfect them. In our political culture it is inconceivable that an effective, high-technology life-saving technique will not become widely disseminated.
9. It would be hard to claim that the passage of the federal HMO Act ten years ago and its subsequent implementation is *responsible* for the current rapid growth in HMO enrolments. Sorting out causal factors in such a complex environment is notoriously difficult.

References

Anderson, C. W. (1978), 'The Logic of Public Problems: Evaluation in Comparative Policy Research', in D. E. Ashford (ed.), *Comparing Public Policies: New Concepts and Methods* (Beverly Hills, CA: Sage) pp. 19–41.

Anderson, C. W. (1979), 'The Place of Principles in Policy Analysis', *American Political Science Review*, 73 (September) pp. 711–23.

Baier, K. (1982), 'Welfare and Preference', in B. Barry and R. Hardin (eds), *Rational Man and Irrational Society?* (Beverly Hills, CA: Sage) pp. 284–95.

Bernstein, B. and B. Ensminger (1983), 'It's Time to Fund Physician Shortage Programs by Abandoning Unrestricted State Subsidies to Medical Schools', *Journal of Health Politics, Policy and Law*, 8 (Summer) pp. 221–34.

Biles, B., C. J. Schramm and J. G. Atkinson (1980), 'Hospital Cost Inflation under State Rate-Setting Programs', *New England Journal of Medicine*, 303 (18 September) pp. 665–8.

Brandon, W. P. (1982), 'Health-Related Tax Subsidies: Government Handouts for the Affluent', *New England Journal of Medicine*, 307 (7 October) pp. 947–50.

Brandon, W. P. (1984), 'Public Policy as the Continuation of Moral Philosophy by Other Means: the Challenge of Allison's Epistemological Models', *Policy Studies Review*, 3 (August).

Brandon, W. P. and E. K. Lee (1984), 'Evaluating Health Planning: Empirical Evidence on HSA Regulation of Prepaid Group Practices', *Journal of Health Politics, Policy and Law*, 9 (Spring) pp. 103–24.

Brazda, J. F. (ed.) (1984), 'Reagan Budget: What's New?', *Washington Report on Medicine and Health/Perspectives*, 38 (6 February) pp. 1–6.

Brazda, J. F. (ed.) (1984a), 'Tax Cap Dealt Double Blow', *Washington Report on Medicine and Health*, 38 (5 March) p. 1.

Brazda, J. F. (ed.) (1984b), 'Conferees Approves [*sic*] Physician Fee Freeze', *Washington Report on Medicine and Health*, 38 (25 June) p. 1.

Cochrane, A. L. (1972), *Effectiveness and Efficiency: Random Reflections on Health Services* (London: Nuffield Provincial Hospitals Trust).

Congressional Budget Office, United States Congress (1982), *Containing Medical Care Costs Through Market Forces* (Washington, DC: Government Printing Office) May.

Coyne, J. S. (1982), 'Hospital Performance in Multihospital Systems: A Comparative Study of System and Independent Hospitals', *Health Services Research*, 17 (Winter) pp. 303–29.

Davis, K. (1975), *National Health Insurance: Benefits, Costs, and Consequences*, Studies in Social Economics (Washington, DC: The Brookings Institution).

Donabedian, A. (1980, 1982), *Explorations in Quality Assessment and Monitoring*, vols 1 and 2 (Ann Arbor, MI: Health Administration Press).

Elnicki, R. A. (1974), 'Hospital Productivity, Service Intensity, and Costs', *Health Services Research*, 9 (Winter) pp. 270–92.

Farley, P. J. and G. R. Wilensky (1983), 'Private Health Insurance: What Benefits do Employees and Their Families Have?', *Health Affairs*, 2 (Spring) pp. 92–101.

Feldstein, M. S. (1971), 'Hospital Cost Inflation: A Study of Nonprofit Price Dynamics', *American Economic Review*, 61 (December) pp. 853–72.

Feldstein, M. S. and A. Taylor (1977), *The Rapid Rise of Hospital Costs*, Staff Report, Council on Wage and Price Stability, Executive Office of the President (Washington, DC: Government Printing Office) January.

Frabotta, J. (ed.) (1984), 'PROs At the Starting Gate', *Washington Report on Medicine and Health/Perspectives*, 38 (5 March) pp. 1–4.

Fuchs, V. (1979), 'Economics, Health and Post-Industrial Society', *Milbank Memorial Fund Quarterly: Health and Society*, 57 (Spring) pp. 153–82.

Gibson, R. M., D. R. Waldo and K. R. Levit (1983), 'National Health Expenditures, 1982', *Health Care Financing Review*, 5 (Fall) pp. 1–31.

Goldberg, L. E. and W. Greenberg (1977), 'The Effect of Physician-Controlled Health Insurance: *U.S. v. Oregon State Medical Society*', *Journal of Health Policy and Law*, 2 (Spring) pp. 48–78.

Hadley, J. (1982), *More Medical Care, Better Health? An Economic Analysis of Mortality Rates* (Washington, DC: Urban Institute Press).

Havighurst, C. C. and J. F. Blumstein (1975), 'Coping With Quality/Cost Trade-Offs in Medical Care: The Role of PSROs', *Northwestern University Law Review*, 70 (March–April) pp. 6–68.

Illich, I. (1976), *Medical Nemesis: The Expropriation of Health* (New York: Pantheon).

Jeffers, J. R. and C. D. Siebert (1974), 'Measurement of Hospital Cost Variation: Case Mix, Service Intensity, and Input Productivity Factors', *Health Services Research*, 9 (Winter) pp. 293–307.

Kidder, D. and D. Sullivan (1982), 'Hospital Payroll Costs, Productivity, and Employment Under Prospective Reimbursement', *Health Care Financing Review*, 4 (December) pp. 89–100.

Kimbell, L. J. and J. H. Lorant (1977), 'Physician Productivity and Returns to Scale', *Health Services Research*, 12 (Winter) pp. 367–79.

Knowles, J. H. (ed.) (1977), 'Doing Better and Feeling Worse: Health in the United States', *Daedalus*, 106 (Winter) pp. v–276.

Lee, R. H. (1984), 'Subsidizing the Affluent: The Case of Medical Education', *Journal of Policy Analysis and Management*, 3 (Winter) pp. 276–84.

May, J. J. (1977), 'Review of Issues Involved in Measuring Hospital Productivity', Unpublished Memorandum to the Board of Directors, Health Research and Education Trust of New Jersey.

McKeown, T. (1979), *The Role of Medicine: Dream Mirage or Nemesis?* (2nd edn) (Princeton, NJ: Princeton University Press).

McKinlay, J. B. and S. M. McKinlay (1977), 'The Questionable Contribution of Medical Measures to the Decline of Mortality in the United States in the Twentieth Century', *Milbank Memorial Fund Quarterly: Health and Society*, 55 (Summer) pp. 405–28.

Northrop, F. S. C. (1946), *The Meeting of East and West* (New York: Macmillan).

Office of Management and Budget, Executive Office of the President (1984), 'Special Analysis G.', *Special Analyses, Budget of the United States Government, Fiscal Year 1984* (Washington, DC: Government Printing Office).

President's Commission for the Study of Ethical Problems in Medicine and Biomedical and Behavioral Research (1983), *Securing Access to Health Care: A Report on the Ethical Implications of Differences in the Availability of Health*

Services, vol. 1: Report (Washington, DC: Government Printing Office) March.

Ruchlin, H. S. and I. Leveson (1974), 'Measuring Hospital Productivity', *Health Sciences Research*, 9 (Winter) pp. 308–23.

Salkever, D. S. and T. W. Bice (1979), *Hospital Certificate-of-Need Controls: Impact on Investment Costs and Use* (Washington, DC: American Enterprise Institute).

Schwartz, W. B. (1981), 'The Regulation Strategy for Controlling Hospital Costs: Problems and Prospects', *New England Journal of Medicine*, 305 (19 November) pp. 1249–55.

Self, P. (1981), 'Planning: Rational or Political?', in P. R. Baehr and B. Wittrock (eds), *Policy Analysis and Policy Innovation: Patterns, Problems and Potentials* (London: Sage) pp. 219–36.

Sloan, F. A. (1983), 'Rate Regulation as a Strategy for Hospital Cost Control: Evidence from the Last Decade', *Milbank Memorial Fund Quarterly: Health and Society*, 61 (Spring) pp. 195–221.

Sloan, F. A. and B. Steinwald (1980), 'Effects of Regulation on Hospital Costs and Input Use', *Journal of Law and Economics*, 23 (April) pp. 81–109.

Starr, P. (1982), *The Social Transformation of American Medicine* (New York: Basic Books).

Stedman, T. L. (1982), *Illustrated Stedman's Medical Dictionary*, 24th edn (Baltimore: Williams & Wilkins) *S.v.* Munchausen syndrome.

Taylor, A. K. and G. R. Wilensky (1983), 'The Effect of Tax Policy on Expenditures for Private Health Insurance', in J. A. Meyers (ed.), *Market Reforms in Health Care: Current Issues, New Directions, Strategic Decisions* (Washington, DC: American Enterprise Institute) pp. 163–84.

Tribe, L. H. (1972), 'Policy Science: Analysis or Ideology', *Philosophy and Public Affairs*, 2 (Fall) pp. 66–110.

Wilensky, G. R. and A. K. Taylor (1982), 'Tax Expenditures and Health Insurance: Limiting Employer-Paid Premiums', *Public Health Reports*, 97 (September–October) pp. 438–44.

Wilensky, G. R. and L. F. Rossiter (1983), 'The Relative Importance of Physician-Induced Demand in the Demand for Medical Care', *Milbank Memorial Fund Quarterly: Health and Society*, 61 (Spring) pp. 252–77.

Wing, K. R. (1984), 'Recent Amendments to the Medicaid Program: Political Implications', *American Journal of Public Health*, 74 (January) pp. 83–4.

Witte, J. (1983), 'The Distribution of Federal Income Tax Expenditures', *Policy Studies Journal*, 12 (September) pp. 131–53.

Wittgenstein, L. (1968), *Philosophical Investigations*, 3rd (revised) edn, translated by G. E. M. Anscombe, edited by G. E. M. Anscombe and R. Rhees (New York: Macmillan).

Part IV
Value Trade-offs and Productivity

9 Local Government Productivity: Efficiency and Equity[1]

Jeffrey L. Brudney and David R. Morgan

As a result of increasing pressures to improve productivity, public organizations may become preoccupied with efficiency at the expense of quality and equity. This chapter reviews previous research on the quality dimension of productivity and develops methods to incorporate equity into performance measurement. Two types of approaches to equity are elaborated: the first relies on evaluation of the severity of pre-service problems of clients, and the second is based on the distribution of services across client groupings. The argument is put forward that equity considerations must become an integral part of productivity analysis.

As local governments struggle with providing services in an era of fiscal constraints, pressures mount to obtain more output from the same or fewer resources. A variety of proposals and schemes for providing more with less are advanced and implemented. In addition to considering alternatives to traditional service delivery, such as contracting to the private sector, a great deal of discussion centres on 'managing for performance' or 'results-orientated management' in the public sector (see Wholey, 1983). Managing for results requires not only agreement on objectives and the development of a system for assessing program performance but also a commitment to enhanced productivity.

Although the goal of improving public sector productivity has gained widespread acceptance, the literature concedes that measuring productivity, especially for service industries, is complex and controversial. Some even contend that measuring services may be impossible; frequently the effort to measure services is reduced to gauging those characteristics that are tangible or quantifiable without regard to their importance. Michael Lipsky, perhaps the foremost proponent of this view, argues (1980, pp. 159–79) that attempts to force greater accountability on lower-level workers through performance measurement may be counter-productive, resulting in an erosion of service quality. He maintains that where efficiency and effectiveness are stressed, employees may adapt their work routines to achieve measurable objectives regardless of client needs, thus sacrificing service quality. If Lipsky is correct – and his observations are not original (see Blau, 1964) – does his argument imply that productivity and genuine service quality are incompatible? Can measures of service quality or effectiveness be devised that take account of the needs of special groups, those who may be disadvantaged or who present especially difficult problems? In effect, can efficiency be made compatible with the quality and equity of service distribution?

The discussion which follows will address certain vital issues evolving out of the growing interest in the quality and equity of local government productivity. We shall examine initially past efforts to measure public sector productivity that explicitly incorporate indicators of effectiveness or quality. Next, we shall consider the arguments in favour of expanding productivity measurement to include the concept of equity. Finally, we shall consider the need for measures that incorporate service quality and equity and present suggestions for creating such measures.

MEASURING PRODUCTIVITY

Measuring private sector productivity has been a relatively straightforward process. The emphasis is primarily on amount produced in relation to resources consumed, with almost no concern for quality or effectiveness. The assumption is that market forces and the price mechanism take care of quality. Government productivity measurement has been much more difficult. In the public sector, productivity has normally been defined to encompass both efficiency (output per unit of input) and effectiveness, the extent to which program objectives are met. Effectiveness may also embrace the quality of the service provided, although distinctions are sometimes made between the two concepts (see Usilaner and Soniat, 1980, pp. 92–3). These are not merely definitions used in academic discussions. When a random sample of 319 local chief administrators were given a choice of 12 competing definitions of productivity, 54 per cent selected the phrase 'the efficiency with which resources are consumed in the effective delivery of services' (Ammons and King, 1983, p. 115).

Despite the increasing acceptance of effectiveness or quality of service as an element of productivity, the actual incorporation of such measures into a single productivity indicator has been problematic. The tendency has been to offer a series of effectiveness measures for a particular service area to be included along with the more traditional efficiency measures. For example, an early report on solid waste collection by the National Commission on Productivity (1973, p. 8) lists five separate productivity measures including total tons collected/crew collection hour, households served/crew collection hour, and cost/tons collected. These would seem to represent rather straightforward technical efficiency criteria for evaluating service performance. Later, Hatry *et al.* (1977, p. 237) recommended adding such data as average litter cleanliness rating (based on trained observer techniques) and the percentage of population expressing satisfaction with collection (based on community sample surveys). These authors present a composite index of productivity that incorporates several efficiency and effectiveness measures, including a cleanliness rating and an indication of customer satisfaction.

Three other attempts to combine efficiency and effectiveness in productivity measures might be considered briefly. Writing in the *Municipal Year Book*, Fukuhara (1977, p. 193) offers a productivity formula that embraces both quality (percentage of consumer, clientele, or community satisfaction) and quantity (the percentage of community need satisfied by the service). Fukuhara recognizes that not all public services can be captured with such a single productivity measure, and that in fact most local governments will probably continue to report efficiency and effectiveness measures separately.

Rosen (1981) has also developed a measure of productivity that explicitly incorporates quality. She contends that administrators need productivity measures that include considerations of quality and yet are simple enough for lay people to understand. In this case, her formula demonstrates that a measure explicitly including quality can be composed of weighted components. For instance, in judging the productivity of mail delivery, she suggests that the relevant quality criteria might be speed, accuracy, and courtesy. Further, it might be decided that speed is the most important criterion (weight 1), accuracy is only half as important (0.5), and courtesy only half as important as accuracy (0.25). Each component is expressed as a ratio of actual accomplishment to predetermined standards and then multiplied together to derive the final measure of quality.

One final illustration of adding quality to the traditional technical-efficiency productivity measure comes from Adam (1979). In developing a Quality Productivity Ratio (QPR), Adam changes the output part of the equation (numerator) to exclude substandard or faulty products. The denominator includes the total number of good and substandard products. The following example shows how the QPR might be calculated:

$$QPR = \frac{\text{Number of buses at final destination on time}}{\begin{pmatrix}\text{Total \#} \\ \text{of bus} \\ \text{destination} \\ \text{route trips}\end{pmatrix} \times \begin{pmatrix}\text{cost per} \\ \text{route} \\ \text{trip}\end{pmatrix} + \begin{pmatrix}\text{\# of buses} \\ \text{not on} \\ \text{time}\end{pmatrix} \times \begin{pmatrix}\text{cost in lost} \\ \text{customer} \\ \text{goodwill per} \\ \text{late bus}\end{pmatrix}}$$

While acknowledging that such efforts as the QPR are an advancement over most previous input/output ratios, Kelly (1980) contends that they still fall short of meeting many of the criticisms of traditional public sector productivity measurement. For example, she argues that the application of a QPR within institutions of higher education would cause wise administrators to adjust admission policies to attract those students most likely to succeed. Students with high entrance exam scores, few financial worries, and good high school grades would be especially attractive. Thus ' "quality" and "productivity" would increase, but equal opportunity and service to the broader community would decrease' (Kelly, 1980, p. 83). In short, most productivity measures that include quality do not take into account the possibility of 'creaming', where program results are skewed because providers prefer to work with those who are most likely to make the quickest and most effective use of the given service.

EQUITY AND PRODUCTIVITY

Although the literature on public sector productivity evinces increasing interest in quality and effectiveness issues, the distribution of goods or services and the social equity of that distribution are rarely considered in productivity assessment (Hatry, 1980, p. 334). In a 1974 article comparing 'Social Equity and Social Service Productivity', Stephen R. Chitwood was skeptical of attempts to integrate these two concepts. Despite certain similarities, social equity centres on the distribution of services and of their effects, while government productivity concentrates on the quantity and/or quality of outputs. Further, whereas equity examines the social groupings from which inputs to the production process were derived, productivity is directed more narrowly to the amount of inputs utilized in monetary terms. As a result of these differences, Chitwood (1974, p. 30) advocates that 'measures of social equity must increasingly accompany measures of productivity in order to assess the adequacy of public services'.

When equity has been considered in government performance measurement, the strategy of separate indicators to assess productivity and distributional aspects has, in fact, been the rule (see, for example, Hatry, 1980; Koss, *et al.*, 1979; Millar, Hatry, and Koss, 1977). Many, if not most, urban researchers share a commitment to the achievement of both values in service delivery. However, even in those instances in which distributional data are available, the danger arises that in an environment characterized by fiscal stringency (especially in the social services), government officials will become increasingly preoccupied with traditional measures of productivity defined as technical efficiency at the expense of distributional issues. A concern with the 'bottom line' – How much was produced at what cost? – may predominate over more elusive questions of social equity – Who received the benefits? Lest one considers this difference to be merely a technical or academic issue, Wilenski (1980–1) has shown that efficiency and equity are 'competing values', which often carry different implications for administrative action and reform. Moreover, 'those who place a high value on equity are continually at a disadvantage in this debate . . . [for] the battle is fought out in a culture where the norms and values of efficiency, economy and productivity predominate' (pp. 1248–9).

Wilenski's argument is borne out by recent proposals to link wages and salaries in the public sector to gains (or losses) in productivity. This plan may, indeed, succeed in controlling inflation and uniting management and labour in pursuit of greater productivity. Yet without equal attention to the distribution of services, it may also strongly cue service agents to apply their efforts to those least in need of assistance in order to demonstrate increases in productivity, at least as measured by the organization. By identifying categories or end-states to which service agents are directed to move clients efficiently as evidence of productivity (for example, 'treated', 'helped', 'self-supporting'), the organization establishes a powerful incentive to work with clients who can reach these states most easily and quickly and to delay treatment or devote less attention to those who are not so fortunate. As a consequence, service agents may choose to work with the blind best suited to adapt to society, Aid to Families with Dependent Children (AFDC) mothers most likely to find jobs, and job trainees with the most skills to bring to the marketplace. In the name of 'productivity', those most in need of treatment – who are likely to be non-white, older, low-income, and women – may receive less assistance than other clients from service agencies.

In order to ameliorate these problems, it is important to elevate equity to equal status with efficiency and effectiveness in the assessment of government productivity. At the conceptual level, Buntz (1981, p. 303) offers a novel definition combining these three values: 'Productivity in the human services refers to the efficiency with which resources are consumed in the effective *and equitable* delivery of human services.' According to this view, efficiency and effectiveness are not sufficient demonstrations of productivity in the delivery of services; the equity of resulting service distributions must also be considered. We share this conception of public sector productivity. The remainder of this chapter develops productivity measures that attempt to take equity into account.

INCORPORATING EQUITY INTO PRODUCTIVITY MEASUREMENT

A concern for equity and allocational issues is certainly not new in the service delivery literature. Research published as early as 1955 by Blau (1964, pp. 44–6) provides an example of how employment counsellors tended to avoid hard-to-place clients when they were evaluated on the basis of successful placements rather than cases handled. More recently, Lipsky (1980) has raised serious objections to the use of performance measures on the grounds that they lead service providers to avoid working with difficult clients. He argues that service quality measures are meaningless without adequate controls for level of difficulty. 'For example, the same student achievement levels might represent excellent work on the part of a teacher of students with learning difficulties and poor work on the part of a teacher with bright and motivated students' (Lipsky, 1980, p. 168). Without such controls for level of difficulty, Lipsky insists that productivity efforts 'may not simply be ineffective but may also lead to an erosion of quality' (p. 159).

Lipsky's objections notwithstanding, some efforts at measuring service productivity have recognized the need to consider allocational and equity issues. Because a substantial research tradition has not been established, attempts to include equity tend to be limited, preliminary, and tentative, but none the less useful. In this section we build upon previous research in this area to develop new approaches.

The Traditional Approach

Like the measures of effectiveness discussed above, the scant research attempting to incorporate equity into productivity measurement relies on a weighting scheme. In this instance the weights require some element of subjective judgement by administrators or other officials of the degree of 'importance' of serving some groups or clients as opposed to others. Krueckeberg and Silvers (1974, pp. 208–10) provide a good example of this concern for the incidence of program impacts in the area of library services. Their illustration assumes that program administrators are able to agree that service to 'low-education' residents is three times as important as services to others. This decision then requires that the amount of service delivered to low-education residents be multiplied by three, and the amount of service to all others multiplied by one. Perhaps the greatest problem with this approach is the necessity for clear specification of target groups and relative weighting of impacts incident to them.

The Perceived Difficulty Approach

Researchers at the Urban Institute have shown interest in categorizing the incoming workload to public organizations according to the perceived difficulty or severity of pre-service problems presented. In the social services, Koss and associates (1979, pp. 68–70) propose the use of subjective ratings of difficulty of initial client problems prior to service delivery; Hatry and associates (1977, pp. 76–9) discuss the need for a 'solvability' index that could be applied to arrest data to adjust for variations in workload difficulty. The rationale underlying these studies is that measures of productivity which ignore the difficulty and mix of the incoming workload may be wholly misleading, reflecting the nature of agency caseloads rather than the quantity and quality of services provided.

The case-severity approach has thus received attention as a technical procedure to correct productivity indexes for workload composition, although formulae by which this objective may be implemented are generally not provided. We suggest that this approach may be used more broadly to incorporate equity concepts into productivity assessment. The difficulty or severity of incoming problems to many agencies constitutes a rough guide to the achievement of equity in service delivery. From the client perspective, a difficult problem or case to the agency often represents an individual or group with special or increased need for services, such as severely disabled people in rehabilitation services or unemployed high school drop-outs in job training programs. If ratings of case difficulty can be interpreted as approximations of clients' needs for services – clients with the most severe problems have the most pressing need for, and claims on, public assistance – then this information can be applied to productivity measures to weight them according to equity criteria. As an example, on a three-point scale of problem severity–client need (minor problem, moderate problem, major problem), treating the most severe cases might be weighted three times as heavily in productivity indexes as helping those with the least serious difficulties. This method could be very useful in overcoming organizational incentives toward 'creaming'. While the approach employs the same type of weighting methodology employed in traditional efforts, in addition to allowing any gradation of need, it has the advantage of changing the basis of weighting from the essentially political criterion of 'importance' (Krueckeberg and Silvers, 1974, p. 209) to the more neutral, less controversial criterion of 'difficulty'.

Moreover, this method can be improved further over the traditional approach. Rather than utilizing arbitrary weights consisting of convenient whole numbers (that is, 1, 2, 3, . . .) with proper data collection, service agencies can validate the weighting scheme against actual outcomes for each 'need' (case difficulty) group. Such research may demonstrate, for instance, that service to clients in the most problematic situations may be 3.7 times less likely to result in 'successful treatment' according to agency definition than service to clients in the least difficult classification. The validated weights, which could be adjusted as frequently as available data or agency preferences require, would replace arbitrary weighting systems in productivity measurement.

By focusing primarily on the difficulty of treatment rather than on the results obtained, the case-severity method may encourage service agents to attend to the most needy clients as anticipated. But it may also establish incentives to give them perfunctory treatment, especially since this group would be expected to demonstrate the least improvement. With service to difficult cases rewarded in productivity indexes, service agents may assist the most needy but do so poorly or in a cursory manner.

One method of compensating for this incentive is to incorporate into productivity analysis not only difficulty but also *effectiveness*, as Kelly (1980, p. 81) advocates. For example, for each level of difficulty of the incoming workload, the degree of effectiveness of outcomes at termi-

nation of services might be graded, so that productivity measures would
increase with treatment to difficult cases but attenuate with poor quality
outcomes. Adam (1979) has called for efforts to measure the degree of
excellence of the characteristics or attributes of the products or services
delivered by public organizations. This method would necessitate a
matrix of case weights associating initial service condition (difficulty)
with final condition (effectiveness); the matrix would provide estimates
of the relative value of each level of accomplishment. While this
procedure will surely confront methodological problems, even in a
policy domain as subjective as mental health, Halpern and Binner (1981)
demonstrate the possibility of rating the level of impairment at
admission (difficulty) and the level of response at discharge (effectiveness) and associating them in a matrix of case weights (see Table 9.1).

Table 9.1   Difficulty by effectiveness matrix*

	Level of response at discharge (effectiveness)				
Level of impairment at admission (difficulty)	(1) Regressed	(2) No change	(3) Slight improvement	(4) Moderate improvement	(5) Marked
Slight (1)	−0.10	0.00	0.10	0.40	0.70
Moderate (2)	−0.10	0.00	0.20	0.50	0.80
Marked (3)	−0.30	0.00	0.30	0.60	0.90
Severe (4)	−0.40	0.00	0.40	0.70	1.00

Source: Adapted from Halpern and Binner (1981, p. 162).

* Entries in table represent weights to apply to cases according to initial difficulty and final
outcome. For example, service to clients with 'moderate' impairment resulting in
'marked' improvement would receive a weight of 0.80.

The Demographic Approach

Millar, Hatry, and Koss (1977, pp. 7–10) discuss a so-called Denver
Inventory of 20 individual characteristics to be used to assess the
potential employability of AFDC clients. Based on characteristics such
as marital status, educational attainment, work experience, and physical
condition, the inventory is intended to yield a measure of case difficulty.
Caseworkers collect the relevant information, which is then used to
derive a total employability score for each client based on a simple
summation across traits. Although the Denver Department of Welfare

has tested the predictive validity of the inventory, Millar and colleagues (1977) point out problems with some of the constituent items. They conclude that this format 'probably merits consideration as a starting point for categorization of clients by difficulty' but present no evidence that such steps have been taken (p. 8).

The use of a demographic inventory offers promise for incorporating equity considerations into productivity assessment. Like the perceptual measures of case difficulty discussed above, the inventory can be employed to approximate client needs for services. In contrast to the assumption of equal weighting of client characteristics to derive the inventory score, however, we suggest the use of a systematic method, such as regression analysis, to estimate empirically the relative weights of the various background variables. In this method, clients' achievement of desired outcome states (for example, self-support, successful completion of job training, and so on) would be regressed on the (independent) demographic characteristics; the resulting weights could be applied to individual clients or client groupings (for example, blacks, women, and so on) to yield composite estimates of case difficulty. As before, these measures would be incorporated into productivity analysis to assign relative values to the cases treated according to the severity of pre-service problems. That is, the efforts of public organizations and their employees would be weighted more heavily to the extent that they served clients in disadvantaged circumstances.

The experience of at least one public agency supports not only the relationship between case severity and equity but also the feasibility of implementing appraisals of difficulty into agency operations. Prior to amendment of the Vocational Rehabilitation Act in 1973, agencies and counsellors in the state-federal rehabilitation program were evaluated according to achievement of 'status 26' case closure (placement of clients in gainful employment) without reference to severity of initial client conditions. Political pressures to increase the number of closures gradually eroded the criterion measure 'to the stage where it only measures the number of people successfully exiting from the rehabilitation system' (Smits and Ledbetter, 1979, p. 81). The 1973 Act requires state agencies to give first priority to the most severely disabled and secondary attention to those with lesser disabilities, an implicit weighting of clients based on case difficulty. Lauth (1981, p. 128) summarizes the implications of this system for the assessment of agency performance: 'This policy change represented for many agencies a dramatic shift in client population from a relatively low cost/high expectation-of-success clientele, to a high cost/low expectation-of-success clientele'.

This change could be instituted in productivity indexes through the use of ratings of initial case severity and resulting client outcomes.

CONCLUSION

'The big tradeoff' is the way economist Arthur Okun (1975) describes the relationship between equity and efficiency. Although we now confront a period in which technical efficiency is clearly in the ascendency, Okun shows that historically American society has also been committed to equality even at some sacrifice in efficiency. No doubt, with a growing concern over this country's capacity to compete in the world marketplace, we will continue to see a considerable emphasis on productivity. Some might assume that a commitment to making the production of goods and services more efficient implies a reduced concern for issues of equity and distribution. But perhaps this need not be the case. For example, Page (1983) maintains that in a variety of ways, greater equality can be achieved with little sacrifice in efficiency. At the least, a good argument can be made that efforts to enhance productivity in the provision of government services should not proceed without explicit and careful attention to the issues of distribution and equity.

This chapter has contended that indeed equity can and should be incorporated as an important criterion in the assessment of government productivity and has discussed several approaches that might accomplish this objective. Because this undertaking is novel, our conclusions should be considered tentative. We have elaborated the traditional method of including equity in cost-benefit analysis and proposed new approaches based on the difficulty or severity of client pre-service problems. These approaches are guided by the assumptions that initial case severity is indicative of client needs for services, and that measures of productivity should reflect the degree to which public organizations and employees attend to the most 'needy' cases. These efforts might be considered as a first but vital step toward instituting equity as a co-equal value with efficiency and effectiveness in the assessment of public sector productivity.

Notes

1. We are grateful to Rita Mae Kelly for her comments and suggestions regarding the development of this article and to Tom Lauth for his useful insights in the analysis. The authors are solely responsible for the contents.

174   *Local Government Productivity: Efficiency and Equity*

References

Adam, E. E., Jr (1979), 'Quality and productivity in delivering and administering public service', *Public Productivity Review*, 3, pp. 26–40.

Ammons, D. and J. King (1983), 'Productivity improvement in local government: Its place among competing priorities', *Public Administration Review*, 43, 113–20.

Blau, P. (1964), *The dynamics of bureaucracy* (revised edn; Chicago: University of Chicago Press).

Buntz, C. G. (1981), 'Problems and issues in human service productivity improvement', *Public Productivity Review*, 5, pp. 299–320.

Chitwood, S. R. (1974), 'Social equity and social service productivity', *Public Administration Review*, 34, pp. 29–35.

Fukuhara, R. S. (1977), 'Productivity improvement in cities', *Municipal Year Book* (Washington, DC: International City Management Association).

Halpern, J. and P. R. Binner (1981), 'A model for an output value analysis of mental health programs', in M. L. Gruber (ed.), *Management systems in the human services* (Philadelphia: Temple University Press), pp. 158–69.

Hatry, H. H. (1980), 'Performance measurement principles and techniques: An overview for local government', *Public Productivity Review*, 4, pp. 312–39.

Hatry, H. P., *et al.* (1977), *How effective are your community services?* (Washington, DC: Urban Institute).

Kelly, R. M. (1980), 'Ideology, effectiveness, and public sector productivity: With illustrations from the field of higher education', *Journal of Social Issues*, 36, pp. 76–95.

Koss, M., *et al.* (1979), *Social services: What happens to the clients?* (Washington, DC: Urban Institute).

Krueckeberg, D. A. and A. L. Silvers (1974), *Urban planning analysis: Methods and models* (New York: John Wiley).

Lauth, T. P. (1981), 'The rehabilitation administrator in the budgetary process: Resource acquisition in a changing environment', in W. G. Emener, R. S. Luck, and S. J. Smith (eds), *Rehabilitation administration and supervision* (Baltimore: University Park Press) pp. 125–45.

Lipsky, M. (1980), *Street-level bureaucracy* (New York: Russell Sage Foundation).

Millar, A., H. Hatry and M. Koss (1977), *Monitoring the outcomes of social services, vol. II: A review of past research and test activities* (Washington, DC: Urban Institute).

National Commission on Productivity (1973), *Opportunities for improving productivity in solid waste collection* (Washington, DC).

Okun, A. M. (1975), *Equality and efficiency: The big tradeoff* (Washington, DC: Brookings Institute).

Page, B. I. (1983), *Who gets what from government* (Berkeley: University of California Press).

Rosen, E. D. (1981), 'O.K. work: Incorporating quality into the production equation', *Public Productivity Review*, 5, pp. 207–17.

Smits, S. J. and J. G. Ledbetter (1979), 'The practice of rehabilitation counselling within the administrative structure of the state-federal program', *Journal of Applied Rehabilitation Counselling*, 10, pp. 78–84.

Usilaner, B. and E. Soniat (1980), 'Productivity measurement', in G. J. Washnis (ed.), *Productivity improvement handbook for state and local government* (New York: John Wiley) pp. 91–114.

Wholey, J. S. (1983), *Evaluation and effective public management* (Boston: Little, Brown).

Wilenski, P. (1980–1), 'Efficiency of equity: Competing values in administrative reform', *Policy Studies Journal* (Special issue # 4), pp. 1239–49.

10 Productivity and Social Goals: A Case Study from Cincinnati, Ohio[1]

Douglas H. Shumavon

This study looks at the tension between productivity and social goals as they are manifested in procurement processes in local government. The renewed interest in productivity (primarily an 'efficiency' goal) and programs designed to achieve social goals provides us with an opportunity to reassess some of the criticisms made by the New Public Administration group in the late 1960s.

The study identifies how upper level administrators pay attention to issues of social equity and societal well-being – primarily because they must attend to the political dimension of their jobs. Administrators and public employees in traditional 'housekeeping' functions (such as procurement) are orientated toward cost savings. The chapter ends with suggestions for how to provide incentives which will allow for greater attention to those programs designed to achieve social goals even within an organizational unit that has efficiency as its ethos.

INTRODUCTION

The issue of government productivity has been at centre stage for some time in a renewed concern for efficiency in the public sector. The cry for more economical efforts on the part of government is not new, however; it has been addressed since the early part of this century when the notions of management were beginning. Government involvement in questions of effectiveness and social equity are, comparatively, a new concern. Since the 1960s specific governmental activities that are designed to achieve social equity have often encountered conflict with questions of efficiency. Taxpayers are interested in reducing costs for goods and services, and our society holds in high regard the efficient use of scarce resources. At times calls for reduced costs and more efficient government neglect the costs attributed to the achievement of social goals. To what extent do these conflicting goals present problems for administrators in the public sector? How attuned to the conflict are public sector employees? What can be done to resolve the tension between these two considerations? This chapter uses a specific case from local government to address the conflict between social goals and questions of productivity and efficiency. It also suggests additional concerns which local officials might wish to consider in attending to both.

'PRODUCTIVITY' DEFINED

'Productivity' has, as with many terms, been used and abused in a variety of ways. Hayward (1980, p. 260) writes that the definition 'implies not only quantity but quality . . . .The inadequacy of the industrial definition (productivity = output/input) to account for effectiveness and quality in the absence of a competitive market is reflected in the breadth of the public sector definition.' Others have defined the term in both an economic and a managerial sense.

> In the economic sense, it refers to the combination of resources used to produce goods and services. In the management sense, the term refers to the adequacy of the way in which a manager uses resources in order to produce specific products and services. (Schott *et al.*, 1977, p. 1)

The General Accounting Office (GAO) has defined it as measuring 'how efficiently or effectively resources are transformed into goods and services. In simpler and more operational terms, it means doing more with the same or fewer resources' (USGAO, 1983, p. 1). These definitions are, of course, somewhat varied. But in all of them the common thread is in determining how one might achieve the goals of the organization by getting more out of the resources with which one must manage.

THE CASE STUDY

The City of Cincinnati, Ohio, addresses the issue of productivity from a somewhat broader definition that still incorporates the idea of cost effectiveness. While marginally different, the issues that could be addressed indicate the similarities between the above definitions and the ways in which productivity is defined in Cincinnati. Specifically, the city has attempted to determine ways in which it could

(a) reduce or eliminate internal red tape,
(b) reduce or eliminate duplication,
(c) improve employee motivation, and
(d) effect cost reductions.

The area of governmental activity that allows us to address both productivity and social goals is the procurement (or purchasing) process. The purchasing of goods and services by the city amounts to an estimated $43 million annually. Several elements that place the purchasing activities in perspective need to be identified at the outset. First, it must be remembered that the purchasing activity itself is an auxiliary function. That is, it is not a line agency directly providing city services to the citizens. Nor is it a staff agency, which makes fundamental decisions, acting as an *alter ego* for the chief executive. The purchasing division performs a 'housekeeping' function. Second, the procurement function has long been centralized so as to serve as a cost-saving activity. Centralized purchasing results in less expensive costs through a variety of mechanisms, most notably competitive bidding for large quantities of goods or services. Unit costs can be reduced by 10 per cent to 15 per cent through centralizing the procurement function (Forbes, 1929, p. viii). Third, the City of Cincinnati has a reputation for leadership in co-operative purchasing agreements (where several jurisdictions join together to derive the cost-savings from competitive bidding by collectively purchasing similarly needed items). Fourth, and most significantly, since the 1960s several policies that aspire to the achievement of social goals have been imposed upon the procurement activities.

Since the early 1960s Equal Employment Opportunity (EEO) programs must be in place and affirmative action is required of firms if deficiencies in their programs are noted when they receive city contracts. More recently, a Minority Business Enterprise (MBE) program has been established to ensure that minority-owned businesses are given an improved opportunity to compete for certain contracts. Both of these programs are designed to achieve goals that are directed toward making changes within the greater community. Both also have considerable economic consequences. At the same time, these two programs have given the procurement function difficulties: the goals to which each is directed conflict with a 'housekeeping' function traditionally assumed to be 'efficiency' orientated.

The items purchased by the City of Cincinnati are quite varied. From specialized goods such as instructional/educational items manufactured by only one firm and costing no more than $15.00 to large items such as fire trucks costing many thousands of dollars, the city handles several thousand transactions each year. There are replenishable items (consumables, such as paper, pencils, paper clips) and items with long durability (such as pumps used in water or sewage treatment plants).

Bid Types

The city distinguishes between three types of invitations to bid, classified by dollar amount and characterized by different bidding requirements. All types of bids are posted in the municipal building. They include specifications for the item(s) desired or the type of construction to be completed, and identify the closing date after which bids cannot be accepted. Category I is for purchases estimated to cost less than $1500. In addition to the requirement that the city post invitations to bid, this category of bid requires the city to select from a list of registered vendors and mail invitations to bid. Category II includes items with an anticipated cost of between $1500 and $25 000 that require a more elaborate process. In this class of purchase a once-only, formal announcement published in the weekly City Bulletin is mandated. As with the posting requirement, this publication includes all the data regarding the specifications for the item(s) desired and the due date for bid submission. The final category is for items or services expected to cost over $25 000. These requests for bids must be published twice in the City Bulletin and advertised in the local daily newspapers. Bids in this category have the additional requirement that they must be publicly opened (City of Cincinnati, Ordinance # 61–1982).

While these three categories of invitations to bid vary by dollar amount and public announcement, they each meet the characteristics of a centralized procurement process. First, each item is identified by the requesting agency (department). Second, the city uses competitive bidding to gain an advantage when like commodities are available from different sources. Third, the bids are assessed so as to determine both the lowest and best bid. This final characteristic is common among public institutions. It allows for factors other than cost to be included in the decision-making process (for example, the quality of the product).

Social Goal Programs

Overarching the procurement processes are two programs designed to achieve social goals. The first is a requirement that the city set aside certain items to be purchased for exclusive bidding by minority business enterprises (MBEs). Specifically, local ordinance requires that 15 per cent of all dollars spent for the purchase of construction, 7 per cent of all contract dollars for supplies and services, and 5 per cent of all professional services contracts be set aside for exclusive bidding (City of Cincinnati, 1983b, Ordinance # 139–1983). Furthermore, for all purchases amounting to more than $5000, the Purchasing Department must certify that the recipient firm (a) is in compliance with EEO standards of '11.8 per cent minority and 6.9 per cent female (of whom one half shall be minorities) in each craft trade in the contractor's aggregate workforce. . .' (City of Cincinnati, 1983a, Resolution # R/32–1983), and (b) has an approved EEO program, or (c) is taking specific affirmative action to employ a greater number of minorities.

In order to achieve the MBE set-aside goals, the city has established procedures whereby as soon as requisitions are received from line agencies they are reviewed to determine if there are registered minority businesses capable of supplying the needed product. If the item requested is available through an MBE, the city will set aside that requisition for exclusive bidding by those minority firms that have expressed an interest in competing for city bids. While the extra step usually does not result in great delay (at most, a day) two phenomena have been identified which create complications in the bidding process. First, if the responding firms are aware that the bid is a set-aside bid, the potential exists for a significant increase in the purchase price (for example, an increase of 50 per cent over the last time the item was bought by the city). Second, the list of MBEs for a particular item may be too generic, while the requisition is fairly specific. This can result in a mismatch where no firms are capable of supplying the specific item while they may provide an item within the generic category. An example here is where the requisition is for a highly specialized pump for sewage treatment generally available from a select group of firms, but the list of minority-owned vendors of 'pumps' does not distinguish between types of pumps available through firms on the list.

If either of these cases manifests itself, the requisition must be removed from the set-aside procedures and new bids solicited. At this point, the process requires several additional delays (for example, the approval to remove from set-aside takes two additional signatures). Once removal from set-aside is approved, the invitations to bid must be reduplicated and mailed to a new list of possible vendors, which does not distinguish MBE from non-MBE firms. If the dollar amount of the items sought is greater than $1500, the invitation to bid will take at least an additional week, since it must be reprinted in the City Bulletin. If the timing is bad (that is, if the submission to the Bulletin does not meet the weekly deadline for publication), the net delay can be an additional two weeks. This will be the case if the deadline is missed by just one day. The consequences of slight errors can result in rather lengthy delays. Compare, for example, the data from Table 10.1 that indicates the average number of work days for direct purchases (for example, sole source providers), for MBE set aside requisitions, and for all bids other than direct and set-aside purchases. The variation runs from nearly two-and-a-half weeks to nearly six weeks.

Table 10.1   Response time

	No. of cases	Percentage of cases	Workdays	Average no. of days per case
All cases	268	100	5781	22
Direct Awards	73	27	918	13
Set-aside	69	26	2011	29
Total less Direct Awards and Set-aside	126	47	2852	23

An example illustrating the confusion and conflict between questions of efficiency and social goals is the requirement of EEO/AA compliance. The city, both by local ordinance and by federal law, is required to ensure that, in cases involving contracts in excess of $5000, recipient firms comply with equal employment guidelines. If they are not in compliance, the firms must take affirmative action to change the composition of their work force. Firms are required to submit data regarding their work force composition at the time a contract is awarded. Thus, even though a firm may be the lowest bidder, that firm must provide information regarding employment mix and could be eliminated from consideration if it is not in compliance. It is the obligation of the Contract Compliance Division of the Purchasing Department to review this data. If the firm has not presented the required data, the Division is responsible for its collection. Delays in either case can slow down the awarding of a contract (because of the arduous and tedious nature of both data collection and analysis). Such delays often result in organizational conflict between the requisitioning agency and the centralized Purchasing Department, and, in examples of construction work, delays can become even more disruptive because of the limited months when weather allows for outdoor work.

In both of the above circumstances there appear to be delays in the purchasing processes attributable to implementation of programs designed to achieve social goals that directly impinge upon the procurement activities. In the MBE set-aside program, it is not always known if a given firm can provide the requested item. If that results in removing an item from the set-aside procedures, the resultant delays may be attributable to the attempt to achieve a social goal. Similarly, in the EEO/AA compliance requirements, the necessary effort to secure the information (raw data) and then assess it also requires additional time – in this example, estimates run as high as one month. As in the previous illustration, delays are attributable to the efforts to achieve social goals.

PERSPECTIVES ON THE PROBLEM

Complaints concerning the inefficiencies of purchasing are common. From outside the organization, criticism is levied against the city because of occasional delays in payment. From within the organization, line agencies are quick to point out the delays in receiving needed equipment. From both directions, the difficulty is perceived as the inability to process paper. As regards the social goals, criticisms are also voiced from both outside and within the organization. The external complaints, ironically, may come from both ends of the political spectrum. Non-MBE firms may complain because the MBE set-aside eliminates them from a chance to bid. Conversely, minority businesses may feel that the city is not progressing satisfactorily toward the set-aside targets. Another concern from the minority businesses is the possibility that some non-MBE owned businesses are trying to classify themselves falsely as MBEs in order to receive special treatment. From within the organization, the concerns about the social goals appear to be addressed from the perspective of explaining the delays in getting needed items. In line agencies the expectation is that the goods are purchased and delivered. Critics of the Purchasing Department who are concerned with large dollar amount purchases or contracts are quick to blame delays on the Contract Compliance Division, which is the division assigned responsibility for the EEO/AA programs in the Purchasing Department. As the expectation is quick delivery of goods, the procedures attributed to the achievement of social goals are an easily identified target.

Requisitioning agencies need materials in a timely fashion. When requisitions move through the procedures smoothly, delays are minimized. Agencies can anticipate depletion of supplies and submit requests for replacements with adequate time. If there are breakdowns or emergencies, all normal procedures can be circumvented; but those circumstances must meet 'emergency' status. As the number of requisitions increases over time and additional demands are placed on Purchasing Department personnel, the ability to reduce the response time diminishes. More importantly, when there is an added set of procedures for the MBE set-aside or EEO/AA, delays are exacerbated. From within the city, it is easy for agency personnel to criticize the programs designed to achieve social goals as being responsible for delays. Most city agency personnel probably do not understand the efficiency costs that accompany achieving such goals nor do they acknowledge the increased demand placed on the Purchasing Department.

The point here is that the City Manager receives pressure to address both the social goals and efficiency/productivity questions. In both cases, the complaints are usually received by upper level management. Centralized housekeeping or support functions are acknowledged as creating additional headaches for management. Conflict resolution by the Chief Administrative Officer (CAO) is called for frequently. Indeed, the complaints by the requesting agencies are directed to the City Manager, or his or her deputy. Furthermore, as the CAO, he or she is responsible for seeing that efficiencies are instituted to save dollars. The external complaints are either directed to the City Council or the CAO – and in either case, it is the City Manager who is asked to respond. The City Manager's political role necessitates a sensitivity to the social goals. As the chief executive he or she is responsible for seeing that programs initiated by the City Council are implemented and the goals of those programs achieved.

Within the Purchasing Department, however, the pressures to resolve problems are perceived almost entirely as efficiency/productivity questions. The pressure is to produce the cost savings and/or reduce or eliminate delays in whatever ways are possible. Whether productivity is defined as more output for the same resources or the same output with reduced resources, the issue for improving productivity becomes 'what causes the delays?' Usually the delays are perceived as a hindrance to improved productivity. Consequently, MBE and EEO/AA are seen as irrelevant to cost savings (the purpose of centralizing the purchasing function in the first place), not as acknowledged costs to achieve social goals.

EFFICIENCY AND SOCIAL GOALS

The New Public Administration group has levied harsh criticism about both the study and practice of public administration. Administrators, they said, were at fault because of their lack of attention to social goals. Harmon (1971) suggested that there was no administrative neutrality and that administrators needed to pay close attention to the social goals. Frederickson (1971) went so far as to suggest that administrators are not only 'not neutral', but that they should be advocates of social equity. The fundamental thrust of the New PA was an across-the-board criticism of the lack of attention to issues involving social equity. Nowhere in their writings did the New PA group suggest that we consider different levels of organizations to understand the extent to which there are (or are not) differences in attachment to social goals.

With the renewed interest in productivity it is possible to reflect again on the potential conflict between social goals and efficiency. Quite possibly we need a reassessment of the charges levied by the New PA group. One useful way of facilitating that reassessment is to acknowledge that upper-level administrators must address pressure from two directions. First, upper-level administrators must be responsive to political officials, with whom they interact regularly. In this example, the CAO responds to external pressures and attends to the social goals. The second set of pressures to which upper-level administrators must address themselves are managerial in nature: that of conducting the business of government. Here, one attends to the efficiency goals. Contrary to the assumptions of the New PA group, sensitivity on the part of top-level administrators is not unidirectional (that is, managerial). Top-level administrators are sensitive to the political dimension, which clamours for attention to the social goals.

From the perspective of lower-level officials – and in this case those employed in auxiliary functions – the pressure is to provide efficiencies to the organization. Their procedures, orientation – indeed, their *raison d'être* – is to save the organization money. When programs designed to achieve social goals are imposed and require procedures that are perceived to be working against the efficiency goals, it is not surprising to find less attachment to social goals than efficiency goals. Their job descriptions are based on the fundamental assumption that they save the city money. Yet with the added burden of attending to the social goals there is a deflection away from an 'efficient' operation (here defined as minimum time to procure needed items). Indeed, most organizations establish merit structures for auxiliary services that reward efficiency. Criticism for failing to achieve the efficiency standard comes from everywhere. Agencies that request purchases are angered by delays. And when explanations are offered which suggest that this is due to attention to social goals, the response is seldom met with understanding or acceptance. Even from outside the organization, criticism is directed at the auxiliary function. Non-MBE owners complain that they are being cut out of the action. Firms that must contend with EEO/AA guidelines are resentful that the city imposes such requirements. In short, the Purchasing Department must shoulder the criticism for the delays (from within) and for the attempt to achieve the social goals (from without).

COPING WITH THE CONFLICT

Any efforts to balance the competing goals of efficiency and social goals must take heed of the inherent tradeoffs. Okun (1975) suggests that there is a direct trade-off – as attention is directed to the social goals, there is a loss of efficiency. If attention is focused on the efficiency question, there is a loss of attention to the social goals. If the primary goal is to increase productivity, attention will be directed toward reducing delays and delivering the service more efficiently. In short, the procedures added to achieve the social goals will be conceived as extraneous. Conversely, if attention is directed toward the social goals, delays may be increased. This appears to hold true when applied to the issue of productivity improvements within procurement. If an MBE program is to be properly run, it may well take longer to process requisitions and greater expenses may be incurred. Additional steps in the process – to identify the minority firms, to decide which requisitions are to be set aside – will result in a longer time period to achieve a healthier business environment for minority firms. If attention is paid to the EEO/AA efforts, the time necessary to achieve a co-operative working relationship with the affected firms may also cause delays in procurement.

To implement changes in the procedures, one must provide appropriate incentives for employees to make adjustments in their traditional practices. Given the current philosophy of the procurement function as one of cost-savings (both in terms of dollars saved by competitive bidding and in terms of limited time to purchase items), the current reward structure (indeed, the ethos of most 'housekeeping' and support services) is based on the most efficient operation. If the attempt is to refocus energies toward the achievement of social goals, there must be a corresponding reward structure that facilitates working toward the social goals. Incentives may take a variety of forms: financial remuneration of achievement of MBE targets is one example. Special training programs might be allowed for those who come closest to or surpass targets. If those training programs are carefully selected, they can also serve as reinforcement. Attendance at seminars designed to achieve the social goals more effectively provides employees with new ideas to be infused into the organization upon their return.

The conflict between social goals and efficiency goals in organizations will continue to be manifested. If we fail to recognize the different orientations within organizations, however, we will exacerbate rather than ameliorate the conflict. If we impose social goals through mechanisms designed to achieve efficiency goals, we must take the steps to see that attention toward those social goals is addressed throughout the organization. This must be the case not only for those auxiliary functions, but for those other parts of the organization that use the auxiliary services as well.

Note

1. The author thanks Professor Michael A. Pagano of Miami University for assistance in clarifying some of the ideas presented herein and for reviewing earlier drafts of this chapter.

References

City of Cincinnati (1982), Ordinance #61–1982.
City of Cincinnati (1983a), Ordinance #32–1983.
City of Cincinnati (1983b), Resolution #R139/1983.
Forbes, R. (1920), *Governmental Purchasing* (New York: Harper and Bros Publishers).
Frederickson, H. G. (1971), 'Toward a new public administration', in Frank Marini (ed.), *Toward a new public administration: The Minnowbrook perspective*, pp. 309–31 (New York: Chandler Publishing Co.).
Harmon, M. M. (1971), 'Normative theory and public administration: Some suggestions for a redefinition of administrative responsibility', in Frank Marini (ed.), *Toward a new public administration: The Minnowbrook perspective*, pp. 172–89 (New York: Chandler Publishing Co.).
Hayward, N. S. (1980), 'The productivity challenge', in Charles H. Levine (ed.), *Managing fiscal stress: The crisis in the public sector*, p. 260 (Chatham: Chatham House Publishers, Inc.).
Okun, A. M. (1975), *Equality and Efficiency: The Big Trade Off* (Washington, DC: The Brookings Institution).

Schott, R. *et al.* (1977), 'Public sector productivity: Background and analysis with special attention to state governments' (Austin: Lyndon B. Johnson School of Public Affairs).

US General Accounting Office (1983), 'Increased use of productivity management can help control government costs' (Washington, DC: US General Accounting Office).

Part V
Human Resources and Productivity

11 Public Sector Productivity and Role Conflicts[1]

Dorothy I. Riddle

This chapter describes the critical roles played by clients and employees in service delivery, as well as the common constraints on optimal participation. The author argues that less-than-optimal productivity is attributable to the complex role of the client both as a 'supervisee', co-producing services in a high-contact service delivery environment, and as a 'supervisor' evaluating satisfaction with the services delivered. An analysis of potential problems that arise from conflicting needs is included as well as a proposed framework for resolution.

Traditional approaches to increasing productivity in the public sector have focused either on decreasing the number of employees necessary to produce the service or on increasing the quantity of services produced by each employee. The government, therefore, has tried to increase productivity through cuts in funding, experiments with consolidating agencies, or 'job rationalization' with standardized times for service encounters – without the desired results. Public service operations are not necessarily overstaffed nor are there necessarily problems with the volume of service production undertaken.

In actual fact, increasing productivity hinges on understanding the complexities of the relationship between client and employee. Public services are, generally speaking 'high contact' service systems – that is, in which there is a necessary interaction between the consumer/client and the producer/employee (Chase, 1978). The co-production literature (for example, Sharp, 1980; Whitaker, 1980) has helped draw attention to the relatively active role played by the client in producing public services; however, the term 'co-production' is misleading. In using the prefix 'co-', theorists correctly imply a necessarily co-operative process. An alternate interpretation – that of co-equal status – is not only not true but lies at the crux of the problem.

In fact, major productivity problems stem from the simultaneously conflicting roles assumed by both client and employee (see Table 11.1). When focusing on the actual production (and hence the efficiency) of service delivery, clients act as 'supervisees' performing (appropriately or inappropriately) under the supervision of the public employee. When, however, one focuses on the effectiveness of the service delivery system, clients assume the role of 'supervisor' evaluating the performance (that is, the quality of the service) of the public employee.

Table 11.1   Role shifts in service production

	Productivity issues	
Roles	*Efficiency*	*Effectiveness*
Client	Supervisee	Supervisor
Employee	Supervisor	Supervisee

Unfortunately, studies of public administrators' perceptions of the productivity issue show little awareness of the importance of the issues raised above. Ammons and King (1983) found that 54 per cent of local government administrators defined productivity as 'the efficiency with which resources are consumed in the effective delivery of services' (p. 114). An additional 17 per cent equated productivity with 'the use . . . of progressive technology' (p. 114), while only 7 per cent related productivity to employee attitudes and job satisfaction. None of the administrators acknowledged the client's role, and 'community relations' was ranked sixth out of ten priorities.

At the heart of the productivity issue, then, is the problem of convincing public administrators that major attention should be paid to the attitudes of both the employees who produce the service and the clients who participate as an unpaid factor of production. Employees can meet client expectations adequately only if they are aware of those expectations and are motivated to meet them. Similarly, clients will only be satisfied with the services delivered if their expectations are realistic and their participation in the service production process results in their needs being met. And finally, both employees and clients must understand that the production of public services requires co-operation between employees and clients, with clients becoming both temporary subordinates and temporary superiors in that production process.

UNDERSTANDING ROLE CONFLICTS BETWEEN EMPLOYEES AND CLIENTS

Co-operation and matched expectations are difficult to achieve for several reasons. The system that delivers public services operates under a series of constraints that can lead to conflicts between employees and clients. In addition, the needs of employees and clients seldom coincide, creating the potential for dissatisfaction on both sides and a resultant loss of productivity.

Constraints on Public Services

Public services have four unique characteristics which must be kept in mind in order to understand the kinds of discontent that can develop among employees and clients (Lynn, 1984; Newman and Wallender, 1978; Rogers, 1981). By their nature, public services are a 'forced purchase'. Whether or not they themselves eventually use the services, citizens pay for them directly through tax dollars, or indirectly through the reduction in funds available for other purposes. Such payment is usually prior to making use of the service and not linked directly to the service itself. Service delivery (for example, police protection) is, in consequence, frequently viewed as 'free', overlooking both the economic price already paid and the other associated costs (for example, effort costs due to limited access).

Most public services undergo constant scrutiny from private citizens, consumer groups, and elected officials. Little discretion is tolerated in discharging responsibilities for fear of favouritism or unwittingly establishing a precedent. The offering or withholding of services is based on statutory authority – that is, employees do what they are directed to do by law. Innovations, apart from direct legal mandates, are not encouraged. New services may be authorized, however, regardless of whether a particular agency and its employees wish, or feel competent, to deliver such services (for example, abortions authorized in county hospitals).

Primary pressure to continue or revise service delivery comes from the public body that allocates revenues. Client, or market, pressure is thus felt only indirectly. In order to survive politically, an agency typically directs its primary marketing efforts at legislators. Marketing to clients or, indeed, to employees is usually overlooked.

Adequately motivating public employees is a real challenge. The nature of the services to be provided within budgetary constraints often results in a sense of helplessness and inadequacy, setting the stage for 'burnout'. Since economic compensation is usually predetermined, and based on credentials and seniority rather than on job performance, the options available to decrease or offset employee frustration are limited (Fottler, 1981; Rainey, 1983).

Implicit Needs of Clients

In order to understand the reasons for role conflicts, we must also understand the motivation, or implicit needs, of both clients and employees. As outlined in Table 11.2, the following discussion will be based on a modification of Maslow's hierarchy of needs (Maslow, 1954).

Table 11.2   Comparing potential needs of clients and employees

Potential needs	Clients	Employees
Survival	Provision of basic needs	
Convenience	Time and place utility	
Security	Fair treatment	Job protection
Belonging		Team membership
Self-esteem	Respect and dignity as individual	Respect as superior
Self-actualization		Improve quality of life

Source: Adapted from A. Maslow, *Motivation and personality* (New York: Harper and Bros., 1954).

When clients make use of public services, it is often with a justifiable sense of entitlement: after all, having paid one's taxes, one has the right to services in return. While public service employees sometimes concede client 'entitlement', they frequently make an exception for users of welfare services and actively discourage the user. In the United States, in particular, there is a strong value bias towards self-sufficiency and away from dependence upon a third party, such as the government, however 'entitled' one is.

Having purchased the public service, clients are in a very real sense the ultimate employers of public employees. As such, they expect to be accorded respect and personal dignity (self-esteem needs). All too often, however, they are viewed as, at best, a nuisance or, at worst, morally inferior for needing public services in the first place. The sense of degradation or humiliation that results when clients are not accorded respect can be thought of as a psychological cost of services purchased (Prottas, 1981).

Public services are established as part of a social contract under which citizens are expected to subsume private interests to the needs of society as a whole. In return, there is an understanding that citizens' needs and rights will be respected and that, as clients, they will be treated fairly (security needs). In addition, citizens in circumstances of extreme hardship must be able to count on the government to provide their basic subsistence (survival needs).

A final need of clients, and probably the most controversial in public service delivery, is the need for time and place utility in the 'purchase' of public services (convenience needs). All too frequently, 'free' public services become extremely expensive in non-monetary costs (El-Ansary and Kramer, 1973). Service locations are often selected to minimize overhead costs or are dictated by existing property holdings, rather than being designed to minimize the effort required from clientele in order to gain access to the service. Depending upon the location of the service, there may be extensive travel costs, both in distance and mode of transportation available. In addition, there may be opportunity costs, especially if the waiting involved is lengthy.

In summary, then, a variety of implicit needs must be met in order for clients to feel that they have received good quality service and to be motivated to co-operate in the production of that service. Clients need to be accorded respect, treated fairly, assured that subsistence needs will be met, and provided with reasonably convenient service delivery locations.

Implicit Needs of Employees

For employees, the motivational picture is somewhat different. They, too, have self-esteem needs, but all too often these involve being respected as a superior. They are likely to respond poorly to clients' sense of entitlement as it conflicts with their own sense of being in charge. When the employee is a professional who has been socialized during professional training to being viewed as the expert, resentment grows if the client attitude is other than the respect of subordinate to superior.

Employees are also motivated by security needs, but again in a different manner than clients. Their security needs centre around job protection; while fair treatment of clients may help ensure job retention, the best insurance is an absolute conformity to procedures (Fottler, 1981). Since human circumstances seldom conform neatly to outlined procedures, there are bound to be many times when 'fair treatment' or basic survival of the client necessitates a bending, or creative interpretation, of the rules, which the employee may be understandably unwilling to undertake. Indeed, a reported difference between public and private employees is that public employees exercise less discretion or influence in the decision-making process (Mirvis and Hackett, 1983).

Another major motivator for many public service employees is the feeling of contributing to society or helping to upgrade the quality of life for all (self-actualization needs; see Downs, 1967). Because of the restrictions placed on discretionary behaviour and the focus of public services away from client needs and towards legislative and bureaucratic concerns, many well-intentioned public employees become extremely frustrated. This frustration, combined with the stresses of continual client interaction, can and does lead to high levels of employee 'brown-out' (lowering of effectiveness) and 'burn-out' (severe dissatisfaction and inefficiency).

Finally, some public employees also have a strong need to feel they are part of a team effort (belonging needs), a need that, if met, can help reduce the potential for burn-out. If such a need is operative, they will be unlikely to take any risks that would jeopardize group acceptance. Such risks might range from treating clients with more respect than is usual to being willing to follow the spirit, rather than the letter, of a regulation.

While most critics of public sector service delivery blame either the employees for exhibiting poor motivation or the system for reinforcing inappropriate behaviour, this chapter argues that the more likely culprit is the built-in conflict between clients and employees. Given the mismatch of implicit needs and the simultaneous supervisee/supervisor roles assumed by the client, it is amazing that the public sector is as productive as it is!

CLIENT AS 'SUPERVISEE'

In reflecting on the co-production process, much of the literature has focused on increasing citizen involvement in the public sector to supplement the efforts of paid public employees (Rich, 1981). Projects such as Detroit's 'Adopt-a-Park' and police reserve (Cheyfitz, 1980) are examples of this approach. Such co-operative behaviour on the part of citizens *does* increase productivity, but usually through providing 'luxury' services to the community. Citizens, when functioning as 'collective co-producers', participate as supplemental unpaid labour in service production. Our concern, however, is with individual citizens/clients who function as 'consumer co-producers' to produce services that they consume as individuals. Such participation, rather than being supplemental, is in fact absolutely necessary for service delivery. The relationship between consumer co-producers and paid public employees is one of interdependence. Traditionally, public employees have seen themselves as having the exclusive responsibility for designing and delivering public services, with clients maintaining a passive role as consumer/recipients. A fundamental shift in perception must take place, then, on the part of both employees and institutions in order to acknowledge clients as 'supervisees' or colleagues in the production process.

Client Skill Level

If we take seriously the fact that clients become temporary employees, then the first issue we must address is the entry-level skills of the clients to receive the service. Clients usually enter a public service delivery system as 'naïve' employees. Unless they have used the system successfully before or are accompanied by a knowledgeable citizen who provides 'on-the-job' orientation, they are usually unaware of the structure of service production and what constitutes appropriate behaviour on their part. Since clients are not commonly viewed as part of the production staff, it is not surprising that job/role descriptions are lacking.

As we would expect, current public service organizations favour clients who already possess the needed skills for efficient production – for example, welfare workers prefer to work with 'employable' clients rather than the hard-core unemployed (Brinkerhoff, 1982). However, public sector agencies are established to provide services equitably to all eligible citizens, without regard to their ability to perform their role in co-production (Buntz, 1981; Chitwood, 1974).

For clients who do not have the optimal skills necessary to perform their co-producer role, several options are available and could be promoted. First, the client role could be redesigned so that clients are more likely to have the necessary skills (for example, by simplifying tax reporting forms). Secondly, clients could be trained to perform the role appropriately (for example, the promotional efforts made when postal

ZIP codes were first introduced). Thirdly, clients could be matched with employees who can enhance client performance (for example, by providing interpreters or patient advocates).

Client Training

In educating clients for their part in service production, it is helpful to distinguish between compliant and co-operative behaviour – that is, between behaviours whose absence can be punished and behaviours which are entirely voluntary. Generally speaking, clients are more aware of necessary compliant behaviour and engage in it at a distance from the service-producing system (for example, traffic regulations in transportation, rubbish (trash) packaging and placement). Appropriate compliance behaviour can be elicited through information about expectations and sanctions, both of which have been established publically and generate little conflict.

Co-operative behaviour, on the other hand, must be obtained through interaction and motivation. One source of difficulties is differences in perceptions between clients and employees regarding what constitutes co-operative behaviour and when it is required. For example, school systems usually expect that parents will supervise their children's homework and castigate parents who do not do so, without recognizing that such behaviour is voluntary rather than required. Schools have no legal sanctions to use against 'unco-operative' parents and hence need to use persuasion rather than coercion (Wittig, 1976).

Recently, researchers have become aware that consumers in 'high-contact' service delivery systems – that is, those in which there is a necessary interaction between the consumer and the producer (Chase, 1978) – must be trained or 'socialized' to perform their role appropriately (Mills, 1984). Inappropriate consumer behaviour – for example, failure to bring the necessary documents, insistence on unique treatment, non-responsiveness to questions, poor implementation of professional recommendations – significantly increases the time required to provide service, increases consumer and producer frustration, and decreases consumer satisfaction.

If clients are apprised of their role in service production *before* they arrive at the service site, the time needed to learn role-appropriate behaviour on-site is reduced and so also is the time in the system. Mailings can inform them not only of how to avoid peak demand times, but also of what materials to bring with them and what to expect on-site. Media advertisements can show model client roles and successful service delivery.

Clients can also be trained to help match demand for services with the agency's ability to deliver them. The aspects of the service delivery process that can be modified to increase the efficiency of service production include the timing of demand for service, the amount of self-service performed, and the use made of intermediaries (Lovelock and Young, 1979). Efforts aimed at changing timing include promotional campaigns such as 'Beat the Peak' to smooth out demand for utilities or 'mail early' campaigns to distribute the enormous flow of mail at Christmas time more uniformly across the month of December. Automobile inspection stations have recorded phone messages informing callers about the waiting time at that facility, in the hopes of shifting demand during rush periods either to other times or to other facilities. Similarly, some welfare offices have experimented with appointments to smooth the demand for services more evenly over the week.

A variety of government services now include a significant component of self-service, ranging from partial assistance in trash removal to complete self-service in the use of postage machines. Even in high-contact services, increasing the self-service component can give both clients and employees a greater sense of control over the process, rather than feeling like passive victims (Ferguson, 1983). Client waiting time can be filled with productive activity (for example, filling out 'interview' forms), and the workload for employees correspondingly reduced. Employees can be rotated through the more frustrating initial client-contact positions of checking the work performed by the client.

The most effort, however, has been directed towards educating clients to use intermediary services to decrease the demand on public employees. Such efforts include recorded phone announcements for a variety of commonly-requested information (such as hours of operation), or obtaining tax forms from banks and public libraries rather than from the Internal Revenue Service. The primary effect of such techniques is to increase the system's ability to service clients because resources are being used at a more constant rate rather than being overutilized at some times and underutilized at others. Secondly, both clients and employees are more satisfied with the service delivery process when the system is not overburdened.

Employee Motivation

In order for service delivery to be effective, not only clients but also employees must be 'socialized' to produce the service appropriately. The primary issue with employees is that of recognizing clients as temporary employees to be supervised with courtesy and treated with respect. One of the difficulties in high-contact services is that the presence of clients as co-producers decreases sharply the amount of control that employees have over the timing of service production. All too often, employees feel that everything would be just fine if it were not for the clients – as illustrated in the following excerpt from an English newspaper:

> Complaints from passengers wishing to use the Bagnall to Greensfield bus service that 'the drivers were speeding past queques of up to 30 people with a smile and a wave of a hand' have been met by a statement pointing out that 'it is impossible for the drivers to keep to their timetables if they have to stop for passengers'.   (cited in Ryan, 1977, p. 140)

As long as the evaluation of employees is based on their performance in isolation from the client, rather than on their ability to co-produce with the client, situations such as the above are the logical result. Thus, incentives must be matched with appropriate job performance.

Having already acknowledged that the self-esteem needs of clients and employees are potentially in conflict, we can extrapolate from the existing literature that employees will be more willing to tolerate a shift in the power balance towards a more co-operative relationship if they feel relatively in control and effective in their jobs. Lopata (1976) has vividly described the pressure for equal-power relationships being brought to bear by clients who are increasingly knowledgeable about their rights to service. At the same time, new employees are being rapidly socialized into rigidly hierarchical behaviour (Brinkerhoff, 1982). Unfortunately, the very employees most likely to be 'supervising' clients are the ones who have the least power themselves and who feel relatively ineffectual in the organization (Gabris and Giles, 1983a).

Clearly, changes must occur at an institutional, not just an individual, level. Needs for control, often met through the denigration of frustrating clients, can be met instead through solicitation from employees of system change recommendations, regular reports to employees of productivity figures, and active career-track planning with employees. Schneider (1980) has demonstrated that, if they are reinforced for quality client service, employees are highly motivated to interact efficiently and effectively with clients. Therefore, if one wants employees to function more productively, one must ensure that in some way they are rewarded for respectful behaviour towards clients or behaviour that clearly reflects an awareness of clients as part of the service production team.

CLIENTS AS 'SUPERVISORS'

In order for services to be effective, they must be perceived as such by clients; hence, the subjective assessment of the quality of service that is received in return for the price paid by the public or the individual client is central to the issue of productivity. No matter how much the quantitative measures of productivity (that is, efficiency) increase, criticisms will continue to be made unless clients feel that they are getting what they are paying for. In a sense, the roles of the employee and the client reverse, and the client becomes the 'supervisor' who evaluates the employee.

Client Expectations

In evaluating the performance of the employee, clients' primary concern is with the employee's attitude towards them (Tansik, 1984). In order to ensure client satisfaction, then, client expectations must be identified and either met or modified.

It is common for non-profit making, especially public, service organizations to focus on the service to be produced and to ignore client needs and expectations (Andreasen, 1982). In reversing this bias, the first problem is to determine accurately clients' implicit needs. The identification process has two separate steps: (a) identify the potential clients; (b) identify the needs of those clients. Realistically, not all citizens are potential clients for a given service. In fact, one may want to differentiate between those citizens likely to make use of the service, and those citizens whom one would wish would make use of the service. El-Ansary and Kramer (1973) give an excellent example of the kind of marketing strategy necessary to ensure that family planning services are used by those who most need to use them, rather than only by those clients already knowledgeable in family planning techniques.

Once the potential clients for the services have been correctly identified, then efforts must be made to understand the heterogeneous nature of that client group. Clients have different needs and must be appealed to in different ways (Lovelock and Young, 1979). For example, in soliciting client co-operation in reducing fire hazards in wilderness areas, some clients will respond best to appeals linking their behaviour to reduced risk (security needs), others will respond to appeals to protect the environment (self-actualization needs), while still others will respond to appeals to 'help keep our area the most beautiful' (self-esteem needs).

It is crucial, also, to keep in mind that appealing to needs and meeting those needs are not synonymous. Service delivery must be structured so that those needs – whether for convenience, survival, security, or self-esteem – are in fact met. In the wilderness area example, if self-esteem needs are being appealed to, the public facilities in the area must be scrupulously maintained to reinforce that feeling of pride and self-esteem. Again, in order for client needs to be met on a consistent basis, employees must be evaluated and rewarded for their ability to identify correctly and meet client needs.

Since so little outreach to clients occurs in the public sector, it is not surprising that clients often approach the wrong agency or believe an agency is capable of providing services that are not within its purview. Until now, consumer advocacy groups have provided virtually the only consumer-orientated education about public services, and their approach is often an adversarial one of demanding 'withheld' services. The response of employees is understandably antagonistic and frustration accelerates.

One approach needed is actively to educate clients about services that are available, realizing that such knowledge may increase the demands placed on already understaffed agencies. However, the alternative of a poorly-informed and hostile public has dire funding consequences in the long run. Included in such educational outreach can be information about peak demand periods and ways for the client to increase the likelihood of satisfactory service.

A related client satisfaction issue has to do with whether adequate access to services is available to all appropriate clients. Access concerns include adequate availability of service providers, accommodation of client needs and schedules, reasonableness of the relationship between price and service, and appropriate matching of client attributes with provider traits (Penchansky and Thomas, 1981). Service locations need to be examined to make sure that race and income differences are not correlated with longer travel and waiting times (Schwartz, 1978). If inequities exist, the result will be lowered service effectiveness, in which case the possibility of opening alternative sites would need to be seriously considered.

A final strategy aimed at increasing client satisfaction is that of increasing perceived client control. Keeping in mind the fact that clients are the employee's 'employer' or 'supervisor', an effective way of accommodating that status shift is through a frequent flow of information regarding service delivery. For example, clients will wait more patiently if informed at regular intervals of any delays and their causes;

otherwise, from 10 per cent to 50 per cent of clients kept waiting will leave angrily before receiving service (Prottas, 1981). Boston's mass transit system, for example, makes announcements periodically to apprise clients of any delays in the subway schedule so that clients can select alternative routes if necessary.

Employee Motivation

No matter what services are legislated for, their actual production depends upon the staff hired to provide them. In other words, in a service organization, whether private or public, productivity and quality control are synonymous with the personnel function (Hostage, 1975). Berry (1981) has suggested that employees be viewed as clients whose goodwill and enthusiasm must continually be solicited.

The most difficult issue to address has to do with the behaviour required of an employee in a high-contact service operation. Hochschild (1983) has pointed out the tremendous emotional strain placed on employees by continual client interaction. Such interaction is a crucial part of satisfactory client service; however, the employees who bear the brunt of such interaction are typically the lower-paid receptionists and lower-status professional staff. Indeed, one of the rewards given for seniority is being protected from direct contact with clients.

As we discussed earlier, the very nature of the constraints in the public sector can result in poor employee morale; therefore, careful attention needs to be paid to ways in which the job can be restructured to enhance employee morale. Davidson (1978) has suggested that the single most useful step management can take to increase productivity is for supervisors periodically to perform their subordinates' jobs in order to have an understanding of the pressures and demands. If such a suggestion were taken seriously in the public sector, not only would the need to decrease, where possible, employee-client interaction become apparent, but also managers/supervisors would have a heightened awareness of the stressful nature of direct client interaction.

Since, in general, public services are not contingent on volume production for continued funding, Prottas (1981) has suggested that the most common way for public service employees to lower job frustration is through 'illegitimate rationing' – that is, discouraging clients from making use of services to which they are entitled. A variety of 'pricing' techniques may be used to create such barriers – for example, demeaning treatment, lengthy delays, monopoly over essential program information. While such techniques may make the job more bearable for the employee and increase their effectiveness with the clients they *do* service, the long-term consequences are an overall decrease in productivity. The restructuring necessary to reduce employee frustration involves acknowledging not only that employees vary in the relative weight which they place on various rewards (Davis and West, 1980), but also that the same employee may need different rewards at different times. Once employee needs have been identified correctly, individual differences need to be accommodated through such concepts as 'flextime' and 'cafeteria benefits', and desired employee behaviour reinforced through direct advertising campaigns.

An alternative consequence of employee frustration is employee burnout because of incongruity between demands on the employee and the employee's expectation of the job. The consequences for the employee include loss of enthusiasm, increased frustration, and apathy (Cherniss, 1980; Edelwick and Brodsky, 1980; Golembiewski, Munzenrider and Carter, 1983). The disillusionment often reported indicates that 'self-actualization needs', in particular, are not being met. Other factors that can contribute to burnout include the characteristically low autonomy and control over service delivery characteristic of the public sector (Rogers, 1981).

Golembiewski *et al.* (1983) have pointed out that, while employees in initial stages of burn-out may be motivated effectively by various forms of job enrichment, employees in more advanced stages would simply feel more overwhelmed. Such employees need a reduction in stimuli and pressures. Since most analyses of how to increase service delivery effectiveness (for example, Lovelock and Young, 1979; Shostack, 1984) emphasize the need to maintain pleasant client relations, a more realistic approach would be to structure jobs so that all employees move back and forth from high-contact to low-contact aspects of service provision. In this fashion, employees are buffered from the more stressful aspects of client interaction for periods of time, and 'burnt-out' employees can be rotated into jobs that provide more distance from clients.

A companion approach involves restructuring employees' job assignments so that there is a clearer link between employee behaviour and client feedback. When approached by a belligerent client demanding an inappropriate service, a natural response for the employee is often to say 'no' – and enjoy the resulting frustration to the client. However, that enjoyment would be short-lived if the tangle of complaints which finally ends up in the office of the funding body were traced. It is not only more effective, but also more productive in the long run, to have employees take the time to educate clients as to how best to get their needs met. For example, SunTran in Tucson, Arizona, rotates bus drivers through the position of answering client questions and complaints so that they can begin to understand the service delivery process from the client's perspective (Tansik, 1984). Some agencies employ ombudspersons to fill such a role, but often it can be done more efficiently by the involved employee.

CONCLUSION

Increasing productivity in the public sector hinges on recognizing the dual role played by clients as 'supervisees' and 'supervisors'. Efficiency of operations is dependent on successfully teaching clients their role as co-producers and reworking the reward structure so that employees are motivated to share power with clients. Effectiveness is closely tied to client expectations and perceptions which must, therefore, be realistically shaped so that they can be met. In addition, structural changes are needed so that employees are able to alternate between high-contact and low-contact tasks to avoid burn-out, while maintaining sufficient client contact to be aware of client problems and perceptions.

Assumptions that productivity in public services can be increased through traditional manipulation of funding or required output levels only exacerbate the problems as they do not acknowledge either the crucial role played by clients in service production, the employee morale issues that affect the quality of service delivery, or the sources of conflict between clients and employees embedded in the system. Without such acknowledgement, potentially productive employees may become disillusioned and apathetic, and even the most dedicated service unit can be hamstrung by unco-operative or disappointed clients.

Note

1. The reader may note that the concepts used in analysis for this chapter are drawn in large part from the literature on internal and external marketing of services.

Bibliography

Ammons, D. N. and J. C. King (1983), 'Productivity improvement in local government: Its place among competing priorities', *Public Administration Review*, 43(2), pp. 113–20.

Andreasen, A. R. (1982), 'Nonprofits: Check your attention to customers', *Harvard Business Review*, 60(3), pp. 105–10.

Berry, L. L. (1981), 'The employee as customer', *Journal of Retail Banking*, 3(1), pp. 33–40.

Bjur, W. E. (1981), 'Coproduction in human services administration', *International Journal of Public Administration*, 3(4), pp. 389–404.

Brinkerhoff, D. W. (1982), 'Linking accountability, client participation, and quality of life in the public sector: A structural framework', *Review of Public Personnel Administration*, 3(1), pp. 67–74.

Brudney, J. L. and R. E. England (1983), 'Toward a definition of the coproduction concept', *Public Administration Review*, 43(1), pp. 59–65.

Buntz, C. G. (1981), 'Problems and issues in human service productivity improvement', *Public Productivity Review*, 5, pp. 299–320.

Capon, N. (1981), 'Marketing strategy differences between state and privately owned corporations: An exploratory analysis', *Journal of Marketing*, 45, pp. 11–18.

Chase, R. B. (1978), 'Where does the customer fit in a service operation?', *Harvard Business Review*, 56(6), pp. 137–42.

Cherniss, C. (1980), *Staff burnout: Job stress in the human services* (Beverly Hills, CA: Sage Publications).

Cheyfitz, K. (1980), 'Self-service. *The New Republic*, November 15, pp. 14–15.

Chitwood, S. R. (1974), 'Social equity and social service productivity', *Public Administration Review*, 34, pp. 29–35.

Davidson, D. S. (1978), 'How to succeed in a service industry. . . Turn the organizational chart upside down', *Management Review*, April, pp. 13–16.

Davis, C. E. and J. P. West, (1980) 'Job reward preferences of Mexican-American and anglo public employees', *Public Productivity Review*, 4, pp. 199–209.

Downs, A. (1967), *Inside bureaucracy* (Boston: Little, Brown).

Edelwich, J. and A. Brodsky, (1980), *Burn-out: Stages of disillusionment in the helping profession* (New York: Human Sciences Press).

El-Ansary, A. I. and O. E. Kramer, Jr (1973), 'Social marketing: The family planning experience', *Journal of Marketing*, 37(7), pp. 1–7.

Ferguson, K. E. (1983), 'Bureaucracy and public life: The feminization of the polity', *Administration and Society*,15(3), pp. 295–322.

Fottler, M. D. (1981), 'Is management really generic?', *Academy of Management Review*, 6(1), pp. 1–12.

Gabris, G. T. and W. A. Giles (1983a), 'Level of management, performance appraisal, and productivity reform in complex public organizations', *Review of Public Personnel Administration*, 3(3), pp. 45–61.

Gabris, G. T. and W. A. Giles (1983b), 'Improving productivity and performance appraisal through the use of non-economic incentives', *Public Productivity Review*, 7, pp. 173–89.

Golembiewski, R. T., R. Munzenrider and D. Carter (1983), 'Phases of progressive burnout and their work site covariants: Critical issues in OD research and praxis', *Journal of Applied Behavioral Science*, 19, pp. 461–81.

Hochschild, A. R. (1983), 'Smile wars: Counting the casualties of emotional labor', *Mother Jones*, December, pp. 35–42.

Hostage, G. M. (1975), 'Quality control in a service business', *Harvard Business Review*, 53(4), pp. 98–106.

Klingner, D. E. (1983), 'What's so important about job satisfaction?' *Review of Public Personnel Administration*, 4(1), pp. 67–77.

Knight, T. (1983), 'An incentive plan program', *Public Productivity Review*, 7(1), pp. 83–4.

Lopata, H. Z. (1976), 'Expertization of everyone and the revolt of the client', *Sociological Quarterly*, 17, pp. 435–47.

Lovelock, C. H. and R. F. Young (1979), 'Look to consumers to increase productivity', *Harvard Business Review*, 57(3), pp. 168–78.

Lynn, L. E., Jr (1984), 'Improving public sector management', *California Management Review*, 26(2), pp. 112–24.

Maslow, A. (1954), *Motivation and personality* (New York: Harper & Bros).

Mills, P. K. (1984), 'The socialization of clients as partial employees', in D. E. Bowen (Chairperson), *Managing employee and client involvement in the creation of service* (Symposium at the annual meeting of the Academy of Management, Boston, August).

Mirvis, P. H. and E. J. Hackett (1983), 'Work and work force characteristics in the nonprofit sector', *Monthly Labor Review*, April, pp. 3–13.

Nalbandian, J. and J. T. Edwards (1983), 'The values of public administrators: A comparison with lawyers, social workers, and business administrators', *Review of Public Personnel Administration*, 4(1), pp. 114–27.

Newman, W. H. and H. W. Wallender, III (1978), 'Managing not-for-profit enterprises', *Academy of Management Review*, 3, pp. 24–31.

Penchansky, R. and J. W. Thomas (1981), 'The concept of access: Definition and relationship to consumer satisfaction', *Medical Care*, 19(2), pp. 127–40.

Prottas, J. M. (1981), 'The cost of free services: Organizational impediments to access to public services', *Public Administration Review*, 41(5), pp. 526–34.

Rainey, H. G. (1982), 'Reward preferences among public and private managers: In search of the service ethic', *American Review of Public Administration*, 16(4), pp. 288–302.

Rainey, H. G. (1983), 'Public agencies and private firms: Incentive structures, goals, and individual roles', *Administration and Society*, 15(2), pp. 207–42.

Rich, R. C. (1981), 'Interaction of the voluntary and governmental sectors: Toward an understanding of the coproduction of municipal services', *Administration and Society*, 13(1), pp. 59–76.

Rogers, D. (1981), 'Managing in the public and private sectors: Similarities and differences', *Management Review*, May, pp. 48–54.

Ryan, P. (1977), 'Get rid of the people, and the system runs fine', *Smithsonian*, August, p. 140.

Schneider, B. (1980), 'The service organization: Climate is crucial', *Organizational Dynamics*, pp. 52–65.

Schwartz, B. (1978), 'The social ecology of time barriers', *Social Forces*, 56, 1203–20.

Sharp, E. B. (1980), 'Toward a new understanding of urban services and citizen participation: The coproduction concept', *Midwest Review of Public Administration*, 14(2), pp. 105–18.

Shostack, G. L. (1984), 'Designing services that deliver', *Harvard Business Review*, 62(1), pp. 133–9.

Smith, R. and M. Waldie, (1983), 'Multi-track career ladders: Maximizing opportunities', *Review of Public Personnel Administration*, 3(2), pp. 15–28.

Tansik, D. A. (1984), 'The customer-server interface: Implications of job design', in D. E. Bowen (Chairperson), *Managing employee and customer involvement in the creation of service* (Symposium conducted at the annual meeting of the Academy of Management, Boston, August).

Tripi, F. J. (1984), 'Client control in organizational settings', *Journal of Applied Behavioral Science*, 20(1), pp. 39–47.

Whitaker, G. P. (1980), 'Coproduction: Citizen participation in service delivery', *Public Administration Review*, 40(3), pp. 240–6.

Wittig, J. (1976), 'Client control and organizational dominance: The school, its students, and their parents', *Social Problems*, 24, pp. 192–203.

12 Policy Initiatives in Worksite Research: Implications from Research on a Phase Model of Burn-out

Robert T. Golembiewski

An evolving research program has isolated a dominant pattern of relationships between four classes of variables: 16 features of the worksite, 8 phases of psychological burn-out, 19 symptoms of physical dis-ease, and several measures of performance and productivity. Causal directions have not been determined. Globally, however, as assignments of individuals progress from Phase I through VIII, regular and usually-robust patterns of association exist: the quality of the worksite deteriorates significantly, physiological symptoms increase in non-random ways, and performance appraisals as well as objectively-measured productivity trend downward.

These relationships imply the significant costs of advanced burn-out and also have two policy-relevant implications. First, technical features of the phase model contraindicate in significant particulars the major evolving policy posture concerning work – for example, the emphasis in *Work in America* on improving the quality of working life by job enrichment and heightened participation. Second, the data suggest the reasonable expansion of the term 'noxious and harmful' work to include psychological burn-out.

An ongoing program of research is demonstrating the usefulness of a phase model of burn-out, and this paper describes that program and also extracts from it brief sets of organizational and policy implications. This dual bottom-line requires two introductory steps: first, conceptual and mensural features of a phase model are described, and, secondly, covariants of the progressive phases will be illustrated. These two introductory efforts permit several extrapolations from empirical data based on the phase model that extend usual thought, but also contraindicate it in particulars.

SKETCHING A PHASE MODEL

Burn-out is attracting considerable attention, and it refers to central human processes. Basically, the world is full of stressors, and these may enrich and enlarge ('eu-stress') or encumber if not herniate ('dis-stress'). Great variability exists about how specific stressors will affect which specific individuals at what times but, generally, herniating stress can cause strain which requires skills and energies for coping. At some point, the strain for individuals can become so great that a coping deficit is experienced, and this energy-drain signals the onset of burn-out. In gross terms, burn-out increases with the deficit and correspondingly burdens an individual's physical and emotional processes. Individuals high on burn-out reflect this syndrome of presenting symptoms: quick-triggered anger and irritability engaged by minor stimuli; pessimism if not despair about making a difference; perhaps working harder and longer but not better; growing alienation from sources of social support; problems with engaging and disengaging from work, which can inspire substance abuse; and so on.

The present research basically seeks a way of distinguishing individuals with different degrees of burn-out from large populations, reliably and conveniently, and several independent research efforts have isolated a strong contender as the bottom-line measure of burn-out. This contender does not focus on either the stressors or individuals, which bias has left much of the stress literature confused and confounded with variability. Rather, this phase approach to burn-out focuses on *the resultant effects* of whatever stressors have been experienced by any individual with their variable inventories of coping skills, attitudes, and situational vulnerabilities.

The phase model of burn-out rests on a paper-and-pencil measure – the Maslach Burnout Inventory, or MBI (Maslach and Jackson, 1981) – which consistently seems to isolate three domains:

(1) *Depersonalization*, high scores on whose component items indicate the tendency of individuals to reify the persons and human relationships in their life space, to consider them as things or objects;
(2) *Personal accomplishment* (REVERSED), low scores on whose component items indicate that persons report doing well on work that they consider worthwhile;
(3) *Emotional exhaustion*, high scores on whose component items indicate that a person is psychologically strained, is 'at the end of the rope' in the sense that an individual's coping systems are not adequate to deal with the stressors experienced.

These domains do not appear to be site-specific. Maslach's subjects are basically 'people-helpers' from public-service occupations; Golembiewski and colleagues focus on subjects from a consumer product-line division of a multinational firm, with respondents representing the range of functions from research through audit. The independent factorial structures share approximately 90 per cent of their variance in common, both in pattern and magnitude (Golembiewski, Munzenrider and Carter, 1983). Rountree (in press) independently corroborates this usefulness of the three MBI dimensions.

Depersonalization is considered the earliest and least potent contributor to burn-out in the phase model. Although some degree of 'distancing' seems useful or even necessary for successful task performance (see, for example, Lief and Fox, 1963), by hypothesis, performance can be affected adversely by too much distancing. The most advanced stages of burn-out would be loaded by emotional exhaustion in this conceptual model of prepotencies.

The present phase model reflects a simple progression. Scores for each of the three MBI domains are distinguished as High and Low; and the three domains, each taken twice, generate eight phases (Table 12.1). Norms developed from a large population ($N = 1565$) permit empirically-grounded High vs. Low distinctions on the three domains (Golembiewski and Munzenrider, 1984). The phase model refers to progressive virulence, rather than to eight stages through which all individuals will pass. The latter seems unlikely, in fact, and testing the relative virulence of the phases constitutes the basic challenge of the research program.

Table 12.1

	Proposed phases of burn-out							
	I	*II*	*III*	*IV*	*V*	*VI*	*VII*	*VIII*
Depersonalization	Lo	Hi	Lo	Hi	Lo	Hi	Lo	Hi
Personal accomplishment (REVERSED)	Lo	Lo	Hi	Hi	Lo	Lo	Hi	Hi
Emotional exhaustion	Lo	Lo	Lo	Lo	Hi	Hi	Hi	Hi

This phase model uses the MBI items in an unconventional way. Most often, research concentrates on the three individual domains, and successfully tests for their covariants (for example, Maslach and Jackson, 1981). One can also calculate a Total Score and test for its interactions with a range of variables, as has been done occasionally (for example, Golembiewski and Munzenrider, 1981). The phase model obviously rests on the three separate domains, and yet transcends them. In addition, Phases I and VIII clearly correspond to the highest and lowest Total Scores. But the internal phases often have phase placements that do not correspond to Total Scores. For example, Phase II and V have similar Total Scores – each having one High and two Low components – but their placement in the sequence of phases clearly differs substantially. Detailed statistical analysis supports this summary (Golembiewski, Munzenrider and Carter, 1983).

NETWORKING THE COVARIANTS OF PROGRESSIVE BURN-OUT

The testing of the usefulness of the phase model is still under way, but existing work permits bold statements about the network of covariants associated with that model. Broadly, the research both rests upon and provides strong support for this network of associations (Figure 12.1). In Figure 12.1 the solid lines represent main effects, while the broken lines depict feedback or reinforcing linkages. 'Worksite descriptors' include as many as 22 variables, such as participation in decisions at work, job tension, and so on (Golembiewski, Munzenrider and Carter, 1983). Physical symptoms are self-reports on 19 indicators (Quinn and Shepard, 1974; Quinn and Staines, 1979). Performance is measured by appraisals, and productivity is tapped by several independent measures of the quality and quantity of output.

Figure 12.1   Network of associations

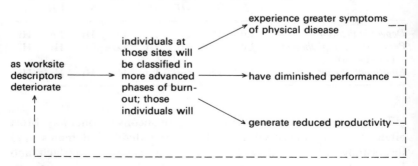

Research on the network is neither complete nor absolutely uniform, but regular and robust covariations definitely dominate. To illustrate this, let us consider physical symptoms. All 19 symptoms worsen significantly by progressive phases of burn-out, but some clusters of symptoms reflect an especially strong pattern of covariation. Table 12.2 establishes the overall covariation between phases of burn-out and five aggregates of symptoms, the latter four of which are isolated by factor analysis.

Table 12.3 provides detail about the regularity and robustness of these overall differences, by summarizing the tests of all possible paired-comparisons of symptoms by phases. For example, are Total Symptoms for Phase I < Phase II, and so on? Patently, the pattern is most pronounced for Total Symptoms, Factor I and Factor II. The data show step-ladder effects between burn-out phases and symptoms, in short, with a very high proportion of significant differences between each of the eight 'steps' or phases.

Note also that those classified in advanced burn-out phases report significantly more aggravated symptoms than two national panels of respondents (Quinn and Shepard, 1974; Quinn and Staines, 1979). So the differences reflected in Tables 12.2 and 12.3 do not appear to be trivial.

Causality has not been established, but the data suggest the usefulness of the network above. Thus worksite descriptors and burn-out phases share over 17 per cent of their variance. In addition, phases and distress have 18 per cent variance in common. Worksite descriptors, however, account for only slightly more than 3 per cent of the variation in the symptoms reported. This suggests the main-line and reinforcing effects in the network of covariants sketched above.

GROUNDING POLICY IN EMPIRICAL FINDINGS[1]

Guidance for both organizational and policy responses inheres in research with the phase model, as the following two sections will show. They ask basic questions. What are we coming to know about burn-out? What constitute reasonable policy responses to what we are coming to know?

What Have We Come to Know?

What we know about the phase model and its covariants can help target organizational practices and public policies. These recent findings

Table 12.2 Symptoms of physical distress by phases of burn-out

	Progressive phases of burn-out								
	I	II	III	IV	V	VI	VII	VIII	F-ratio
	LoLoLo	HiLoLo	LoHiLo	HiHiLo	LoLoHi	HiLoHi	LoHiHi	HiHiHi	
Aggregates of Symptoms	(352)	(107)	(193)	(129)	(107)	(176)	(109)	(367)	
Total Symptoms	33.5	34.2	33.9	35.5	38.7	40.1	40.5	42.6	39.628*
Factor I: General enervation and agitation	17.0	17.1	17.1	18.1	20.0	20.5	21.2	22.2	54.995*
Stomach pains
Headaches
Cough-colds
Fatigue
Trouble getting up
Sweaty hands
Nervous
Worn-out
Poor appetite

Factor II: Cardio-vascular complaints	5.9	6.2	5.9	6.3	7.0	7.1	7.4	7.5	17.134*
Heart pain									
Tightness in chest									
Trouble breathing									
Heart pounding									
Factor III: Non-cardiac pains	7.1	7.2	7.6	7.3	7.8	8.2	8.0	8.3	7.766*
Leg cramps									
Swollen ankles									
Stiffness									
Factor IV: Sleeplessness	3.6	3.5	3.5	4.0	3.9	4.3	4.0	4.6	15.421*
Getting to sleep									
Staying asleep									

* p< 0.001.

Table 12.3 Summary of paired-comparisons, physical symptoms by phases of burn-out

	In expected direction (%)	In expected direction and statistically significant (%)*	In contrary direction (%)	In contrary direction and statistically significant (%)*
Total symptoms	96.4	60.4	3.6	0
Factor I	96.4	64.3	3.6	0
Factor II	92.9	42.9	7.1	0
Factor III	92.9	17.9	7.1	0
Factor IV	71.5	32.1	28.5	0

* As defined by the 0.05 level on the Least Significant Difference test, modified for unequal sub-population sizes.

can be summarized briefly under four headings: virulence, incidence, persistence, and locus.

(1) Virulence

The virulence of the advanced stages of burn-out seems substantial. The present research program has associated burn-out differences with regular and robust variations in features of the worksite, in physical symptoms, as well as in performance and productivity (Golembiewski and Munzenrider, in preparation). These effects are consistent with the broader array of personal and organizational deficits generally associated with burn-out (for example, Cherniss, 1980; Maslach, 1982), but transcend and detail them.

(2) Incidence

Estimates of the incidence of burn-out stages must now rely on a few organizational surveys, but Table 12.4 suggests the value of substantial attention to this frequency-charting. Three organizations are profiled in the table, and they suggest that the situation is worse than most estimate, even under favourable conditions. The first case in Table 12.4 refers to a firm that is, in most respects, a model of good human practices – a long-standing concern for people, personnel policies and practices that are 'modern' and in cases precedent-setting, with excellent compensation and benefits packages. Even in this firm, over 22 per cent of the cases fall in the highest three phases of burn-out, that is, greater by a factor of 2 or 3 than executives of the firm consider a tolerable incidence, given their understanding of the phase model and its probable covariants, as balanced by the reality that 'some problems will always exist'. The second case is a mid-level slice from a federal service agency, where substantial stress and job pressures exist. Here 42.5 per cent of the cases are in the three most-advanced phases (Golembiewski and Munzenrider, 1984). A third case involves the multiple sites of a health-care service for the elderly, and it presently constitutes the most advanced profile of the distribution of phases of burn-out observed in an organization.

These limited data urge prompt attention to both empirical and normative issues concerning the incidence of burn-out. Two questions are central.

(i) What is the empirical incidence of phases of burn-out? We do not know whether Table 12.4 reflects the 'best' and the 'worst' of worksite conditions, but the following two points seem non-controversial. Thus

Table 12.4 Incidence of burn-out phases in three organizations

	Distribution of phases (%)							
	I	II	III	IV	V	VI	VII	VIII	Total
Organization I (N = 274)	40.9	10.6	7.7	4.7	13.9	9.1	7.3	5.8	100.0
Organization II (N = 1534)	22.9	7.0	12.6	8.1	7.0	11.5	7.1	23.9	100.1
Organization III (N = 2389)	29.1	0.0	0.0	14.1	0.0	18.5	9.5	26.9	100.1

the phase approach provides a reasonable vehicle for generating such information. Moreover, the data suggest that lack of attention to burn-out has great personal and organizational costs, even in 'good' settings.

(ii) What incidence of advanced phases of burn-out is too great? Here a blend of normative and empirical perspectives will be required. In part, working answers will come from a clearer sense of burn-out consequences and their claims. Those answers also will rest critically on our ethical and value sensitivities.

(3) Persistence

The persistence of the phases of burn-out has both practical and theoretical significance, and what little we know is troubling. It appears that most cases of burn-out can be considered chronic, rather than acute. If effective remedial action is absent, the personal and organizational deficits associated with advanced burn-out will not be transitory: in most cases, those effects will persist over substantial periods, if available evidence is at all representative.

Specifically, in two observations bracketing a one-year interval, people remained in the three highest and three lowest burn-out phases in about 70 per cent of the cases (Golembiewski, 1984). In contrast, Phases IV and V are transitional. About 10 per cent of the incumbents remained in those two phases, and the other 90 per cent moved about equally to more or less advanced phases.

Time does not seem to heal advanced burn-out in most cases and, despite the sparse data, this urges two initiatives. First, organizational policies and procedures must be developed to actively maintain and support low-levels of burn-out where they exist. Reasonable guidance (Golembiewski, 1982) is available concerning both the range of potential stressors in organizations and useful approaches for moderating them.

Second, we know little about how to reduce already high levels of burn-out, and nature clearly requires assistance in this regard. Consider depth-interviews of people who 'switch' phases over time, for example. Such longitudinal attention would permit greater clarity about both contributors to advanced burn-out, as well as about 'natural' amelioratives which could inform conscious remedial efforts.

(4) Locus

The locus of advanced burn-out has a patent relevance, but opinions vary. Thus some observers (for example, Freudenberger, 1980) focus on burn-out as a disease of the young and idealistic; others see 'people-helpers' as being at special risk (for example, Maslach, 1982).

The phase model suggests, but does not yet establish, three major aspects of burn-out loci that have significance for both theory and practice. First, although several generic loci no doubt contribute to burn-out, the immediate work group seems most potent (Golembiewski, 1983). The original research on this point receives powerful and independent reinforcement from research with a larger population (Rountree, in press). Few work groups evidence mixed distributions of burn-out phases, in short. About 70 per cent of all respondents in one organization, for example, were in groups of first-reports, *most* of whose members were classified in Phases I–III or VI–VIII. This suggests the significance of supervisory style and immediate work practices in inducing burn-out, and helps credibly explain the generally-chronic character of burn-out.

Some burn-out no doubt derives from two other sources: personality features, and specific life events. Preliminary efforts to test for such effects do not suggest major covariation with burn-out phases, however (Golembiewski and Munzenrider, in preparation).

At a practical level, the apparent centrality of the immediate work unit urges caution about 'stranger workshops' on stress management, a common response to burn-out. If work-group membership is in fact central in burn-out, 'stranger' experiences will be misdirected in that they avoid the issue of changing the work context. Paradoxically, indeed, such workshops may prove counter-productive. Even as such experiences succeed, to suggest the point, they may enhance coping skills for attendees which, in turn, may well be translated into even greater stress-inducing demands on *all* members back at the workshop. In relation to this point, in one case we advertised a stress management workshop and asked for volunteers who wished to attend. Who volunteered? The record does not encourage optimism. Nearly 90 per cent of the volunteers were in Phases I–III, which contained less than 50 per cent of the respondents.

Second, a broad range of demographics, at most, account for only a percentage point or so of the total variance in burn-out phases (Golembiewski and Scicchitano, 1983). The demographics cover a broad range: the normal ones of age, sex, race, and so on; and organizational variables such as hierarchical level, history of promotions, and the like.

This urges caution in accepting the common view that certain sub-populations are at special risk. Even if this view *is* correct, moreover, that should not encourage neglect of the far broader incidence of burn-out.

Third, the dimensions of the MBI seem quite stable in different contexts (for example, Golembiewski, Munzenrider and Carter, 1983). Although the virulence of burn-out may differ – for example, in people-helping organizations vs. profit-making enterprises – burn-out seems dimensionally quite similar in 'different' contexts.

What Constitute Reasonable Policy Responses?

Given its various development unevennesses, existing research on the phases of burn-out encourages contemplating some departures from accepted policies and procedures, as well as some extensions of long-run developments. Four themes are emphasized in this chapter:

(1) the need to modify certain policy biases, which have gained national prominence in America only recently and elsewhere a little earlier;
(2) a two-track model for organizational policies and practices for ameliorating burn-out;
(3) expanding the definition of 'unsafe, hazardous, or harmful';
(4) a new work ethic, including a growing freedom from noxious worksites.

(1)   The phase model of burn-out implies the need to modify significant worksite policies, only recently mobilized and now gaining national visibility.

The phase approach to burn-out immediately raises profound questions about policies and practices intended to improve the quality of working-life such as the widely-accepted prescriptions in *Work in America*. Consider a worksite with this profile: low involvement in work; low satisfaction with task components; unwillingness to disagree with supervisors; and so on. Conventional prescriptions focus on a variety of stimulus-enhancers: increased participation in decisions; enriched jobs that permit greater senses of achievement and personal responsibility; interpersonal confrontation to clarify communications; reliance on such systems as Management by Objectives (MBO); and so on through a longish catalogue. Individuals reporting advanced phases of burn-out characterize their worksites in terms of just such a 'bad' profile but, in opposition to the conventional wisdom, advanced burn-out implies the common need for stimulus-reduction. For those with advanced burn-out, in short, 'good practice' might lead to tragic stimulus overload.

The critical point may be put in another way. Those things that lead to advanced burn-out, if reversed, will not necessarily reduce burn-out; indeed, they might exacerbate it. Directly, stimulus-enhancing prescriptions – interpersonal confrontations to 'tell it like it is', job enrichment to tap unused capabilities, and so on – have similar requirements. All these interventions presuppose a degree of emotional and physical 'slack': they require high levels of energy; they imply a new commitment and involvement in work; and they would be well served by a sense of efficacy and self-esteem concerning the probability of making desired things happen; and so on.

The general point should be clear. Individuals with low burn-out may supply such requirements. But clearly the present model suggests that individuals at advanced stages of burn-out will have little of the necessary slack, if not actual deficits in it. Phases VI through VIII, that is, imply: low levels of energy not already committed to everyday coping, and perhaps an actual energy deficit for coping with everyday stressors; low commitment to and involvement in work; and a diluted sense of efficacy and self-esteem.

The usefulness of a phase model in the present regard deserves to be highlighted. We know two things about such prescriptions as interpersonal confrontation and job enrichment: they 'work' sometimes; and at other times they do not. Differing levels of burn-out seem a reasonable contributor to differentiating both types of effects, for understanding them, and especially for consciously planning interventions with burn-out differences in mind.

The stakes here may well be far larger than the success or failure of an organization intervention. Interventions like job enrichment are only a technical expression of a broad belief system reflected in such movements as 'industrial democracy' or 'organizational humanism'. Hence failures of the interventions, without sensitivity to possible burn-out effects, may paradoxically result in 'blaming the victim'. That is, some may see such interventions as 'not working' because individuals lack the skills, interests, and motivations for informed and active participation at the worksite: 'they' are a hedonistic and mindless rabble, if sometimes a troublesome rabble, from this point of view.

Consider the gravity of 'blaming the victim' in this case. More and more observers (for example, Elden, 1981; and Mason, 1982) are coming to believe that, if responsible freedom cannot be achieved in the organizations in which so many spend such a great proportion of their waking lives, representative political institutions will be eroded. Illustratively, take away day-to-day opportunities for meaningful participation in micro-settings, and people will lack relevant skills and attitudes concerning effective political participation, and they may well lack a sense of efficacy about making a difference in the broader political arenas. Interventions like job enrichment, in effect, provide training for citizenship, as well as serve more immediate needs for quality and production. The general failure of such interventions could well be read as having very broad implications, not only for the possibility of developing worksites that are more broadly responsive to people and their needs. In the broadest compass, indeed, such failures might also undercut that optimistic view of people on which representative political systems are based – a view already very easy to denigrate.

Without overdramatizing the point, then, the recognition of burn-out effects may have implications far beyond recognizing them as a significant intervening variable in theoretical models of organization behaviour.

(2)   Relatedly, the phase model of burn-out suggests the usefulness of a two-track model for ameliorative efforts.

Ameliorative strategies for progressive phases of burn-out can only be dimly envisioned now, but two points seem clear enough. First, the preferred strategy is to keep already-low burn-out where it is. Fortunately, quite a bit is known about the panoply of organizational approaches – ideally dealing with interaction, structure and design, as well as appropriate policies and procedures (for example, Golembiewski, 1982) – for avoiding unnecessary stressors and hence limiting the psychological strain that is reflected in burn-out.

Second, for those individuals or groups already characterized by advanced stages of burn-out, an alternative track with two stages seems reasonable. Initially, Stage I efforts should be made to reduce levels of burn-out via a variety of low-stimulus designs. In the most extreme cases, extended leave from the worksite may be required. For other cases, various 'time out' designs may be useful or even necessary. Job rotation may be used in certain stressful roles, for example: umpires, air traffic controllers, Veterans Administration employees, and so on, in their several ways often rely on such an accommodation. Many other low-stimulus designs exist that have a broader applicability: flexible workhours programs have numerous attractions for both individuals and organizations (Golembiewski and Proehl, 1978), with low costs and substantial benefits; role negotiation designs (Harrison, 1972) can deal with the major stressors inherent in incongruencies, overlap, or overload in roles.

Only when 'manageable' levels of burn-out are attained for individuals or groups would the broad range of designs for managing stressors become appropriate. This is Stage II.

These two tracks imply a major reorientation in almost all organizations. Today, the most enlightened organizations tend to follow the first track – as in sponsoring Quality of Working Life (QWL) ventures – but even they neglect differences in burn-out that may be critical. Most organizations follow neither track.

(3)   The work on burn-out represents another step toward expanding the definition of 'unsafe, hazardous, or harmful' conditions at work.

Arguably, at least, a society can expect effective contributions from a broad range of participants over the long run only to the degree that they see their work as responsive to a broadening spectrum of human needs and conditions. Even a supporting 'work ethic' is not likely to maintain labour when that implies 'killing one's self', physically or psychologically. No doubt, the expanding views of what constitutes killing or deadening work are closely tied to the 'educated society' we are becoming, with increments in knowledge and desires raising the ante for what qualifies as 'acceptable work'.

Movement toward such an expanded definition proceeds with two goals in mind. The research so far implies that burn-out can be measured in large populations – validly, reliably, and conveniently. Hence burn-out is not merely faddish, or 'in the air'. In addition, the correlates of burn-out represent an unattractive catalogue, which it seems useful to avoid by prudent expansion of what constitutes 'unsafe, hazardous, or harmful'.

This expanded definition is more incremental than radical, for we are far removed from the germ-specific view of disease that earlier constituted both progress and cop-out in Flexner's 1910 report on medical schools. No doubt that view improved medical practice in many regards, but it also discouraged attention to environmental contributors to disease – such as pollution, industrial practices, and carcinogenic materials – and may indeed have been intended to do so (Applebaum, 1981, p. 143). The battles still range on many fronts, to be sure, but several states already recognize a variety of features of work – including stress or tension – in workers' compensation claims.

The present research encourages a further extension of the definition of 'unsafe, hazardous, or harmful', and provides a useful measurement tool for monitoring work environments. This could help both employees and managers, as is implicit in the network of covariants in which the phase model is imbedded.

(4) In the broadest sense, finally, research on burn-out encourages further movement toward a 'fifth freedom' – freedom from noxious and stultifying worksites.

This would complement and reinforce those 'four freedoms' articulated by Franklin D. Roosevelt: freedom of speech and expression, freedom of worship, freedom from want, and freedom from fear.

This fifth freedom could constitute part of a new work ethic, arguably much needed to sustain effort toward what needs doing in today's world. That new work ethic also could help legitimate a new role for both management and labour, who would serve as prime implementors of this fifth freedom. Progress toward this fifth freedom has been made over the centuries, and present purposes can be met by simply underscoring the fact that growing knowledge goads further progress.

The contribution to the legitimacy of authority figures might also profit well from brief discussion. The theme is not a new one, of course, but that does not solve the problem but rather testifies to its significance and intractability. By whose warrant does a manager exercise control over others? The owner-capitalist had a far clearer claim to such legitimacy than almost all of today's managers. Few contemporary managers can say: 'You do it because I say so. I own the enterprise, and you do as I say or leave my property'. The legitimation consistent with the present approach would take some such form as: managerial authority derives in part from success in inducing the kind of work settings that increasingly meet human needs at work while contributing to more efficient performance.

In conclusion, several stages in the evolution of such a fifth freedom can be envisaged. They involve: heightening consciousness about burn-out; monitoring existing levels of burn-out, and moderating the effects of burn-out by private and public initiatives.

CONCLUSION

In sum, the thrust of this brief extrapolation from limited but intriguing data-bases can be framed in terms of the three stages sketched above. The phase model of burn-out contributes to the first stage; it might well help spearhead the second; and it could help act as mid-wife to the third stage.

Note

1. An earlier version of this section appeared as 'Organizational and Policy Implications of A Phase Model of Burn-out', in L. R. Moise, Bruce Kemelgor, Robert St. Clair, and Stephen Spangehl (eds), *Organizational Policy and Development* (in press).

References

Applebaum, S. H. (1981), *Stress management* (Rockville, MD: Aspen Systems Corp.).

Cherniss, G. (1980), *Staff burnout: Job stress in the human services* (Beverly Hills, CA: Sage Publications).

Elden, J. M. (1981), 'Political efficacy at work', *American Political Science Review*, 75 (March) pp. 43–58.

Freudenberger, H. J. (1980), *Burn-out: The high cost of high achievement* (Garden City, NY: Anchor Press).

Golembiewski, R. T. (1982), 'Organizational development (OD) interventions: Changing interaction, structures, and policies', in W. S. Paine (ed.), *Job Stress and Burnout* (Los Angeles, CA: Sage Focus Editions) pp. 229–53.

Golembiewski, R. T. (1983), 'The distribution of burn-out among work groups', in D. D. Van Fleet (ed.), *1983 Proceedings* (Houston, TX: Annual Meeting of the Southwestern Division, Academy of Management) pp. 158–63.

Golembiewski, R. T. (1984), 'The persistence of burn-out', in L. M. Calvert (ed.), *1984 Proceedings* (San Antonio, TX: Annual Meeting of the Southwestern Division, Academy of Management) pp. 300–4.

Golembiewski, R. T. and R. Munzenrider (1981), 'Efficacy of three versions of one burn-out measure: The MBI as total score, sub-scale scores, or phases?' *Journal of Health and Human Resources Administration*, 4 (Winter) pp. 228–46.

Golembiewski, R. T. and R. Munzenrider (1984), 'Phases of psychological burn-out and organizational covariants: A replication using norms from a large population', *Journal of Health and Human Resources Administration*, 6 (Winter) pp. 290–323.

Golembiewski, R. T. and R. Munzenrider (in preparation), *Toward a phase model of burn-out: Research developments in mid-stream*.

Golembiewski, R. T., R. Munzenrider and D. Carter (1983), 'Phases of progressive burn-out and their worksite covariants', *Journal of Applied Behavioral Science*, 19 (November), pp. 461–82.

Golembiewski, R. T. and C. W. Proehl, Jr (1978), 'A survey of the empirical literature on flexible workhours: Character and consequences of a major innovation', *Academy of Management Review*, 3 (October) pp. 837–53.

Golembiewski, R. T. and M. Scicchitano (1983), 'Some demographics of psychological burn-out', *International Journal of Public Administration*, 5, pp. 435–47.

Harrison, R. (1972), 'Role negotiation', in W. W. Burke and H. Hornstein (eds), *The Social Technology of Organization Development* (Washington, DC: NTL Learning Resources) pp. 84–96.

Lief, H. I. and R. C. Fox (1963), 'Training for "detached concern" in medical students', in H. I. Lief, V. F. Lief and N. R. Lief (eds), *The Psychological Bases of Medical Practice* (New York: Harper & Row) pp. 12–35.

Maslach, C. (1982), *Burnout: The cost of caring* (Englewood Cliffs, NJ: Prentice Hall).

Maslach, C. and S. E. Jackson (1981), 'The measurement of experienced burnout', *Journal of Occupational Behaviour*, 2, pp. 99–113.

Mason, R. M. (1982), *Participatory and workplace democracy* (Carbondale: ILL: Southern Illinois University Press).

Quinn, R. P. and L. J. Shepard (1974), *The 1972–73 quality of employment survey* (Ann Arbor, MI: Survey Research Center, University of Michigan).

Quinn, R. P. and G. L. Staines (1979), *The 1977 quality of employment survey* (Ann Arbor, MI: Survey Research Center, University of Michigan).

Rountree, B. H. (in press), 'Burnout in work groups in a health-care setting', *Journal of Health and Human Resources Administration*.

Part VI
Conclusions about Promoting Productivity in the Public Sector

13 The New Productivity

Stuart S. Nagel

'The New Productivity' in the context of this chapter refers to a set of ideas including the following.

(1) Productivity should include all cost items, not just labour items.
(2) Productivity should include both monetary and non-monetary benefits and costs.
(3) Productivity should be thought of in a societal sense, not just in terms of individuals, business firms, government agencies, and other sub-societal units.
(4) Productivity should be partly stimulated by a careful allocation of government subsidies and tax breaks.
(5) The new productivity implies enabling people to be better off through an increase in the total national product, as contrasted with a redistributional approach.
(6) The new productivity is part of a cycle of alternating periods of growth and equality in American history.
(7) The new productivity seeks to decrease inflation by providing more for one's money, and to decrease unemployment by enabling workers to produce and earn more in less hours, thereby making more jobs available.
(8) The new productivity applies to stimulating productivity in all segments of society including public aid recipients, union members, white collar workers, public sector employees, and corporate executives.
(9) An emphasis on technological innovation and diffusion.
(10) A motivation to increase the ability of the United States and other countries to compete well in international markets.
(11) An emphasis on the development of new and useful ideas through university research.
(12) An emphasis on developing better decision-making methods.
(13) An emphasis on productivity in public policy-making so as to deal more effectively with social problems.
(14) Productivity improvement as a bipartisan and liberal–conservative joint activity.

Socio-economic reforms can be readily adopted when they are supported by both liberals and conservatives, although they may not support them for the same reasons. Examples include some aspects of the criminal justice system. For instance, in the last few years, there has been a substantial change across the country, decreasing criminal sentencing discretion. Liberals perceive the previous discretion as resulting in sentences that are discriminatory along class, race, sex, and other lines. Conservatives perceive the previous discretion as resulting in sentences that have been unduly lenient. As a result, one finds liberals like Senator Kennedy joining with conservatives like Senator Thurmond to support decreased sentencing discretion in the federal courts.

DEFINITIONS AND HISTORICAL CONTEXT

The field of productivity may be an even better example. Liberals and conservatives are in agreement that the nation would be better off if it were more productive. Virtually everyone would endorse the idea of being able to produce 20 units of desired output with only 5 units of effort, rather than 10 units of effort. Likewise virtually everyone would endorse the idea of being able to get as much as 30 output units, rather than 20, for 10 units of effort. This may have been the main appeal of the Reagan campaign, namely, the idea of increased productivity and creativity for the United States. The Carter campaign may have made the mistake of overemphasizing the traditional Democratic party concern for equalizing the pie, when the American people were more concerned with having a bigger pie to equalize.

American history seems to involve alternating periods of growth and equalization. We were in a period of industrial and geographical development from the end of the equalizing Reconstruction Era to the administrations of Theodore Roosevelt and Woodrow Wilson. Both these presidencies pushed the progressive income tax and forms of economic regulation that were consumer-orientated. The 1920s resumed business growth, and the Depression and the Second World War also focused more on growth than equality. The 1960s was a period of equalizing with regard to poverty, civil rights, women, gays, handicapped people, old people, children, and even animals, although further equality of opportunity still needed to be obtained. That period extended until about 1980. We now seem to be re-entering an era in which the emphasis will again be on bipartisan growth and productivity. The periods of growth are not necessarily Republican periods, and the periods of equalization are not necessarily Democratic periods. The growth in the late 1800s was promoted by both Cleveland and McKinley. The equality of the early 1900s was associated with both

Theodore Roosevelt and Woodrow Wilson. The renewed emphasis on growth from 1920 to 1960 involved both Republican and Democrat presidents, as did the equalization period from 1960 to 1980.

A concern for productivity may occur especially in times of inflation when prices are rising with nothing to show for the price increases in terms of a better quantity or quality of products. Wage and price increases are justifiable and acceptable if they are based on increased productivity. If a worker who was formerly being paid $3 an hour now produces twice as much in an hour, he or she should receive $6 an hour, although something may have to be deducted to cover the cost of buying and maintaining capital equipment which may have made possible that increased productivity. Likewise, if a $1 head of lettuce spoils in a week, and a new technology is developed that will enable lettuce to last for a month, the seller should be entitled to charge more, especially if there are additional costs involved, but also because there will be increased demand due to the better product. A strong concern for productivity also occurs in time of recession or depression when so many potentially productive people are not producing in accordance with their skills. Keynesian fiscal policy and Friedmanite monetary policy may be relevant to dealing with inflation and unemployment, but such policies are too broad relative to policies that are specifically focused on improving productivity.

The forthcoming era of new productivity might also be called the era of new incentives. The concept of 'incentives', however, emphasizes the main means of bringing about the new productivity, rather than the goals toward which those means are directed. By 'incentives' in this context are meant government policies designed to reward various segments of the population for doing things that increase productivity, as contrasted with a regulatory approach which emphasizes controls and penalties. Tax incentives are the main incentives that government has available for stimulating the new productivity. This is especially true of the federal government, given its control of corporate and individual income taxes, but is also true of state and local governments, with their control of property taxes. Foregoing tax is also more politically feasible than outright cash grants since taxpayers are more willing to support government policies that do not involve explicit government expenditures. It also enables the recipients of the incentives to preserve their self-respect more than if they were receiving an outright cash grant, just as farmers prefer indirect price supports to the direct subsidies associated with the Brannan Plan.

SPECIFIC MEANS AND GOALS

The federal government can develop a list of business activities that will increase national productivity in which business firms might otherwise not engage. Engaging in these can then entitle participating firms to various types of tax breaks including depreciation or expense allowances, tax credits, or even tax exemption under special circumstances. A good example of such an activity might be hiring willing and able people who are otherwise unemployed. This may be true of many welfare recipients including those who are receiving aid to the aged, disabled, or unemployed, or those caring for dependent children. If through a tax subsidy a business firm can be encouraged to hire such a person who otherwise would be unemployed, then society is better off in two ways. First, the individual is adding to the gross national product which constitutes an increased benefit to society's benefits and costs. Second, the subsidy is probably costing society less than the former welfare payments, which means a societal cost reduction.

This example helps clarify what increased productivity means. In a general sense, it means increasing societal benefits or income, while holding constant or decreasing societal costs. It can also mean holding constant societal benefits, while decreasing societal costs. In either situation, the positive difference between societal benefits and societal costs has been increased. The term 'productivity' is also sometimes defined so as to refer just to increased benefits regardless of costs, or benefits divided by costs, but benefits minus costs is the preferred criterion when those criteria conflict. Society would prefer a situation involving $100 in benefits and $60 in costs for a net gain of $40, rather than $10 in benefits and $3 in costs for a net gain of only $7, even though the latter situation involves a 10/3 benefit/cost ratio and the former situation involves a worse 10/6 ratio. Other terms besides 'productivity' are used to refer to improving benefits minus costs, such as profitability, net benefits, efficiency, or effectiveness, but productivity has the semantic advantage of arousing more positive connotations than the other concepts, as well as being more commonly understood.

Other business activities that it seems appropriate to stimulate through tax subsidies include:

(1) *Developing and implementing new technologies*   When a new technology is developed that enables workers to produce more with less labour, this usually means an increase in the quantity and possibly the quality of the products produced, with the cost per item produced being less than the former more labour-intensive cost.

(2) *Locating plants and job opportunities in high unemployment areas* This is like putting welfare recipients to work. The marginal rate of return tends to be higher in moving someone from unemployment to employment, as contrasted with a move from one form of employment to another. Stimulating business firms to locate in such areas can be aided by local property-tax exemption, as well as federal income tax incentives.

(3) *Subsidizing business firms to engage in programs designed to upgrade the work of groups (such as blacks, handicapped people, and the elderly) who have traditionally been discriminated against in obtaining jobs commensurate with their skills* The subsidies would cover advertising available jobs in media likely to reach those groups. The subsidies might also be designed to facilitate transportation and housing patterns to bring people who are discriminated against, under-employed, or unemployed closer to the job opportunities.

(4) *Expanding business operations as a result of technological developments that enable prices to be reduced so that larger quantities could be sold* – as contrasted with seeking expansion through increased advertising.

(5) *Developing training programs* – so as to upgrade the skills of workers and thereby make them more productive, with the cost of training generally being substantially less than the increased product which the workers are able to produce.

The above business activities cluster around two kinds of activities. One relates to technological development as emphasized in points (1) and (4). The other relates to a more productive hiring and training as emphasized in points (2), (3) and (5) and the earlier point about welfare recipients. In order to make the hiring and training opportunities more meaningful, it is desirable not only to stimulate business to make them available, but also to stimulate the potential worker participants to take advantage of those opportunities. In the case of welfare recipients, this may mean offering such incentives as being able to keep the first $60 or so earned each month, and about $1 out of every $2 earned until a welfare cutoff figure is reached. This kind of system clearly makes more sense than deducting from the welfare payments every dollar that a welfare recipient earns (as was done prior to the late 1960s), or having an exemption substantially less than about $60 or $1 out of every $2 earned (which is the current system). The Nixon–Moynihan family assistance plan originally proposed such incentives for encouraging productive work on the part of welfare recipients, but the plan was never passed, due partly to Watergate distractions, and it was not combined with a business incentives program to provide jobs for welfare recipients and other unemployed and underemployed people.

In order to make the technological incentives more meaningful, it is desirable to stimulate basic research in the universities. Business firms do have the capability to implement new technologies, especially with tax subsidies to cover the costs. Business firms do not do so well though in running departments of physics, genetics, psychology, or other fields of knowledge; this is the province of universities. American universities have been successful in producing basic research and teaching, as indicated by where the Nobel prize winners are and where international students choose to go. Unfortunately, American industry has not taken sufficient advantage of the creativity of American academic research. It is ironic that Japanese industry is more computerized than American industry in spite of the fact that much of the basic computer technology was developed in American universities. Getting American business to implement new research ideas can be done partly through tax subsidies, but there is also a need for further stimulation of basic research, especially in these times of tight academic budgets. Tax exemption for American universities is not the answer – they are already tax-exempt. What can be done, however, is to allow tax credits to people who make university contributions. Under the present system a person earning $10 who contributes $1 to his or her favourite university receives an itemized deduction bringing his or her net taxable income down to $9. If the tax rate is 20 per cent, the tax in this hypothetical situation is $1.80. If, however, the government were to provide a $1 tax credit in addition to the $1 deduction, then the tax to be paid would only be 80¢. This kind of tax credit could provide a strong incentive to contribute much needed funding from private individuals and business firms to American universities. The tax law could also specify that the contributions must be earmarked for research purposes rather than athletic, dormitory, or other university activities.

The above analysis emphasizes the role of business, welfare recipients, and universities in the new productivity. What, however, is the role of the great mass of middle-class people who are not business executives, welfare recipients, or professors? Their role is mainly to be the beneficiaries of the increased GNP at lower cost, that these incentives can bring about. This increased GNP gets widely spread, partly because middle-class people tend to work for the business firms that are in a position to benefit from these subsidies and to use the subsidies to increase their productivity and the income of their workers. That includes large and small businesses, since both are capable of improving their hiring practices and of adopting improved technologies. The bulk of the American population could also benefit from the new productivity by virtue of having a reduced working week if the new productivity can result in producing as much or more with a 30-35-hour work week as was formerly produced with a 40-hour working week. If each person were working less but was still as productive and therefore still earning the same or more income, this would also enable more jobs to be spread around. Ordinary middle-class people can also take advantage of the tax subsidies by investing their money in activities that would entitle them to tax deductions or tax credits. At the present time, there may be an over-investment on the part of middle-class people in real estate because of the real estate tax breaks. Money tied up in real estate may represent lost opportunities to society, as those funds could be invested in more productive technological development.

ALTERNATIVES TO AN INCENTIVES-PRODUCTIVITY PROGRAM

It is important to distinguish the above incentives-productivity program from related programs that emphasize governmental tax cuts. The key distinction is that the tax cuts described here are made in return for the taxpayers doing things considered helpful to national productivity. The proposed Kemp–Roth legislation involves a 30 per cent tax cut across the board without strings attached. Such legislation may, if there are no productivity strings attached to the tax cut, miss a tremendous opportunity of using a large quantity of potential rewards. The taxes saved may go into savings or consumption that could stimulate the economy – although possibly in an inflationary way if the increased attempt to consume is not adequately met by increased production. Much of the taxes saved may go into increased dividends, real estate purchases, and other purchases that in themselves contribute little if anything toward increased productivity. Likewise increased property-tax reductions and restrictions like those associated with California Proposition 13 do little for increased productivity unless strings are attached whereby property holders are required to do something worthwhile in return for the tax reductions. That something might include changing the insulation or the heating system of their property so as better to conserve energy and thereby reduce society's energy costs. The property tax reductions could also be more selective so as to encourage property development in depressed areas or residential development in areas that have job opportunities but lack adequate housing for a local labour force.

There are basically two alternatives to the above incentives program for seeking increased societal productivity. One is to try to achieve it through controls and penalties for lack of productivity. This does not work well: one can generally encourage socially desired behaviour better through rewards, than punishments. This may even be true of traditional criminal law. The main reason middle-class people do not commit robberies is not because they are so afraid of the jail penalties, which they may not receive for a first offence, in any case. What keeps them in line may mainly be the available career opportunities that would be lost to them if they were arrested for a robbery. On the other hand, poor teenage blacks and whites do not have such rewards for good behaviour so readily available. For them, committing a mugging may often be a wise entrepreneurial decision, given the alternative incentives available. Regardless of how meaningful penalties like jail and fines are in the traditional criminal context, they do not generally work well in the realm of economic matters like occupational safety, environmental protection, and increased productivity. They especially lack effectiveness when they require expensive, time-consuming, and difficult litigation in order to be enforced.

The second basic alternative for obtaining increased societal productivity is to leave the matter to the marketplace. This also does not work well, either with regard to improved technology or to improved hiring practices. The new technologies often require massive investment which takes years to pay off. American business and possibly business in general does not want to wait that long for a large capital investment to become profitable, and even large business firms may not have the kind of capital available for developing and implementing large-scale modern technologies. As a result, there may be a need for government financial resources to facilitate the development and implementation of new technologies, especially through the indirect approach of tax breaks, rather than through outright government expenditures. Likewise with regard to hiring practices, business firms may not have much incentive for hiring welfare recipients, locating in high unemployment areas, or developing outreach programs to attract groups previously discriminated against, unless there is some kind of government subsidy to do so. Engaging in those hiring practices may be beneficial to society, but not necessarily to the individual business firm, and firms are geared towards being profitable, not idealistic. In other words, hiring a welfare recipient produces an external benefit-minus-cost, but not necessarily an internal one. If society wants those external benefits-minus-costs, then it should be willing to pay for them in the form of a tax reduction. That is especially true if a relatively small tax reduction can produce a relatively large increase in output and also a reduction in other societal costs like welfare payment costs. One effect of marketplace competition that is contrary to the new productivity is the stimulus that it gives to American business to ask for tariff protection from foreign competition. That kind of government policy runs contrary to a policy of stimulating new technology for increased productivity, as contrasted with sheltering American business from foreign business firms which have adopted new technologies. In the long run, all nations would be better off if they were to follow incentive programs of stimulating their respective national productivities so each country would be doing well whatever it does best relative to other countries.

DECISION SCIENCE AND PRODUCTIVITY IMPROVEMENT

Decision science can be defined as a set of methods for deciding which of various decisions or policies will maximize or increase benefits-minus-costs in achieving a given set of goals in the light of the relations between the alternative decisions and the goals. Decision-science methods tend to fall into five categories that relate to benefit-cost analysis, decision theory, optimum-level analysis, allocation theory, and time-optimization methods.

Basic benefit-cost analysis involves making an optimum choice among discrete alternatives without probabilities. Discrete alternatives in this context mean alternatives where each one is a lump-sum project in the sense that a government agency can meaningfully adopt all or nothing of a project, not multiple units and not fractions of units. Each project is thus basically a yes–no matter. Under these circumstances, an agency that is interested in maximizing the good that it does should spend its whole budget for each of the alternative projects in the order of their benefit/cost ratios. This situation can be illustrated by the example of choosing the optimum combination of a set of notification procedures for notifying defendants to appear in court, or a combination of dam-building projects. Other examples include excluding illegally seized evidence, allowing abortions, or allowing teacher-led prayer in public schools.

Optimum level analysis involves finding an optimum policy where doing too much or too little is undesirable. These situations involve policies which produce benefits at first, but then the benefits reach a peak, and start to fall off. The object in such situations is to find the point on a policy continuum where the benefits are maximized. These situations may also involve policies that reduce costs at first, but then the costs reach a bottom, and start to rise. The object then is to find the point on a policy continuum where the costs are minimized. That situation can be illustrated by the problem of deciding the optimum percentage of defendants to hold in jail prior to trial, the optimum level of pollution, or the optimum speed limit on city highways.

Allocation theory or optimum mix analysis involves allocating scarce resources across activities, places, people, or other objects of allocation. The overall goal is generally to allocate one's scarce resources in such a way as to (1) use all the available budget, while (2) equalizing the marginal rates-of-return of the activities or places so that nothing is to be gained by switching from one activity or place to another. That kind of allocation recognizes that a good activity or place should not be given too much because after a while the diminishing marginal rate-of-return becomes smaller than what can be gained by shifting a dollar or unit of effort to another normally less productive activity or place. This situation can be illustrated by the example of allocating the resources of the Legal Services Corporation between routine cases handling and law reform activities, or allocating anti-crime dollars of the Law Enforcement Assistance Administration across a set of cities.

Time-optimization models involve decision-making systems designed to minimize time consumption. Time-optimization models often involve variations on optimum choice, risk, level, or mix analysis, but applied to situations in which the goal is to minimize time. Some time-optimization models are peculiar to a temporal subject matter such as (1) queuing theory for predicting and reducing waiting time and backlogs from information on arrival and service rates, (2) optimum sequencing for determining the order in which matters should be processed so as to minimize the average waiting time, and (3) critical-path analysis for determining what paths from start to finish are especially worth concentrating on with regard to delay-reduction efforts.

In general, public policy evaluation based on decision-science methods seems capable of improving decision-making processes so that decisions are more likely to be arrived at which will maximize or at least increase societal benefits minus costs. Those decision-making methods may be even more important than worker motivation or technological innovation in productivity improvement. Hard work means little if the wrong products are being produced in terms of societal benefits and costs. Likewise, the right policies are needed to maximize technological innovation, which is not so likely to occur without an appropriate public policy environment.

SOCIETAL PRODUCTIVITY AND PUBLIC POLICY PROBLEMS

Societal productivity affects every public policy problem, and public policy is highly important to substantially improving societal productivity. With regard to societal policy problems, a typical list of the top five problems might include defence, inflation/unemployment, crime, civil liberties, and health. Others might have a different top five. The important point is that societal productivity is relevant to whatever policy problems might be included. For example, a key problem in the realm of *defence* policy relates to how to develop more effective defences for the United States at reduced costs. Both liberals and conservatives question how effective our defences are, and they both question even more the extent to which we are buying defence efficiently. Increased productivity in that context does not just mean having an MX missile system at as low a cost as possible. It also means making the right decisions in terms of benefits-minus-costs in choosing the MX system over alternative defence systems. On an even higher level, one can talk about how wasteful any defence expenditures are in comparison with using the money for societal goods and services if we could develop alternative means of decreasing the probability of an attack on ourselves or our allies.

The *inflation* of rising prices and wages would be no problem if productivity were increasing simultaneously so that people would be receiving more benefits for the increased prices and so that workers would be producing more output for the increased wages. There would likewise be no *unemployment* problem and a substantial reduction in poverty if we could arrange for people to be employed more productively in a more organized economy. Such an economy would see to it that all people had jobs which they could perform, including older people, women, minorities, handicapped people, less-educated people, and others. There is obviously much waste in the *crime* field, not in the relatively trivial sense of police officers sleeping in squad cars, but in the more important sense of society's resources being wasted on prisons, police activities, and losses due to crime which could possibly be prevented through a more productive societal anti-crime program that provides more productive alternatives to crime-committing. Productivity in the *civil liberties* context especially refers to how to stimulate more freedom of speech and unconventional advocacy which would encourage the development and diffusion of innovative ideas. On the matter of *health*, a key problem is how to enable society to be more productive through the distribution of better health care in order to prevent and cure ailments that decrease societal productivity.

PUBLIC POLICY FOR IMPROVING SOCIETAL PRODUCTIVITY

On the point that public policy is important to substantially improving societal productivity, even conservatives recognize that without an appropriate public policy environment, business would be unable to innovate and improve its ability to produce. Appropriate public policies from a conservative perspective might emphasize:

(1) police protection of property
(2) enforcement of contract rights through the courts
(3) maintenance of a money system
(4) limited liability for corporations
(5) protection of patents, copyrights, and trademarks
(6) uniform standards concerning weights and measures
(7) census and other statistical information
(8) good roads, harbours, airports, and other transportation facilities
(9) protection of US business activities abroad
(10) loans to various business activities including housing, farming, exporting, and small business
(11) special rates for business bulk mail
(12) business bankruptcy proceedings that allow creditors to collect something and businesses to have a fresh start
(13) special tax treatment in terms of business deductions
(14) government purchases from business
(15) government policy that benefits the economy as a whole, including monetary and fiscal policy.

Appropriate public policy for stimulating societal productivity from a liberal perspective might emphasize the need for the government to:

(1) encourage the stimulus of international competition by refraining from adopting tariffs or other restrictions on international trade;

(2) play a greater role in long-term societal investment decisions in partnership with business and labour, in the way that the Japanese government does;

(3) stimulate better relations between business and academia by subsidizing two-way exchanges of personnel, relevant conferences, mid-career training, and information systems whereby business is better informed of relevant developments in academia, and academics are better informed of business needs;

(4) help pay for the dismantling and replacement of obsolete industrial equipment;

(5) put more emphasis on positive incentives to make business perform socially desired activities instead of relying on regulation, litigation, and negative sanctions which generate negative relations between business and government;

(6) have a more vigorous policy of providing job security, retraining, and loans to start new business/jobs, so as to lessen the anxieties of American workers who feel threatened by technological innovation;

(7) actively pursue means for reducing arms expenditures between the US and the Soviet Union in order to free billions of dollars in potential capital for implementing productive new ideas.

Instead of talking about public policy toward increased productivity from a conservative and liberal perspective, one could discuss the subject in terms of the key elements of productivity. Those elements are generally referred to as land, labour, capital, and management, and the organization of those elements. *Land* or natural resources is an important element, but it is not so subject to being improved through public policy, although the government can encourage conservation and the development of synthetic alternatives to natural resources. On the matter of *labour*, some of the productivity improvement suggestions have included (1) the need for more education, especially with regard to technical skills, (2) the need for more worker input in making management decisions, and (3) more sensitivity to worker morale among public employees. It is, however, often felt that workers can be more productive with good technology or *capital* equipment with which to work even if they lack strong motivation, as compared to strongly motivated workers who lack good technology. To stimulate good technology, both liberals and conservatives endorse tax-break incentives. Conservatives may, however, have more faith in across-the-board tax cuts like the 30 per cent tax cut of the Reagan Administration. Liberals tend to advocate ear-marked tax breaks which require specific productivity-increasing activities in order to earn the tax breaks. A key problem in American technology may be the need for business to be better at implementing innovative ideas. The US does seem to do well on creativity, especially in university research, but may not be as efficient in implementing new ideas as the Japanese are.

Good *management* and leadership are important for choosing decisions that will maximize productivity. There may be a need for better training of both public and private managers with regard to practical decision-making methods. On the matter of stimulating more productive *organization*, that may mean stimulating more competition in the private sector, especially where business units can be relatively small and efficient. The matter of having a more productive organization of labour, capital, and management often raises the issues of governmental versus private implementation. Those issues in the past have taken the form of emotional disputes over socialism versus capitalism. In recent years there has been a movement on the part of socialists to concede the need for more decentralization of decision-making, and to show more concern with increasing national income as a way of reducing poverty, rather than emphasizing income redistribution. Likewise, there has been a movement on the part of capitalists to concede the need for more governmental co-ordination, at least in the ways mentioned above, and to show more sensitivity to the need for equality of opportunity, with both co-ordination and equality directed toward increased productivity.

POLICY ANALYSIS AND PARTNERSHIP

In order to make these new productivity ideas more effective, it may also be necessary for the government to be more productive in choosing among alternative governmental programs in fields like housing, transportation, poverty, economic regulation, criminal justice, and so on. Doing so may require the development and implementation of methods for more meaningfully evaluating alternative programs and policies regarding their ability to achieve their goals effectively and efficiently. Those methods are being increasingly developed in interdisciplinary policy analysis programs and social science departments at universities across the country. Government budget cutbacks have been a stimulus to that development in recent years, since they often necessitate an evaluation of existing programs to determine which ones should be cut. Unfortunately, budget cutbacks have generated a negative atmosphere in policy evaluation, emphasizing the need to reduce government output in the light of reduced budgets. What may be needed in the public sector is a more positive attitude emphasizing the need to try to get more government output from those reduced budgets. In other words, a reduced budget can be viewed as a half-empty bottle, emphasizing what is missing and the need to cut back on what can be accomplished. Alternatively, it can be viewed as a half-full bottle, emphasizing what is there and the need to maximize what can be accomplished with the resources available.

In the light of the above analysis, one can conclude that we may indeed be entering an era of new productivity involving a partnership between (1) the public sector of government agencies using tax reduction incentives to encourage productive behaviour, (2) the private sector of business firms taking advantage of those incentives to increase their productivity, and (3) the not-for-profit sector including the academic world seeking to develop new knowledge relative to improved technologies, industrial psychology, public administration, and other relevant fields. That kind of productive partnership can mean increased societal benefits and reduced societal costs, which in turn can greatly expand the cornucopia of societal goodies, and lead to the next cycles of equalization and growth further down the line of American political history.

Suggested Reading

Dogramaci, A. (1981), *Productivity analysis: A range of perspectives* (Boston: Martinus Nijhoff).

Greiner, J., *et al.* (1981), *Productivity and motivation: A review of state and local government initiatives* (Washington, DC: Urban Institute).

Johnson, C. (ed.) (1984), *The industrial policy debate* (Institute for Contemporary Studies).

LeBoeuf, M. (1982), *The productivity challenge: How to make it work for America and you* (New York: McGraw-Hill).

Lowi, T. and A. Stone (eds) (1978), *Nationalizing government: Public policies in America* (Beverly Hills, CA: Sage).

Magaziner, I. and R. Reich (1982), *Minding America's business: The decline and rise of the American economy* (San Diego, CA: Harcourt Brace Jovanovich).

Mitnick, B. (1980), *The political economy of regulation* (New York: Columbia Press).

Nagel, S. and M. Neef (1979), *Decision theory and the legal process* (Lexington, MA: Lexington-Heath).

Public Productivity Review (1976–   ).

Roucek, J. (ed.) (1978), *Social control for the 1980s: A handbook for order in a democratic society* (Westport, CT: Greenwood).

Schwartz, G. and P. Choate (1980), *Being number one: Rebuilding the U.S. economy* (Lexington, MA: Lexington-Heath).

Sternlieb, G. and D. Listokin (eds) (1981), *New tools for economic development: The Enterprise Zone, Development Bank, and RFC* (New Brunswick, NJ: Rutgers University).

Thurow, L. (1980), *The zero-sum society: Distribution and the possibilities for economic change* (New York: Basic Books).

Tornatzky, L., *et al.* (1980), *Innovation and social processes: National experiment in implementing social technology* (New York: Pergamon).

White, M., *et al.* (1980), *Managing public systems: Analytic techniques for public administration* (North Scituate, MA: Duxbury).

Index